Violence Workers

Violence Workers

Police Torturers and Murderers Reconstruct Brazilian Atrocities

Martha K. Huggins

Mika Haritos-Fatouros

and Philip G. Zimbardo

UNIVERSITY OF CALIFORNIA PRESS

Berkeley / Los Angeles / London

University of California Press
Berkeley and Los Angeles, California

University of California Press, Ltd.
London, England

©2002 by The Regents of the University of California

Library of Congress Cataloging-in-Publication Data

Huggins, Martha Knisely, 1944–
    Violence workers : police torturers and murderers reconstruct
Brazilian atrocities / Martha K. Huggins, Mika Haritos-Fatouros,
Philip G. Zimbardo.
        p.   cm.
    ISBN 0–520–23446–4 (alk. paper) — ISBN 0–520–23447–2 (alk. paper)
    1. Police brutality — Brazil.   2.   Political atrocities — Brazil
3. Torture — Brazil.   I. Haritos-Fatouros, Mika 1930–
II. Zimbardo, Philip G. III. Title.

HV8183.H84 2002
323'.044'0981–dc21   2002022331

Printed in the United States of America

9 8 7 6 5 4 3 2 1

The paper used in this publication meets the minimum requirements
of American National Standards for Information Sciences — Permanence
of Paper for printed Library Materials, ANSI Z39-48-1984.

To Andrea Klein Willison, whose own tortured mental illness led to her suicide. Andrea's poetry (The Only True Power Is in Connection, *White Wing Press, 1998) and her powerful activism for peace, justice, and on behalf of those with mental illness demonstrate the enduring resilience of the human spirit.*

— MARTHA K. HUGGINS

To the members of Brazil's FENAPOL dissident police organization. Although your organization no longer exists, your human rights spirit left an indelible mark on the Brazilian police systems that you struggled to change.

— MIKA HARITOS-FATOUROS

To the perfection, perversity, and resiliency of the human spirit, which I have come to appreciate so much now that I have begun to understand the dynamics of torture from my experience in this research team.

— PHILIP G. ZIMBARDO

Contents

List of Tables, Figures, and Photographs

Tables

Figures

Photographs

Acknowledgments

The book's first author, Martha Huggins, spent three and a half months in the field in Brazil, working closely with the study's translators. She took primary responsibility for analysis, and wrote the Preface, Introduction, and the first ten of the book's eleven chapters. Haritos-Fatouros had primary responsibility for Chapter 11 and Zimbardo for the Conclusion. Haritos-Fatouros's and Zimbardo's oral and written input on the data analyses and writing has clearly put their personal and professional imprint on *Violence Workers*.

Having been in the field the longest and taken primary responsibility for writing *Violence Workers*, Huggins has the most people and organizations to thank. However, before all else the research team recognizes that this study would not have been possible without generous funding from Hamburg Germany's Hamburger Stiftung zur Förderung von Wissenschaft und Kultur. In particular, we wish to thank Jan Phillip Reemtsma for having the faith in our project and for committing such generous funding to it. The Hamburger Stiftung grant would not have been possible in the first place without the grant securing and writing skills of Mika Haritos-Fatouros.

Haritos-Fatouros's original grant had proposed a comparative analysis of Greek and Brazilian torturers, a study that was to build on her own research on Greek torturers, now being published as *The Psychological Origins of Institutionalized Torture* (Routledge, 2002). At the time, Huggins was writing *Political Policing* (Duke, 1998), about U.S. training of Latin American police, a study that documents the U.S. role in facilitating atrocities in Latin America. Knowing that Huggins's research for *Political Policing* was examining torture, Haritos-Fatouros recognized that this research would interface well with her work on the training of Greek torturers. But as our research began to take shape, it became clear that before any comparative analysis could be effectively undertaken, we needed to understand the scope and dimensions of the Brazilian story. With such a book in mind, it made sense for the Brazil specialist on the research team, Martha Huggins, to take primary responsibility for writing our book.

Huggins and Haritos-Fatouros recognized very early in the planning stages of the research that the best person to enrich our research collaboration was Philip G. Zimbardo, whose recognized scientific research and theoretical scholarship on obedience to authority and associated violence—brilliantly illustrated in the Stanford Prison Experiment (Zimbardo 1973; Haney, Banks, and Zimbardo 1977; and Zimbardo, Maslach, and Haney 2000)—would be absolutely essential to the success of our research outcomes. We formally began our three person research collaboration in August 1994, in São Paulo, during several planning sessions prior to beginning the interviews. Then, in July 1994, at Haritos-Fatouros's home on Greece's Hydra Island, we spent four days discussing interviews and reviewing the interview data, examining our research perspectives, and planning the final research report for the Hamburger Stiftung. Two of Haritos-Fatouros's graduate assistants, Despina Karabatzaki and Nikos Bozatzis, proved invaluable at that time and throughout our collaboration, helping Haritos-Fatouros to organize interview data analytically and to suggest tabular presentations.

The research for *Violence Workers* officially began in São Paulo, Brazil, in August 1993. Our assumption at that time was that we would use São Paulo as our initial interview base, beginning the interviews on the day after our arrival. Huggins—having worked with Brazilian police for a decade at that point—was less optimistic about this time frame, but began seeking interviewees the next day just the same. We learned very quickly that interviews with police would be extremely difficult to obtain and that finding police who were willing to admit to having tortured would be almost impossible. We would have to cast a broad net—requesting interviews with any police who had served during Brazil's military period—and hope that some torturers would end up in the net. Before long, through a number of Huggins's research associates in São Paulo, the team began securing interviewees there—although without any guarantee that they were torturers. Chapters 2 and 3 give the full story of our problems obtaining Brazilian police interviewees and getting them to tell us about themselves and their and others' violence.

During the month that Haritos-Fatouros and Zimbardo were in São Paulo and Rio de Janeiro, they carried out three interviews through our translator and transcriber, William Shelton. Over the next three months, Huggins conducted another twenty interviews during her research trips to São Paulo, Rio de Janeiro, Brasília, Recife, and Pôrto Alegre. By December 1994 we had turned the twenty-three interviews over to William Shelton, our translator. Over the next year and a half, Shelton transcribed all twenty-three interviews and translated nineteen. Without Shelton's careful attention to our project and his unflagging enthusiasm about it, the researchers' own passion might have declined over the years following the initial interviews. The four interview translations that Shelton did not complete were done by international educator and linguist Donald Occhiuzzo. His skill at translating and his willingness to take on this task in addition to his administrative duties at São Paulo's Associação Alumni Bi-Cultural Center are greatly appreciated.

In the five years of stealing time from teaching and other research commitments to carry out analysis and writing, a number of people helped move *Violence Workers* forward. However, because we must maintain the anonymity of those who helped us secure police interviewees, we will indicate their names without their essential contribution to this project. Without the help of these people, this project simply would not have been possible. Recognizing that our support has come primarily from four countries, Brazil, the United States, Holland, and Greece, we will indicate our gratitude by country.

Among the colleagues in Brazil who helped move our research forward were sociologists and human rights advocates Sérgio Adorno and Myriam Mesquita; sociologist and police specialist Guaracy Mingardi; political scientist and human rights scholar and advocate Paulo Sérgio Pinheiro; historian Beth Cancelli; Rio de Janeiro police official, scholar, and friend Carlos Cerqueira; scholars and then justice administrators Nilo Batista and Julieta Lemgruber; lawyer and human rights scholar and advocate Ester Kosovski; *Jornal do Brasil* journalist Fabiano Lana, and educational administrators Caio Cardoso, Kathy Harrington, and Donald Occhiuzzo.

In the United States, Huggins owes special thanks to Union College for financial and sabbatical support, especially through her endowed Roger Thayer Stone Chair in Sociology. The Stone endowment was essential as years of writing and research depleted our funding from the Hamburger Stiftung.

A number of U.S. colleagues who conduct research on atrocity have also provided inspiration: David Chandler, Leigh A. Payne, and Darius Rejali. Specialists in police and prison research pointed to sources and supportively critiqued our thinking, including especially David Bayley and Graeme Newman.

We could not have refined our burnout analysis without the careful reading and insightful suggestions of Christina Maslach. Andrew Feffer and Matthew Leavy, intellectual historians, and Mark Walker, a historian of Germany, suggested ways of writing our story. Aaron Broadwell offered his considerable linguistic skills at several points in the discourse analysis; two other anthropologists, Karen Brison and David Hess, provided excellent direction on secrecy. Tom McGee and Judith Willison gave inestimable insights about remembering and writing atrocity. Ruth Stevenson researched and provided rich quotations from William Shakespeare.

The professional oversight, assistance, and enthusiasm of Union College's Schaffer Library reference librarians moved forward the research and writing, with considerable assistance especially from Donna Burton, Mary Cahill, Bruce Connolly, and David Gerhan. Several Union College undergraduates fact-checked material and located bibliographic citations, among them Dapo Akinleye, Saima Husain, Erika Migliaccio, Jessica MacTurk, and Sarah Osowski. Some Internet research and a good deal of computer assistance came from Janet McQuade. Besides typing several drafts of the early manuscript, Carolyn Micklas took great care and advised on the final assembling of *Violence Workers*.

Several conferences, three U.S. and one international, were particularly important in helping to focus aspects of Huggins's analysis and writing: the University of Wisconsin–Ford Foundation 1998 workshop "Legacies of Authoritarianism"; the New School for Social Research/Janey Program/Sawyer 1998 seminar "Coercion, Violence, and Rights in the Americas"; the University of Chicago's 1999 conference "Investigating and Combating Torture"; the 1999 Rutgers University/Cuernavaca Center for Hemispheric Studies conference "Cultura, Ciudadania y Violencia"; and presentations at the Netherlands Institute of Human Rights and the Hague School of Social Science Research.

At the University of Utrecht's School of Human Rights Research (SIM), three Dutch colleagues with whom Huggins worked, Niels Uildriks, Piet Van Reenen, and Hans Werdmolder, provided invaluable intellectual input at the last stages of this project. Considerable infrastructural support was provided in the final stages of manuscript preparation by the School of Human Rights Research, where Huggins spent three months in Spring 2001 as a visiting research fellow.

In Greece, our gratitude is given to Maria Papathanassiou, who oversaw with professional care various stages of Mika Haritos-Fatouros's contributions to the manuscript. Our gratitude is given to Dr. Nicos Bozatzis and two advanced graduate students, Despina Karabatzaki and Dina Diamantidou, whose work on various stages of tabular organization, as well as on Haritos-Fatouros's theoretical thinking, was invaluable.

We are deeply indebted to Van Nath and the Phnom Penh Tuol Sleng Prison Museum, especially its director, Chey Sopheara, for their permission to use a photograph of Nath's painting in this book. Nath, one of seven to survive—among thousands who, like himself, were tortured at Pol Pot's infamous Tuol Sleng Prison—has painted dramatic and troubling images of brutalities he saw. Our book is also enriched by a painting at the Ho Chi Minh City Vietnam War Remnants Museum. We are grateful to the museum's director, Nguyen Quoc Hung, and vice director, Huynh Ngoc Van, for permission to use the Fine Arts School student's rendition of torture. Two powerful Brazilian images of atrocity were made available by the *Folha de São Paulo* newspaper. We especially thank *Folha* photographers C. Leite and Z. Guimarães for the haunting photographic images of execution victims. To Union College biologist Dr. Twitty Styles we offer gratitude for a photograph of hope—those who keep vigil at São Paulo's Praça de Sé to publicize the struggle for missing loved ones.

The authors wish to thank the three anonymous readers whose often painful critiques and always valuable insights undoubtedly improved the final quality of our written story. Our gratitude is great to Stanley Holwitz, associate editor of the University of California Press. Without his faith in this project and his guidance along the way, *Violence Workers* would not have been published. The quality of the manuscript was improved greatly by the careful and insightful copyediting of Gregor Everitt of Impressions Book and Journal Services, Inc. We, of course, accept full responsibility for any omissions or oversights in the final product.

Finally, the research team is greatly indebted to Malcolm Willison for his academically and intellectually inspired editing of each of the many versions of this book's chapters. Without Willison's sometimes difficult and always theoretically rich and creative questions and feedback, *Violence Workers* could not have been written.

Preface

In 1991 a videotape of Los Angeles police violently beating Rodney King was broadcast worldwide. This book's Brazilianist author, then teaching on police violence in Latin America at the University of São Paulo's Center for the Study of Violence, was asked by her students if U.S. police could possibly be as violent as they knew Brazilian police to be. Would there in fact be more excesses if the United States did not have more strict civilian supervision and legal accountability? Did the subsequent exoneration of all the filmed police by a suburban all-white jury, however, raise questions about U.S. police accountability?

The Brazilian students pointed to the more numerous and dramatic police abuses in their own country. Indeed, in late 1992 just outside São Paulo City an elite unit of São Paulo State Militarized Police (*Polícia Militar*) stormed Carandiru Prison and gunned down 111 inmates— most already subdued and on their knees. Even though members of the militarized SWAT team had summarily executed prisoners under their superior's orders, as of June 2001, no one—neither the unit, nor its members, nor its commander—had been held legally accountable for what is still Brazil's worst prison massacre. Brazil's police, dubbed by Amnesty International the most violent in the Western Hemisphere, continue to mete out violence with impunity.

The violent reality of policing in Brazil was again demonstrated when late one night in July 1993, nine Rio de Janeiro off-duty police and their vigilante associates fired from their cars into a crowd of seventy-two street children sleeping as they always did in front of Rio's Candelária

Cathedral. World sentiment brought heavy pressure on Rio's justice system to identify and prosecute the perpetrators, thereby starting a reduction of police and vigilante violence. Nevertheless, not even by the first year of this new millennium had more than four of the many perpetrators been indicted and imprisoned.

In August 1993, as we began our own interviews with Brazilian police who had beaten, tortured, and murdered "subversive" suspects during that country's military period (1964–1985), we pondered the complicated causes of and supports for police violence. Had the organizational and operational dynamics of the Candalária and Carandiru massacres also operated in atrocities during Brazil's military past? Did the Rodney King beating suggest similarities even for police violence in military Brazil? To what extent are the police who carry out extreme violence essentially different from those who do not? What role in such violence is played by those members of a police unit who are less immediately involved? How do a police unit's immediate supervisors contribute to its violence? What role do political and high-level police officials play in fostering police violence? Considering our questions about possible similarities between seemingly unrelated cases of police violence, we needed to widen our theoretical system to include not just the immediate perpetrators of violence but also its facilitators—colleagues, supervisors, and officials—who ignore, excuse, support, or even reward it.

Beyond these insights about the various actors and roles in an atrocity system, our research was beginning to suggest how organizational systems themselves, especially in conjunction with certain kinds of ideological constructions, might foster and excuse police atrocities. A particularly dramatic example of this came in early 1999 in the United States when New York City police gunned down African immigrant Amadou Diallo with over forty-one bullets. This police team—known as "the Commandos of the NYPD" (Morales 1999: 3)—charged with hunting alleged robbers, muggers, and rapists in a "war against crime," had been challenged by New York City political and police officials to pursue its battle as local conditions seemed to require. Night after night, in the course of confronting the real and constructed dangers giving the unit its raison d'etre, this insular elite police team—whose T-shirts read "There is no hunting like the hunting of men" and whose battle cry was "We own the night" (Morales 1999: 3)—had developed its own specialized "professional" police culture, an organizational dynamic that clearly contributed to Diallo's shooting.

Despite the unit's temporary suspension, no hard questions were ever addressed publicly about the role that creating such organized units has in fostering police violence among those charged with reducing community crime. The Diallo shooting was explained instead by the same crime model that had legitimized the police unit in the first place: where urban violence is supposedly rampant and everyone a potential criminal, anyone—especially a black man—is presumed to be a potential threat. Because of this presumption, an innocent man reaching into his pocket for identification was shot to death on the grounds that he must be pulling out a gun. No policeman was convicted for Diallo's death, another parallel between such apparently different legal cultures as in Brazil and the United States.

Back in Los Angeles at the millennium, another U.S. police scandal further highlighted our awareness of a complicated atrocity dynamic that may transcend societal settings and historical periods. Free rein was given by Los Angeles administrative and police officials to a special Los Angeles Police Department Community Resources against Street Hoodlums (CRASH) antigang unit in the Rampart District. With a mandate to rid the downtown area of street gangs, this unit quickly evolved into a police operations group with few connections even to other police divisions. The CRASH unit engaged in extortion and fabricated evidence, shot alleged criminals outright, and beat and tortured suspects. In the end, just one policeman—labeled its only "out of control" cop—was convicted for the unit's far-reaching illegalities. The upper-level political, justice, and police officials who had promoted and excused the CRASH unit's violence completely escaped formal blame, as did the very political and organizational structures that seem to have made its violence practically inevitable.

As *Violence Workers* was being prepared to go to press, the United Nations released its Year 2000 Report on torture in Brazil. This demonstrated that in major cities throughout Brazil—in police stations, prisons, and even orphans' facilities—psychological terror and brutal physical torture are still routinely practiced. Among the 138 cases of torture documented by United Nations Special Rapporteur on Torture Sir Nigel Rodley was that of a young Rio de Janeiro boy who was beaten in prison with boards for over an hour and then thrown into the deep end of a swimming pool. Left to sink or swim, the young boy succeeded, bruised and broken, to dog-paddle his way to safety in the pool's shallow end only to be driven back three times more into deep water before he was allowed to return to his small dark cell. In another case of torture in Rio de Janeiro, police brutalized a man for six hours—alternating beating him on the head and neck and holding his head under water until his lungs felt they would burst. As these cases suggest, the purpose of much torture in democratic Brazil is instilling terror in its victims, clearly one function of torture during Brazil's military period as well. However, even more to the point, and for whatever designated function, torture is still widely used in democratic Brazil years after the end of authoritarian military rule.

These few examples from Brazil and the United States suggest that the formal political structure itself—authoritarian, democratizing, or solidly democratic—may not determine where police torture and murder will occur. However, our examples do suggest several factors common to "atrocity environments": police excesses have occurred in a sociopolitical climate of public and/or police fear tied to an assumption that police were "at war" against some segment of the population—designated as "enemies of the state." In each case, a small or elite and often militarized police unit had operational independence, sometimes even from the rest of its own formal police organizations when carrying out numerous brutalities, often without close oversight even by their low-level police supervisors, yet nearly always, paradoxically, with the tacit approval of higher organizational and political officials. While a few of the (less powerful) direct perpetrators of atrocity were occasionally—although rarely—punished at law for their brutalities, their more powerful facilitators were almost never held accountable and the operational systems that had engendered and fostered police violence almost always escaped analytical and legal culpability.

Our own case study of police atrocity during Brazil's military period postulates that a search for the causes of atrocity—whether in military authoritarian states or in emerging or consolidated democracies—must go beyond simplistic personalistic "bad apple" and vague "unique" society-wide "culture of violence" perspectives: neither the psycho-biological or the general cultural determinist perspective accounts for the effects of the bureaucratized systems that permit or encourage the social-psychological and cultural mechanisms that can engender violent police conduct and grant impunity to perpetrators and facilitators alike. Some research on police violence in the United States has pointed to a few viable explanatory alternatives to these inadequate perspectives—e.g., situating police violence within "operational cultures," "leadership styles," and "organizational mandates." Yet, while most of these provide an immediate understanding of some police violence situations, they do not very effectively explain the larger-scale structural supports for security force atrocities. Instead, less viable perspectives dominate most media explanations of police atrocities, inform some academic analyses, and often shape the legal arguments for defending or prosecuting violent police.

While a study of police torture and murder during Brazil's military authoritarian dictatorship may seem at first glance tangential to expanding our own knowledge about police brutality in democratizing states and especially in consolidated democracies, for several reasons this study may help do just that. In the first place, we will show that even those Brazilian police in special units who perpetrated some of the most egregious barbarities for the state were not initially different socially and psychologically from the police who might have been in a position to do so but did not. Thus, second, if the worst police violence can be shown to have been shaped by certain kinds of broader social-psychological and organizational processes, then it may be possible that less dramatic police violence (less publicly visible though more widespread) is shaped by these processes as well. Finally, perhaps, both types of violence can be reduced by deliberate policy manipulation of the factors we will identify in this study. Theorists and practitioners might then use our findings to predict and prevent state-related and socially structured security force violence in contexts in and outside post-military Brazil.

Applying insights from a study of police atrocities in military Brazil to other social, political, and historical contexts may therefore have considerable value. The Holocaust teaches us that the real danger of totalitarianism is not its unique forms of domination but the banality of its normal processes and structures. Even for those within democratic contexts such immoral and even illegal processes may be tempting to enact and apply where there is political and social pressure to solve crime, eliminate subversion, or deal with terrorist threats. The possibility of a totalitarian dynamic made up of ordinary citizen bystanders, atrocity facilitators who are not directly violent, as well as of the perpetrators of direct violence indeed exists for democracies, to their peril. If we do not recognize the ways that the past has shaped, or finds disturbing parallels in, the present, we are bound to revisit its most evil outcomes. Thus, we hope that by systematically investigating a sample of Brazilian police violence workers—torturers and death squad murderers—we will contribute to an understanding of the transformations that make such men into perpetrators of evil, while also making more transparent the broader social and political contexts that facilitate the production of state-sanctioned evil.

Introduction

Why do ordinary men torture and murder for the state? How do atrocity perpetrators explain and justify their violence? What is the result of their murderous deeds—for their victims, themselves, and their society? What memories of their atrocities do they admit, and which become public history? *Violence Workers* provides a means to answer these and related questions about official violence and about the evil men whose acts remain buried in the secret recesses of their minds. Systematic interviews were conducted in 1993 with twenty-three Brazilian policemen, fourteen of whom were identified as official or semi-official torturers and murderers for the state—men we designate as *direct perpetrators* of violence, the violence workers of this book's title. Through the reports of these direct perpetrators, and by sometimes comparing them with the nine other interviewees whom we label *atrocity facilitators* for their having participated indirectly in violence, we can learn about and then reconstruct social memory about state-sanctioned violence in Brazil.

The two groups of policemen's careers span a period of some thirty years, from the late 1950s through the mid-1980s, including the twenty-one years of rule by Brazil's military (1964–1985). The twenty-three interviewed policemen were affiliated with one of Brazil's two main police organizations—either the Civil Police or the Militarized Police. The latter is a uniformed state police force with jurisdiction over first-response street policing. To avoid any confusion that a strict English-language translation of *Polícia Militar* (literally, "Military Police") might create in readers' minds, we have labeled this police organization the Militarized Police to lessen possibility of its being seen as an arm of the military itself.

The Civil Police (*Polícia Civil*), a judicial police force, has jurisdiction over postarrest investigations of crime. Prior to 1968, each police force was under the control of state or local civil officials; between that date and the mid-to-late 1980s, both police organizations were formally subordinated to the Brazilian armed forces. After the military period formally ended, so did strict military control of these police forces, except that the Militarized Police continues to have its crimes adjudicated by military tribunals.

By exploring how men from Brazil's two main police forces describe their careers, explain police behavior, and justify their violence, we will penetrate the secrets of those who carried out torture and murder for the state, explore how they came to perpetrate atrocity, and probe the personal consequences of their complicity with the official program of state-sponsored violence that they may have carried with them all these years.

In pursuing these objectives, *Violence Workers* weaves together four interrelated patterns that structured the lives especially of the direct perpetrators of state-sponsored violence and explores how these patterns influenced their memories about atrocity and shaped our reconstructing of it. These four themes are secrecy, occupational insularity through professional and institutional isolation, organizational fragmentation through the division of labor for violence, and personal isolation through social separation from significant others in their daily lives. However, woven throughout these themes themselves is a fifth one: how changes in the Brazilian state may have intersected with violence workers' biographies and influenced their moralities about torture and murder. Taken together, these five themes are powerful tools for assessing why and how ordinary men are transformed into state torturers and murderers, how they justify such violence, and what impact violence work has had on them.

The first of these patterns, secrecy, is the most ubiquitous: whether securing interviewees, getting their responses to potentially threatening questions, documenting their atrocities, or analyzing and writing about the horrors of state-sanctioned violence, secrecy had to be reckoned with in both interviewer and interviewee, or else this study could not have proceeded. The other three patterns—occupational insularity, personal isolation, and organizational fragmentation—normalize moralities about atrocity by eliminating the wider ethical and legal standards and implications that could call security force violence into question. Pointing to the role of occupational insularity in violence work, when such work becomes a full-time preoccupation in a state's "war against" crime and subversion, the only people with whom some violence workers associated were other violence workers. Such occupational insularity in turn nurtured personal isolation, where separation—whether physical, psychological, or both—from family and nonpolice friends was so extreme that the violence worker had no social contacts outside the violent system itself. Within this violence worker's occupational environment, the system's organizational fragmentation masked personal contributions to and responsibility for violence and its effects. With violence work fragmented and subdivided such that each policeman's personal contribution to atrocity was masked (misrecognized personally and socially) as something other than what it was, avoiding personal or political responsibility for atrocity was easy. Within such a system of secrecy, occupational insularity, personal isolation, and organizational fragmentation, a climate is created that powerfully structures not only the business of state violence but also social accounting of it.

Organization of Our Story

Chapter 1, "Violent Lives," follows the lives of four emblematic police torturers and murderers during crucial periods in the thirty years from 1957 to 1987—from seven years before the military coup into a short period after Brazil's 1985 postmilitary redemocratization.

Chapter 2, "Reconstructing Atrocity," elaborates the theoretical and methodological questions associated with our broadest objective—to reconstruct social memory about atrocity: Do different styles of human rights record keeping influence social memory about state violence? Does the social and research perception of atrocity workers—as perpetrators or as victims—influence how their violence is written about and remembered? Does the moral sensitivity of researchers to writing an ethnography of atrocity shape what they write and become the "facts" of public knowledge?

Chapter 3, "Locating Torturers and Murderers," lays out the strategies for locating and interviewing the Brazilian police who had carried out state-sponsored atrocities. We disclose the scope and characteristics of our sample, along with the methodological challenges associated with studying police in general and police atrocity perpetrators in particular.

Chapter 4, "Deposing Atrocity and Managing Secrecy," illustrates how secrecy simultaneously structured violence workers' disclosures about atrocity and shaped interviewers' understanding and subsequent presentation of their violence. We suggest that documenting atrocity creates an interactive and self-reinforcing relationship between interviewer and interviewee that produces a jointly constructed memory.

Chapter 5, "Biography Intersects History," lays out the historical foundation for understanding state-sponsored torture and murder in Brazil by weaving violence workers' biographies into the three decades of Brazilian history covered by this study.

Chapter 6, "Personalistic Masculinity," begins a three-chapter exploration of the modal masculinity presentations of the violence workers. We dispute the popular idea that all atrocity perpetrators have or adopt a common, stereotypic, sadistic masculinity; in fact, a variety of masculinities were demonstrated among the Brazilian violence workers. We explore in this chapter how the first of these three modal masculinities, that of the "personalistic" police, presented themselves, discussed their relations with others, and depicted violence.

Chapter 7, "Bureaucratizing Masculinity," looks at the violence workers who presented their masculinity as an extension of "rational," bureaucratic police organization. These "institutional functionary" police subordinated "unprofessional" feminine or masculine passions to a supposedly dispassionate internal security system and state.

Chapter 8, "Blended Masculinity," introduces the violence workers whose masculinity presentations were a combination of personalistic and institutional functionary masculinities as well as a new synthesis of them. Attempting to make theoretical sense out of the three modal masculinity presentations, in this chapter's conclusion we address how the multiplicity of masculinities within Brazil's atrocity system functioned to obscure and legitimize official violence by structuring images of the state's relationship to it.

Chapter 9, "Shaping Identities and Obedience: A Murderous Dynamic," explores, through a comparison of direct perpetrators of violence and indirect atrocity facilitators, how some kinds of police training and its most visible component, hazing, may have contributed especially to shaping a Militarized Police murder dynamic.

Chapter 10, "Secret and Insular Worlds of Serial Torturers and Executioners," explores the interaction among secrecy, occupational insularity, organizational fragmentation, and personal isolation that shaped and facilitated *serial* torture and execution.

Chapter 11, "Moral Universes of Torturers and Murderers," uncovers violence workers' retrospective social control moralities about their work.

The moral universes of violence workers, having been shaped during the military period by national security ideologies and then nurtured by occupational insularity and personal isolation, have been restructured in the present to render atrocity justifications compatible with Brazil's postmilitary sociopolitical climate.

Chapter 12, "Hung Out to Dry," examines one result of carrying out sustained occupational violence—burnout and the personal, social, and occupational factors related to it.

The Conclusion, "The Alchemy of Torture and Execution: Transforming Ordinary Men into Violence Perpetrators," ties Brazilian atrocity to the social psychological literatures about authority and obedience, linking this in turn to questions about how relatively ordinary men in a variety of historical and social contexts have become perpetrators of unspeakable horrors in their roles as violence workers.

CHAPTER I

Violent Lives

---

*[There is] that strange impulse of indiscretion, common to men who
live secret lives, and accounting for the invariable existence of
"compromising documents" in all the plots and conspiracies of history.*
Joseph Conrad, *Under Western Eyes*

Things past redress are now with me past care.
William Shakespeare, *King Richard II*

In the pages that follow we place human faces on the facts, statistics, and
labels that others have used to paint one kind of picture of atrocity
workers. This chapter looks specifically at four representative lives from
among the fourteen who carried out unspeakable violence both for their
government and parallel to the government's own security services.

To maintain the anonymity of all interviewees, those included in this
book have been assigned a pseudonym that matches in no way their
own first name. Although we do include the cities and states where
some interviewees worked, we have tried to disguise as much as possible
other biographical information about them. No doubt, some interviewees will recognize themselves in the Portuguese version of this book, but
we do not anticipate that anyone other than their closest work associates
(often equally violent) will recognize them in these pages. We assume
that the violence workers' pasts will in any case keep them from identifying their testimonies to other Brazilians.

Like the fourteen direct perpetrators of violence, of which the four violence workers introduced in this chapter are a subset, each violent life

represents a different "generation" of police work, with two among the four from the military government generation. By examining these generational panoramas sequentially, we have created a documentary picture of some of the men who carried out atrocities in Brazil over a thirty-five-year period. We discovered by analyzing these case studies that this chapter's four violence workers' stories suggest a series of questions that are further addressed throughout this book. How do violence workers manage their secrets about atrocity? How do they account for, explain, and excuse violence work? How do secrecy, training, ideology, and organizational insularity interact to shape, promote, and support violent conduct? How does work in repression create personal and public identities? What physical and psychological impact does violence work have on its perpetrators? This chapter hints at the initial answers to these and other questions that will be discussed in greater detail later.

Generational Panoramas

The recruitment of the twenty-three police who were interviewed for this study (see Chapter 3) can be divided into three historical periods. Focusing specifically on the fourteen men among the twenty-three—the former we label *violence workers*—we discovered that the first "generation" of six among them all joined the Civil Police between the late 1950s and early 1960s. The majority in this generation of violence workers, illustrated in this chapter by Márcio, were policemen for up to seven years before Brazil's military took power.

The second generation of violence workers includes six policemen who joined and carried out their police careers almost exclusively under Brazil's military state. Illustrated in this chapter by Civil Policeman Eduardo and by Militarized Policeman Armando, this group contains three militarized and three civil policeman in all.

Among the last generation of violence workers, illustrated in this chapter by Civil Policeman Ernesto, there were two policemen overall. Both joined their police force after Brazil's military regime had formally ended. Of these violence workers, one is militarized police (Roberto) and the other is a civil policeman (Ernesto).

Among the first generation of violence workers, all but one higher-ranking policemen, the motivation to join the force was a mix of economic need, family ties, and crime-fighting images. Although it might be expected that cold war politics had stimulated the second generation of violence workers to join the police force and fight against "subversion," in fact most of these men saw police work, like those in the generation before them, as merely a form of steady employment, a family occupation, and a way of improving society by fighting crime. The third generation of policemen, which includes two men who grew up under dictatorship, was different in this way from most of those in the two generations of violence workers before them. However, like the others, this postmilitary generation was not initially motivated by a war ideology to join the police, having been drawn to policing by family ties, economics, and citizen protection and assistance ideals.

Police Lives with Violence

Márcio, in the first generation of violence workers, is now retired. At twenty-four, in 1957, Márcio joined his state's Civil Police. There had never been a policeman in Márcio's upper middle-class family. His father, a dentist, and his mother, a housewife, thought that being a policeman was "almost worse than being a thief." But Márcio had come to see the "superior character" of the São Paulo Civil Police during several years as a crime reporter for a major Brazilian newspaper. Wanting to be a part of the Civil Police organization, Márcio studied law while still working as a reporter. After taking a short criminology course and passing competitive examinations, he became a Civil Police *delegado*—a station or regional police chief with a law degree.

His first post was in a small rural town in the interior of his state. Márcio recalls favorably the respect that townspeople gave him, although he disliked the extreme geographic, cultural, and social isolation of the area. Because Márcio believed it essential to remain professionally and socially aloof—"If you get very friendly with one group, the other political boss will say that you're favoring the other political group"—he had almost no friends nearby. With few associates whom Márcio believed he could trust and without a wife, Márcio felt cut off from people most of the time; however, he found some social support from the fact that "back then, there was...a statewide network of *delegados* who helped each other out with information."

Márcio was quickly promoted from this small-town assignment to the capital city, where in 1958 he was made head of the city's notoriously violent civil police motorized night patrols, the Rondas Noturnas Especiaís da Polícia Civil (RONE). Police officials liked and trusted Márcio: he'd interviewed them as a reporter, and they liked his "objective" presentation of their work. These officials apparently believed that Márcio's newspaper experience would help promote a positive image of the bloody night patrols. Over a series of years, Márcio was directly involved with police patrols known for a shoot-to-kill policy and supervised policemen who, both inside RONE and in associated death squads, were infamous for torture and murder.

During Márcio's almost thirty years in the São Paulo State Civil Police, he worked in violent police squads and openly admits to having tortured. He reports having commanded men who carried out violence, including torture and murder. Yet, as we shall see in Chapter 7, Márcio sees himself as a police "professional" who used violence legitimately in the line of police duty. On those allegedly rare occasions when Márcio went too far, this was either the result of his youthful (preprofessional) indiscretion or an instance of something other than torture—for example, psychological "persuasion"—and therefore not unprofessional torture at all.

Among the second generation of violence workers, Eduardo joined his center-west state's Civil Police at the age of nineteen; it was 1968. Rather than becoming a policeman to carry out political repression, Eduardo just took "the first competitive civil service examination to come along, [which happened to be for] a Civil Police investigator." Having just been discharged from the army for health problems, the unemployed Eduardo needed a stable job. A police career was familiar to him because his father was a civil policeman and Eduardo had grown up surrounded by his father's police friends. Although Eduardo's father "wasn't overly supportive" of his son's entering the police, his father "didn't create any problems either."

After studying for six months in day classes at his state's new Civil Police academy, Eduardo was assigned to the Social and Political Police (Departamento de Ordem Político e Social, or DOPS). Political turmoil was growing in Brazil, and Eduardo was to secretly infiltrate the student movement: "I think they chose me because I had a baby face; because I was very young, I could pass myself off as a student." Eduardo, who mostly worked alone, remembers being teamed up with an older policeman early in his career. Looking forward to learning infiltration techniques from this man, Eduardo instead almost lost his life. When students recognized the older policeman, Eduardo and this partner were almost lynched. Resolving that this would not happen again, Eduardo says that he taught himself how to conduct infiltrations. This meant starting out with "missions that required less knowledge, less experience,...and getting experience little by little." Always afraid that he would be murdered, Eduardo nevertheless spent most of his eight years in DOPS "in the midst of the students, listening, going to the campus, and staying there."

Using his cover to promote his own career, Eduardo studied law while investigating student groups. Finding it difficult to concentrate and study, Eduardo began doing "poorly in the law course because [he] traveled a lot." Eduardo remembers that his boss always needed him for out-of-town operations, and Eduardo "never told him 'no.'" This took a serious toll on his law studies, but Eduardo is proud that he was always ready to serve. For having rendered such loyal service to DOPS intelligence, Eduardo was transferred in the early 1970s to an important city. At the university there, while continuing his police work on student organizations, Eduardo resumed law studies. He finally earned his law degree after almost a decade of mixing intelligence missions with academic study.

Recounting his career in intelligence, Eduardo recalls that his police team sometimes interfaced with DOI/CODI, an internal security organization made up of Information and Operations Detachments (DOI), coordinated by Internal Defense Operations Commands (CODI). The DOI/CODI internal security organization was infamous for its torture and murder. Eduardo remembers positively one combined DOI/CODI–DOPS agitprop mission in a small rural town. Eduardo's role was to hang out in a bar and spread rumors that a local high school principal "was a leftist,...immoral,...a homosexual, something like that." Eduardo recalls this as the most tranquil mission he had had up to that point: he could pass time in a bar "where prostitutes hung out." This was "a good mission; the state paid us to drink beer and spread a rumor."

Two years into this life of secret infiltrations and agitprop operations, Eduardo began to recognize that he was drinking excessively. Spending much of his time in bohemian (i.e., prostitution) zones, Eduardo recalls feeling peer pressure to drink because policemen who did not drink were marginalized by their peers. Eduardo believes that the stress of work contributed to his excessive drinking: "When there was a strike, we'd work straight through. We'd sleep, but very little, and go back to work. So we didn't have much time off." Eduardo remembers getting into a lot of fights during that period of constant and stressful work. "I shot at people several times, always drunk during those scrapes." Thus, even though Eduardo maintains that he liked this work, he also developed emotional problems from the risks he took. Eduardo, at the ripe old age of twenty-two, was already suffering from hypertension and insomnia just three years after entering the Civil Police DOPS.

Leading a double life as student and secret police infiltrator did not leave much time for Eduardo to meet a woman and marry. He took up with a prostitute and police informant "from a night-time environment"—the perfect fusion of Eduardo's two personas. He had met his future wife while on DOPS undercover duty, so she knew that Eduardo was a policeman on clandestine missions. It helped that Eduardo did not have to hide his work from her, but Eduardo's marriage still "had serious problems" because he had to work at night and spend many nights away from his wife. She was jealous and did not trust him.

In 1974, with his alcoholism, an intense work schedule, serious unhappiness at home, and a law degree, Eduardo took the examination to become a member of the Federal Police, Brazil's FBI-like police organization. When he flunked the medical examination owing to hypertension and other stress maladies resulting from his life in intelligence, Eduardo became "really revolted and upset." His insomnia increased and his hypertension worsened. Next, Eduardo was nominated for a position in Brazil's important National Information Service (SNI), but he lost this opportunity as well because he had not lived in Brasília for two years. Deeply disappointed, Eduardo spent the next six years on call twenty-four hours a day, seven days a week as an official in the Civil Police's robberies-and-thefts division—known for its violence, including the liberal use of torture, especially to obtain information about stolen cars. Eduardo finally earned the political appointment as chief of Civil Police for an important Brazilian city.

Eduardo, a quintessential police bureaucrat who has learned to keep parts of his various lives and jobs separate, claims that he himself never tortured anyone. In fact, he denies ever even having seen torture and maintains that his "job was just to look for information." Eduardo does not recognize that the information he collected and the arrests his team made often led to his captives being tortured by others. Bureaucratically separating repressive work in a way that divorces him from responsibility for its violent outcomes, Eduardo claims that "we made our report and turned it in to our boss." When talking about the shootings that he took part in, Eduardo allows that much gunfire occurred, but mostly when he was drunk—on or off duty. Situating this violence in the passive voice—it just "occurred"—Eduardo places the murders outside his own direct action. As double proof of his own lack of responsibility for murder, he relegates any residual murders to the action of a different part of his compartmentalized self: some shooting took place when Eduardo was drunk. But Eduardo's boss forgave the mistakes he made off-duty in bar fights. As for the violent work that Eduardo necessarily carried out while on duty, it was legitimated by Brazil's state of war: "We were patriots; we were defending our country," a sweeping ideological justification for any professional violence that Eduardo had to perpetrate. In his explanations of such on-duty violence, Eduardo focuses on his own and his work team's bureaucratically subdivided professionalized *performance,* as if it were without significant moral consequences.

Armando, another second-generation violence worker, joined his state's Militarized Police in November 1964, just eight months after Brazil's military coup. At twenty-one, Armando was taking a preparatory course to enter a university engineering program, but "the police examinations came up," and he reasoned that "by joining the police, [he would] be able to help his family more quickly than if [he] waited five years to become an engineer." Although practicality seems to have dictated Armando's taking the Militarized Police examinations, in fact Armando also remembers that he "really wanted to be in the military: helping people had always attracted [him]." Armando wanted to be "useful to the population." Although Brazil's police had not yet been subordinated to the armed forces, Armando hints at his philosophy of policing by referring to his state's Militarized Police as "the military."

Ranking first in his Militarized Police qualifying examinations, Armando's initial post was an important one. In an elite Shock Battalion organized to operate like a Special Weapons and Tactics (SWAT) team, Armando explains that the battalion's role was to "react to masses, mobs, large tumults, and other such disorders." Thinking like the commander of an invading army, Armando disembodies people into sets of problems to be managed and eliminated.

Like the violence bureaucrat that he was, Armando describes the Militarized Police as having "a hierarchal regimen." Explaining this further, he argues that "a soldier has to obey the hierarchy and the discipline. . . . Whoever has a higher rank in the hierarchy has power." Because of the way that hierarchy dictates a policeman's behavior, Armando asserts that someone in his position could not have taken part in atrocities: "The Militarized Police don't have the mission of interrogating anyone," so they could not possibly torture them. Armando would kill only if it "protected a greater good more than what [would] be lost by [killing]"—a justification that uses "national security" to explain any police transgressions that might have been outside his official jurisdiction.

Armando's prestigious career in Militarized Police operations obviously paid off. Selected toward the end of his police career to head judicial security for a major Brazilian city, Armando then parlayed this high-profile political post into an even more important one. In the early 1990s, he was appointed by the city's mayor—a former classmate from his Militarized Police Academy days—to head the city's Municipal Guard. Armando was to make this civil police force "dynamic by training it along the lines the Mayor wanted." Having headed his own private security business for years, Armando would bring his connections (and allegiance) to private interests to this prestigious new post—a characteristic very common among the following generation of police.

Ernesto, among the third generation of violence workers, joined his state's Civil Police in mid-1985, just months after Brazil's formal redemocratization had begun. Ernesto's father did not want his son to pursue such a career, arguing that he had "spent a lot of money so that Ernesto could go to college...and become a doctor, not a policeman." Having to choose between his birth family's wishes and his own, Ernesto left home. College degree in hand, Ernesto was first assigned as a detective in the Civil Police Robbery Division, where his coworkers gave him instant grief: The older police teased Ernesto ruthlessly, making him the brunt of jokes, playing pranks on him, and "not taking what [he] did seriously." Ernesto found it difficult to develop friends and allies among his colleagues in the division.

Yet apparently Ernesto was an effective policeman, because promotions came regularly. Ernesto describes police work as "being intelligent; it involves using reasoning [to crack a case]." Therefore, Ernesto believes that a policeman should not "mix such things" as emotions and reason: "You shouldn't get emotionally involved in police work." For example, Ernesto admits to having killed seventeen people in the "legitimate line of duty." Yet in recalling each of these, Ernesto says that firing his gun was "instinctive, quick: You don't think too much about making an arrest." Recognizing that each of the seventeen killings ultimately boiled down to "instinctive" action, Ernesto admits that even rational police can be momentarily irrational. However, Ernesto's killings were legal: his was a response to criminals' "acts of resistance" and therefore strictly by the book.

Serving time in jail for having kidnapped and tortured a suspected robber, Ernesto criticizes himself in that case for having demonstrated extreme irrationality. He "captured" a drug dealer and got himself into trouble because he let his anger overcome intelligence. Just the same, Ernesto believes that if a crime is "really horrible"—for example, if someone were to rob his house—he could appropriately use violence out of blinding rage. Such a crime would motivate him to punish the perpetrator—for example, make Ernesto "angry enough to [legitimately] beat him." Describing his arrest of the alleged robber, Ernesto says that he grabbed the "perp," handcuffed him, and threw him blindfolded in the trunk of his car. "Blinded by...hatred, [Ernesto] was going to kill" this perpetrator, so he drove the man to "someplace really dark in the woods, pulled him out of the trunk, and said, 'Now, you're really going to die.'" Ernesto was going to make good his threat—he had the intended victim all tied up—but the police caught him before he could carry out the murder.

Ernesto maintains that he later learned that his supervisor was in the drug business with the criminal he had kidnapped. Knowing that Ernesto wanted revenge against the perpetrator, Ernesto's supervisor must have called the perpetrator's lawyer. Ernesto's supervisor also "activated police in the entire state" to capture and convict Ernesto, a move to protect the supervisor's own reputation and drug profits.

Justifying his sometimes irrational violence, Ernesto explains that he "became very violent, very aggressive on the job" because the situations in which he found himself required this attitude. Ernesto argues that the type of environment in which police live every day "contaminates you little by little without your feeling it." Ernesto also blames the police organization itself for his violence: as a policeman he was "subordinated to an immediate boss" in a "bureaucracy that keeps you from escaping supervision." This is a problem for Ernesto because he does not trust most police officials: when they catch a lower-ranking policeman in an illegality, police officials have a "real carnival," even though they themselves are corrupt. Distrusting ordinary police as well, Ernesto points out that in day-to-day policing, if "the policeman at your side is involved with the corrupt faction that you've bothered, your partner will...eliminate you."

Yet, even through Ernesto lacks confidence in the police system and its hierarchy, he still relies on police bureaucratic criteria for distinguishing between legitimate murders in the line of duty and illegitimate killings that result from blinding passion and are carried out by police who behave like vigilantes. Ultimately, however, according to Ernesto, the system decides if a killing falls into one category or the other—with the majority of the murders that Ernesto committed apparently adjudged to have been "legal...in the line of duty." Indeed, although in prison for attempted murder, Ernesto points out that he is the only imprisoned policeman at his facility who has been convicted of a crime, is still in the police, and has even gotten a promotion while in prison.

Violent Life Themes

Two of the four profiled violence workers—Márcio and Ernesto—chose to become policemen, were educated in law, and were (or became) police officials. Among the other two violence workers discussed here, Eduardo, an officer, entered the police because he was unemployed and he needed a regular salary. Armando, an officer, saw policing as the quickest way to contribute to his family's maintenance and to improve society. None of these four violence workers had been motivated initially to become policemen because of appeals to defend national security or some other "just war" concern. Yet, in spite of their initial lack of political passion, the three violence workers who served during Brazil's military period—Márcio, Armando, and Eduardo—became enthusiastic operatives for the military's national security state. The fourth policeman, Ernesto, who did not enter the police until Brazil had begun redemocratization, became passionate instead about controlling crime.

Three of the four violence workers lacked initial training for their job, learning what they needed to know as they went along. Being thrown quickly and fully into intelligence and operations, these three reported experiencing stress and fear on the job. Involvement in the nonstop pursuit of so-called subversives and bandits contributed to all four violence workers' becoming completely absorbed by their jobs—spending day and night at them, sometimes supplemented, especially in Ernesto's case, by death squad moonlighting.

Although these violence workers remained generally enthusiastic about serving Brazil's government, whether military or democratizing, in three of the four cases the work took a visible toll on their mental and physical health. Nonstop work in repression made interaction with family and nonpolice friends almost impossible. The policemen manifested such stress-related symptoms as insomnia, hypertension, fear, and depression; they suffered marital discord and divorce. These violence workers' stress was exacerbated by an inability to talk about their work with family and close friends. Vociferously rejecting these outcomes in his own case, Armando—who maintains forcefully that the system has not made him "a victim"—says that he was "very conscious of [his] choice[s]." Because Armando "*chose* to leave [his] family...days and nights," he does not see himself as a victim of a system that "robot-ized" him.

Enveloped within a closed system of work that was organized around secrecy, anonymity, and violence, these men lived an almost cultlike existence. They paid allegiance to a distant, seemingly omnipresent, violence-facilitating authority. Their daily lives were mediated by rela-tively faceless officials who fostered and condoned their atrocities—the police, justice, and political officials who gave orders, punished their misconduct, inconsistently defined "acceptable" behavior, and rewarded what served their or the state's interests. In the end, a culture of fear—which the violence workers had helped to nurture and sustain—came to envelop and victimize them as well. Fear and secrecy lubricated the Brazilian state's repressive machinery, shaped the social memory of this historical period, and greatly influenced what we as researchers could learn, as Chapter 4 in particular illustrates.

These realities of Brazil's atrocity system unexpectedly raised difficult philosophical questions for us as researchers: Why study those who have committed unspeakable acts of violence? Would it not be better to ex-amine those whom the system has victimized? Having answered these questions to our satisfaction and dedicated ourselves to studying the perpetrators of atrocity, we then faced a series of even more challenging philosophical and methodological dilemmas. These are elaborated and discussed in Chapter 2.

CHAPTER 2

Reconstructing Atrocity

What's past is prologue.
William Shakespeare,
The Tempest

Countries undergoing redemocratization from military dictatorships—as throughout Latin America in the last sixteen years—have to consider the aftereffects of the state-sponsored torture and executions that had been systematic government practices. In these transitional nations, forgetting as well as remembering has both personal and political dimensions. Those who have experienced an authoritarian past can deal with it personally in very different ways. And how the evolving politics of revived democracies takes up painful memories influences whether the dictatorship's torturers and murderers are simply ignored, receive blanket amnesty, make some general public acknowledgment of their acts, submit individually to a formal commission of inquiry, or undergo judicial trial.

These various courses of action shape personal and political healing among participants in different ways. Blanket amnesty for those who have been in violent security forces may demoralize their victims while providing a political bargain that promotes a stable transfer of power from military to civilian rule. Conversely, punishing atrocity perpetrators too early can be politically destabilizing (Payne 2000b). And human rights investigative commissions and threatened or real punishments can result in the once-violent security forces all the more deeply repressing their own memories (or silencing their own voices) to avoid becoming victimized by their victims.

Moving too slowly with investigative commissions and punishments for human rights violators may suppress or discourage victims' recall of their memories (see Payne 2000a). Indeed, it is likely that the healing process of victims is aided by political trials or any public discussion of wrongdoing by perpetrators of state-sanctioned violence. To be sure, information gained from uncovering atrocities can provide the evidence that victims' families need for obtaining their loved ones' death certificates. This can facilitate burial and personal and familial acceptance of a loved one's passing (see Payne 1999) and begin the process of families' obtaining access to the personal estate, where one exists.

At the same time, publicly exposing past atrocities may block the accused's participation in the new regime, which in most cases is not desired by victims but can be useful for promoting some kinds of political transitions (Payne 2000b). However, such a political bargain must recognize that even confessions before investigation commissions may not lead to perpetrators' transformation into respectable and respectful participants in a more democratic system.

In the end, any of the alternative policies for reconciliation or punishment may suppress social memory in one way or another. However, if the ultimate goal of resurrecting memories about atrocities is to make sure that brutal regimes do not gain ground and flourish in the future and to make clear that those who do a state's dirty work will be held accountable, then the projects dedicated to retrieving and documenting memories of atrocity must continue.

Using memory construction as a backdrop for this chapter's analyses, we begin our discussion of Brazilian state-sponsored torture and murder by addressing the theoretical questions associated with the book's broadest objective—to reconstruct and write social memory about state violence: Do different styles of human rights record keeping and organization influence social memory about state violence? Does the traditional binary distinction between victims and perpetrators influence research participants' memory and shape what is written about atrocity? Does the social and research perception of atrocity workers—as perpetrators or victims—influence how their violence is written about and remembered? Does researchers' moral sensitivity to writing an ethnography of atrocity shape what they write and which facts become public record? Can researchers' moral sensitivity to an ethnography about perpetrators inhibit certain forms of knowledge about these actors' roles in repression?

Thinking about State Violence

It is not just the behavior of victims, perpetrators, and their governments that shapes social memory about atrocity; how scholars and human rights workers conceptualize and study atrocity can influence the content and scope of memory construction as well. Different styles of human rights record collecting and organizing—through statistical stockpiling or narrative storytelling—can shape what a country's social memory becomes in the first place. John Collins (1998), building on the earlier work of Walter Benjamin (1968), explains that each of these traditions produces different patterns of discourse about human violence and that each reflects and creates different systems of meaning about violence.

STOCKPILING

According to our understanding of Collins's framework, stockpiling emphasizes the collection and dissemination of facts about atrocity.[1] As a conscious attempt to pile up statistical information about the present or past (Benjamin 1968; Collins 1998), stockpiling has implications for social action based on the "reality" it creates.

In the first place, it could be argued that stockpiling alone—particularly where state violence is involved—may generate a mere statistical array of abhorrent acts. This inadvertently supports the repressive system's hegemony over the collective memory of its violence. Second, statistical facts about atrocity can make subordinate nonvictims feel impotent through their horror at cruelty against others. These feelings are exacerbated by the apparent implacability of the perpetrators who still live among them, unpunished. The victimizing of some is a constant reminder of what could happen to others. Third, the victims themselves—reduced

1. One of the three anonymous readers of this book argues that Collins meant to use the stockpiling and storytelling concepts somewhat differently than we have employed them. According to this reader, Collins intends "to speak to the issue of raising international attention to human rights abuses, contrasting the importance of numbers of atrocities, photos of atrocities, and other forms of stockpiling for mobilizing international attention [with] 'storytelling.'" This, according to the anonymous reviewer's understanding of Collins, "mobilizes local groups around trickster myths and other struggles of survival." Not only do we not find any great distortion in our understanding of Collins, but we also believe that our discussion has expanded and enriched Collins's existing scheme by pointing to additional ways that these two strategies—whether for raising international attention or for mobilizing oppressed communities—can undermine each of their operational objectives.

to the status of homogenized cases—are rendered relatively powerless by their statistical visibility only as victims. By emphasizing the reality of what power has done to them, stockpiling can further disempower ordinary citizens by formulating into public record—and in the victims' and their fellow citizens' consciousness—the ineffectual reality of their status. In effect, those defined as victims, as well as those who fear becoming victims, may accept their victimhood, making them too demoralized to struggle against any repression that might exist. Finally, stockpiling often reduces the great varieties of modes of repression to a few statistically communicable categories.

As a result of stockpiling's homogenization of violence, only certain kinds of victims and victimhood are included in any collection of data, and only certain categories of perpetrators and victims enter public consciousness—sadistic fiends and hapless innocents. In particular, those who perpetrated atrocity are shielded by their own homogenization into psychologized categories, especially those that link their violence to pathological sadism. This helps to guarantee both the relative invisibility of the indirect facilitators of violence and the structural processes that have given direct perpetrators their power to violate others.

Michel Foucault (1979) suggests this homogenizing of victim and perpetrator in his analysis of carceral discipline. This is the societal structuring of groups not only through physically visible repression—bars, uniforms, guns, electronic surveillance—but also by less visible and less visibly repressive means—statistical accounting and measuring, categorizing, and recording—what Foucault calls "normalizing judgment." For example, statistical documentation transforms the enormous breadth of individual variation into a manageable bureaucratic case record. And when victims become mere cases, they enter a particular "state of conscious and permanent visibility that assures the autonomous functioning of power" (Foucault 1979:201). Foucault's argument is relevant for memory construction through stockpiling. Treating atrocity simply as a set of statistics—as a system of official and academic research and record keeping—transforms the emotional human experience of personal violence into a dispassionate public record of its effects on enumerated subjects. By collectivizing victim status into a few case types, these subjects of repression become more visible than their tormentors and, as such, more politically manageable. Their control is facilitated by their objectification.

As we have said, most stockpiling of state violence makes only, or at least primarily, the most dramatic perpetrators statistically visible. Data collection of this sort seldom gives much more than lip service to

Families of disappeared victims gather at São Paulo's Praça de Sé Cathedral to remember and challenge violence. Twitty Styles, photographer.

the various associated actors in a torture system—high-level state officials who facilitate violence by ordering torture or failing to prevent it. Also hidden in stockpiled records is the faceless but vital role played by the doctors, nurses, notaries, engineers, administrators, guards, and other factotums who keep the system running efficiently. These actors facilitate, disguise, promote, and even participate directly in the violence of the statistically more highlighted and homogenized agents of repression. Focusing only on the most visible "stars,"—who, in fact, are often politically much less powerful than the supporting cast of facilitators—helps guarantee the secrecy, anonymity, protection, and continued power of both those who order and those who support state violence.

Foucault (1979) might argue that stockpiling torture atrocities has the effect of backlighting and thus obscuring the violence of the more powerful individuals. Moreover, by focusing on the seemingly exceptional brutality of a few highly visible people, the larger system of which these actors are a part escapes serious examination and documentation. This fosters the institutionalizing and even perpetuation of the repressive regime's practices by guaranteeing that the systemic nature of its violence remains outside the historical, academic, and journalistic record.

STORYTELLING

An alternative way of reconstructing memory is the storytelling approach, which focuses on how people experience the past by producing social memory out of their own and others' everyday experiences. Storytelling by victims of systemic violence can take the form of sardonic jokes about the powerful or their own ways of coping with violence. Storytelling seeks an "internally circulating narrative of 'getting-by'" (Collins 1998: 11) among those whom stockpilers would designate merely as victims. Collins argues that to overlook the coping strategies of subordinate groups obscures a part of the memory of their day-to-day experiences. This incompleteness can inhibit learning and promote "certain kinds of collective remembering [that] circumscribe the possibility of political resistance" (11).

One product of storytelling research on atrocity is an analog picture of the resistance, struggle, and strategies of survival that the stockpiling statistical tradition overlooks in its digital rendition of reality. Some past storytelling research on those traditionally considered victims has focused on homeless Brazilian youths' organizing themselves for life on the street (Hecht 1998; Rodrigues and Huggins 1999); the poor's modes of struggle for resources and their adaptations to poverty (Bourgeois 1995; Stack 1974); prostitutes' daily coping mechanisms (Cronin 1999; Rosen 1982); how the very ill live with physical deterioration (Frank 1995); the collective jokes of West Bank Palestinians about Israelis (Collins 1998); and the struggles of concentration camp internees (Levi 1995).

Perhaps owing to what Becker (1967) labels "hierarchies of credibility" and Clendinnen (1998) calls the "moral sensitivity exclusion," there has been great reluctance among human rights scholars to conduct storytelling research on the perpetrators of atrocity. Unique among such potential research is the study of Greek torturers by Haritos-Fatouros (2002). Our own research on Brazilian violence workers expands upon Haritos-Fatouros's research.

However, in the process of relating either victims' or perpetrators' accounts about atrocity, there is a danger of overemphasizing resistance and underplaying structural power; the powerful and their subordinate victims may be perceived as relatively equal in a given violent interaction. This can deny organizational power or underplay its socially structured impact. In fact, of course, the personal resistance of subordinates is not politically equivalent to the action of state agents against them. Not only do officials and officers ordinarily have decidedly more power than their victims, but they and their minions can also use political force to structure whether subordinates are able to resist in the first place and whether any resistance is even revealed to outsiders who might attempt to publicize it. In other words, storytelling can involve the ideological downplaying of unequal socially structured power; this may mask the political realities behind the moves and countermoves of the dominant and the subordinate, with the dominant initiating and the subordinate reacting. Because the powerful are in a position to negate, discount, or rewrite stories about others' resistance to their violence, they can structure how such resistance is written about, read, understood, and subsequently incorporated into social memory.

Only when used in harmony do the storytelling and stockpiling traditions contribute the necessary ingredients for the final stew of reconstructing social memory about state violence. Stockpiling uses statistics about victimization to paint the overall horror of atrocity (see Amnesty International 1984, 2001b; Huggins and Mesquita 1995; United Nations Commission on Human Rights 2000); storytelling turns the victims of stockpiling into actors whose accounts point to various direct and indirect forms of subordinate resistance. Although the social memory about victims and perpetrators of state violence is enhanced when the two traditions are used together, even such an integrated approach does not sufficiently grapple with very tough questions about the essence and possibly shifting nature of victim and perpetrator classifications.

Deconstructing Status: Victims and Perpetrators

Memory construction about state violence requires taking a hard look at victim and perpetrator labels. In the first place, much can be learned about victims' positions within the larger torture system by recognizing the relevance of victim status for more than just the immediate subjects of system terror. For example, if *victim* is taken to mean "a recipient of some undeserved harm," then researchers must recognize that many Latin Americans now seen as having been victims of state repression would not have been placed in that category during their nation's dirty war. At that time, it was common in many Latin American countries for state agents and some citizens to distinguish between the innocent victims of systemic terror—who had been mistakenly or unfairly tortured—and the violent activist "subversives" who—as perpetrators of violence against the military state and fellow citizens—presumably deserved what they had gotten. Moreover, it is common today for some police and military from formerly authoritarian regimes to see themselves as victims of truth commissions or as persecuted by human rights groups (see Payne 1999, 2000a). We illustrate in Chapter 11 that many police violence workers in this study routinely assigned some torture and murder victims to perpetrator status; Chapter 4 shows that some atrocity perpetrators defined themselves as victims.

In a more recent example of victim-perpetrator fluidity, people living with AIDS have been divided in the Western world into its innocent victims—heterosexuals, hemophiliacs, and health care workers—and the tainted ones who were infected through their "deviant" sexuality or by "shooting" illegal drugs. The latter set have been just as likely to be seen as perpetrators as victims. Among this group, those who deliberately or through oversight or ignorance have infected others are even explicitly labeled as criminals. Thus, although some victims slip easily into the perpetrator category, the reverse also holds true. There is already a precedent in U.S. law for certain kinds of abusers to be given a lesser penalty when their own abuse can be demonstrated to have caused them to abuse others. All of this demonstrates that there can be crossover or overlapping in such value-laden categories as victim and perpetrator, with various political and moral measuring sticks—often accepted only implicitly—shaping social consciousness about who appropriately belongs in them.

Without excusing the egregious violence of torturers and murderers, the researcher may be better able to probe the range of roles associated with both statuses and thus to document and reconstruct the systemic aspects of violence work by abandoning a strict dichotomy between victims and perpetrators. We argue that restricting the study of atrocity to this traditional binary division may limit research primarily to these two complementary yet narrowly defined statuses. In the process, traditional victims are often atomized, individualized, and rendered passive, while traditional perpetrators—a limited "other" status over and against the victim—are overly empowered. Such perpetrators are seen as qualitatively and morally distinct from victims—and as uniquely and perhaps inherently evil. Seen to be motivated largely by internal psychological and biological factors, the sadistic out-of-control torturer or emotionless executioner is branded a monster.

Yet perpetrators may be more productively understood as sharing in victim status themselves. By studying the victimizing inherent in perpetrator status, as we do throughout our book, other new statuses are revealed along with their supportive relationships with one another—for example, that of violence facilitators who order, train, and assist the perpetrators and the interaction of these primary and facilitator statuses within a larger socio-organizational system that justifies, nurtures, and protects them. Such a broader conceptualization opens the door to seeing "perpetrator" as an *achieved status* that is earned through often-victimizing rites of passage and status degradation ceremonies (see Haritos-Fatouros 2002; Haney, Banks, and Zimbardo 1973). Once the victimizing aspects of perpetrator status are recognized, it is possible to analyze the impact of violence training, and of violence work itself, on its willing and not-so-willing agents. But such an analysis cannot proceed until researchers come to terms with the profoundly disturbing impact of the narrative they will hear.

Listening to Atrocity

How are researchers to listen to violence workers' atrocity accounts? Does skepticism about the ability of perpetrators to be honest, along with real fear of them personally, influence what scholars research and write about? Can the emotionally devastating impact of atrocity stories shape research narratives about state violence? What is the appropriate role for the interviewer who documents atrocity—that of objective observer maintaining distance from subjects and subject matter or of subjective participant in the perpetrator's ethnographic worldview? Failure to address these pressing questions has very probably contributed to the relative absence of careful research on this subject. In any case, these challenges are likely to result in an interviewer's feeling great pressure to remain distanced emotionally, politically, and socially from a violence perpetrator's accounts. The interviewer may resist their storytelling versions of reality, believing it more objective and politically respectable to stockpile their atrocities. Interviewers may assume that an investigation based on interviewee storytelling might raise questions about researchers' methodologies, their findings, and even their values and political loyalties—a less likely outcome in research on atrocity victims. As Robben (1995: 84) points out, there is "more sympathy for unmasking the abusers of power than doubting the words of their victims."

Indeed, in contrast to the permissibility of empathic witnessing in research with atrocity survivors—where an interviewer can accept taking simultaneously the roles of observer and victim (see Gunn 1997) and be morally transformed by such embodied involvement in atrocity survivors' accounts (Frank 1995; Gunn 1997)—the researcher working in this field must solicit the accounts of morally indefensible violence perpetrators. But how can researchers interview and engage in collaborative deep listening (Gunn 1997) with people who have carried out unspeakable acts of violence? Can these perpetrators' memories of atrocity be anything but elaborate justifications for their violence? Can their testimonies be considered credible?

Moral Exclusion

Such questions have kept many scholars from considering any research on violence perpetrators to be legitimate, a phenomenon that Clendinnen (1998) identifies as a "moral sensitivity exclusion." For example, in Holocaust research there is an assumption that even to attempt to understand Nazis is to risk contamination by them (see Clendinnen 1998). Putting this another way, Howard Becker (1967) argues that studying groups labeled "deviant" may evoke the suspicion that the researchers accept the deviant group's illegitimate point of view, placing them in the position of being labeled "biased" or even "deviant" themselves. The assumption behind such charges seems to be that understanding the perpetrators of violence necessitates an acceptance of their actions. This, of course, militates against wanting to reproduce perpetrators' stories: Why would anyone be interested in, and why is it useful to know, how torturers and murderers experienced their bloody pasts? Why are their stories and personal accounts about getting by in the torture system scientifically or even politically useful? Can anything be learned about torture and murder from their coping strategies?

Of course, academic silence about state violence has also been promoted by the power of atrocity perpetrators and their higher-level state-linked associates to keep their violence out of public record and social consciousness. Researchers who seek to tell their stories have been threatened and even murdered. At the very least, memory construction about state violence can be hampered by the resistance of torturers and murderers to disclosing their secrets, as our study will shortly demonstrate.

Yet, although researchers must continue to pressure the powerful and their associates to talk about the state-sponsored violence they ordered or committed, it is equally important to recognize and challenge the implicit research assumptions and processes that silence researchers and encourage their producing some kinds of memory over others. Researchers must select a strategy for studying state violence—stockpiling, storytelling, or a combination of these. They must eliminate the binary categories of victim and perpetrator and come to terms with the moral sensitivity exclusion that encourages some actor's voices and eliminates others'. Finally, researchers must consider how implicitly held beliefs regarding who should be considered credible shape hearing and writing social memory about atrocity.

Hierarchies of Credibility

A socially constructed and implicitly accepted hierarchy of credibility presupposes that "in any system of ranked groups, participants take it as given that members of the highest group have the right" to be believed (Becker 1967: 241). Their versions of reality are considered objective and legitimate; these become official public memory. In contrast, the memories of groups situated socially and morally lower in the hierarchy of credibility—particularly when these actors disagree with official versions of reality—are considered less believable. The result is that the stories of lower-ranked deviant groups are disparaged and usually omitted from supposedly legitimate reconstructions of social consciousness. Ironically, in the case of state-sponsored violence, it is often only the accounts of a few sacrificed lower-ranked violence workers that enter into public memory. The upper-level facilitators who order and promote torture and murder, and sometimes even carry it out themselves, are able to manipulate and control the definition of truth so that any information that threatens their secrets is labeled "illegitimate" and "against the national interest." Researchers need to recognize that a complicated set of silences is fostered by traditional assumptions about credibility and truth.

The relative lack of storytelling scholarship on violence perpetrators (see, for example, Conroy 2000; Huggins and Haritos-Fatouros 1998; Johnson 1997; Payne 1998; Scully and Marolla 1984) or on the victimization inherent in perpetrator status (see Haritos-Fatouros 2002) makes storytelling information about perpetrators very useful for fleshing out social memory about state violence. The study that follows, based on interview interactions with Brazilian torturers and murderers, relies primarily on storytelling to discover how police carried out torture and executions and then coped with what they had done. In the process, we learned that documenting violence workers' atrocities involved mediating identities and secrecy—a process including both interviewer and interviewee, which began with the secrecy that often delayed or totally blocked securing police interviewees for this study, as our discussion of methods in Chapters 3 and 4 illustrates.

CHAPTER 3

Locating Torturers and Murderers

Recipe for rabbit stew: first, catch one rabbit.
old cookbook recipe

Preparing for this project a year before our research began, we decided that the sample should include police who were known to have engaged in torture or murder. In the field it became immediately clear that this "wish list" would be exceedingly difficult to obtain. The potentially easiest group to identify, those listed by human rights groups and who had been denounced by their victims, were the most resistant of all to granting an interview. Having been exposed for their atrocities, with many still vehemently denying them just the same, these men did not want to participate in any project that might further increase their and their family's pain.

Although Brazil had granted amnesty to known official (e.g., military and police) torturers and killers, we knew of no official public list of those who had applied for or received amnesty. And because of their distrust of any researchers and of the government itself—suspecting that some new regime might take action to hold them retroactively responsible for past deeds—even the amnestied torturers and murderers would not identify themselves by confession or other self-revelation. These former agents of Brazil's national security state just wanted to put this part of their lives behind them.

However, we knew that most police atrocity perpetrators had not even used the amnesty process. Because their secrets about violence had been hidden successfully for over a decade and given the statute of limitations on murder, for example, twenty years—with many having carried out their summary executions only ten or fifteen years earlier—some police perpetrators of atrocity could in theory still be held liable for their homicides. At the very least, they feared that human rights groups might find out and publicize their admitted past misdeeds. In either case, they would be turned into victims by a system that they had once (albeit under a different government) loyally and honestly served.

To overcome these stumbling blocks to locating torturers and killers, we designed a method for finding these police indirectly. This included employing an organizational strategy, identifying regional targets, and selecting imprisoned police. We assumed that potential interviewees who had been in the police during Brazil's military period might be more likely than those who had not to have committed atrocities. This led to our initially limiting the sample to those who had been in a police force during the period from 1964 to 1985. Within this group, we attempted to locate interviewees who had been in units known to have carried out the heaviest repression, including torture and murder. Such units included the Social and Political Police (DOPS), Civil Police criminal investigations units (e.g., the Division of Crimes against Patrimony [Departamento Estadual de Investigações Criminais, or DEIC] in São Paulo), the Civil Police homicide and property crimes divisions, Civil and Militarized Police motorized patrols and SWAT and riot teams, and the Militarized Police intelligence division (P-2). We also sought police from the special operations and intelligence squads that combined Civil Police, Militarized Police, and the military itself (e.g., Grupo de Operações Especiaís [GOE], Operação Bandeirantes [OBAN], and the Information and Operations Detachments and Commands [DOI/CODI]). We reasoned that someone who had been in any of these violent units would have either himself committed violence or been present when such violence had taken place—in other words, would have been at least a silent participant in, or a witness to, brutality, torture, and murder.

A complementary strategy for securing police who had tortured or murdered was to locate potential interviewees in Brazilian regions that had experienced the greatest political repression. These were, in particular, Brazil's south-central cities of São Paulo and Rio de Janeiro, the southern city of Pôrto Alegre, Recife in the northeast, and the federal capital Brasília, in the north-central region.

Finally, suspecting that those who did not identify strongly with their police organization might talk more openly about violence, we sought interviews at a special section of a Rio de Janeiro prison for convicted militarized and civil police—although its roughly two hundred and fifty inmates very seldom had been incarcerated for having tortured or murdered during the military period. Nevertheless, our assumption (whether accurate or not—see the following section) was that being in prison, these police might feel that they had little to lose by speaking about the violence they had committed. State prison officials seemed to consider the incarcerated police so discredited by their conviction that they apparently did not feel threatened by our conducting interviews.

Assembling the Sample

Our final sample was assembled according to the previously mentioned criteria through a "snowball" technique. In each target city, the snowball began with the Brazilianist interviewer's contacts with academic police specialists, criminal justice professionals, and Brazilian police themselves. Having taught classes or delivered public lectures on comparative policing—for government personnel and at Brazilian universities—in which at least half of the students or other auditors were from the Militarized or Civil Police, the Brazilianist researcher had a ready pool of potential contacts and of interviewees themselves in each city. After each interview, according to the snowball design, an interviewee was asked to suggest other police—usually his close friends or colleagues—who might participate in our study. Through the confidence established by an interviewee's having already met professionally or heard a lecture by the Brazilianist or just from having been interviewed, the interviewer was able to get introductions to other prospective police interviewees. Regardless of the strategy used to create an interviewee sample, it was common for several interviews to be conducted before a suspected torturer and murderer was uncovered. However, after locating one of these violence workers, the interviewer was sure to ask that person to suggest at least one police colleague with whom he had worked closely.

Several factors influenced whether an interview was secured and how it progressed. It is very likely that the primary interviewer's gender, insider knowledge, professional status, class, color, and temporary residence in Brazil—the latter making her a cultural outsider—combined to help secure some interviewees and to produce among them some greater openness and some silences. Because most of the interviews were conducted by one woman, with not enough interviews conducted by the other researchers (one male, one female) to use them as a control group, it is difficult to assess exactly how the Brazilianist interviewer's personality and gender alone influenced the male interviewees' willingness to participate in the study or to talk openly about their and others' atrocities. The Brazilianist female interviewer suspected that some interviewee information came more slowly and perhaps with more concern for her "feminine sensibilities," as defined in Brazil, than would have been the case if she had been a man. For example, the relative absence of graphic descriptions of scenes of torture or murder may have resulted from the male policemen's belief that a woman should not hear such things. Yet, at the same time, being a woman may have actually led to her being seen as more forgiving and nurturing, thus possibly inviting interviewees to disclose emotions about their violence that they might not have shared with a male interviewer. But no matter how much the interviewees may have attempted to shelter the female interviewer, they still disclosed a great deal about many aspects of their human rights atrocities, with such success possibly based on several convergent factors of the primary interviewer's status.

For example, the primary interviewer's academic knowledge about policing, both in Brazil and elsewhere, may have made her work easier. As a police specialist, Huggins has noticed that in a variety of cultural settings, if those interviewing police are recognized as insiders—with police themselves, of course, being the most legitimate of such insiders—the interviewer will be more readily accepted by prospective police interviewees. Although an academic specialist on the police may not ever be a real insider, having this status to at least some degree seems to have been perceived by the Brazilian police interviewees as preferable to being a total outsider. Just the same, the primary researcher's being a woman studying a predominantly male institution may have still limited how much she could ever be a full occupational insider, whatever academic knowledge of policing she could demonstrate to interviewees.

The fact that the interviewer was primarily academic clearly opened some doors: at least half of the interviewees remarked that they would accept being interviewed by the researcher because, as an academic, she was objective and journalists and human rights activists are not. This greater trust in university interviewers was also encountered by Payne (2000b) in her research on Latin American participants in violent "uncivil movements." Nevertheless, as we shall illustrate in Chapter 4, if an academic is willing to use journalistic exposé methods, information can be gained that value-free academic research might not be able to secure—which is precisely one reason why interviewees said they did not trust journalists. We did not employ such methods, selecting instead more ethical and subtle interview strategies.

The Brazilianist interviewer, being a university-trained expert and social superior and also assumed to be a "wealthy foreigner," was accorded some positive social distance and much respect. Such class and status combinations may have, on the one hand, spared her from hearing some unpleasant things and, on the other, given her entrée—as one of the powerful and respected—into other kinds of information.

Color differences and concomitant Brazilian definitions of relative respectability very likely also structured interviewer acceptability and interviewee openness. Although much of Brazil's population is black, in fact, all but two of the interviewees (neither of them atrocity perpetrators) were white or light-to-medium brown. It is not clear how the color difference between interviewees and interviewer affected interview outcomes, but the interviewer's Anglo whiteness—in a sociocultural system that values light skin and associated physical characteristics above darker skin colors—may have added to the primary interviewer's presumed higher-status position relative to interviewees. However, the impact of such a difference in and of itself on interviewees' willingness to participate in the study and their openness during the interview itself is not entirely clear.

The fact that the interviewer was not Brazilian and therefore would be taking her interview disclosures away to the United States very likely did contribute to interviewees' openness. Although the interviewees were assured that the authors would not use their real names in their book, it could have increased interviewees' confidence that before any book could be written, the researchers had to spend a good deal of time in their own countries, rather than staying in Brazil and possibly coming into contact with journalists or human rights activists who would want their information immediately. In other words, the interviewer's status as a limited cultural outsider may have made interviewees more willing to open up to her.

In the end, it is our assumption that a combination of characteristics associated with the primary interviewer's status—being female, foreign, an academic whose work was known to some prospective interviewees, of a higher social class, and of a socially valued skin color—helped the primary interviewer secure interviewees and promoted somewhat greater willingness among them to disclose valued secrets about their and others' police atrocities. Much like a bartender or beautician, the primary interviewer took the role of a friendly stranger. As such, she was very likely seen as relatively unthreatening, and interviewees felt that they could disclose their feelings, complaints, and deepest secrets with relative security that the interviewer would keep their confidences. Whether such assumptions were accurate, believing them apparently led interviewees to open up in ways that they might not have otherwise. Thus, although we cannot assess in the end exactly how gender, insider occupational knowledge, status as an academic, the combined variables of class and color, and the Brazilianist interviewer's position as a cultural outsider influenced interviewees' willingness to be interviewed and shaped the amount and types of disclosures they made, clearly the combination of these factors positively determined interview outcomes—an assumption supported by the wealth of important disclosures in this book. However, as Chapter 4 explains, an absolutely crucial factor that structured interview outcomes was the interviewers' skill at penetrating the overall dynamic of secrecy.

Interview Procedures

Secrecy powerfully influenced how much we told prospective interviewees about our research objectives. For example, our initial explanations to interviewees about this research were true though necessarily incomplete. Knowing that the majority of prospective interviewees would not grant an interview if we began by stating that we were studying police torture and murder during Brazil's military period, we told them that we were conducting a comparative study about policemen's lives in times of conflict and crisis. This was indeed the case. We further explained that we were examining the careers of Brazilian police who had been in service at some time between the 1950s and the 1980s. This, too, was correct because our study required information from the periods before, during, and after the military regime about interviewees' personal lives, education, police recruitment and training experience, daily work, and career changes.

Each interview took at least three hours of face-to-face interaction. In two cases, the interviewee who agreed to a second round was interviewed for another three hours or so. Only after we had established rapport with a police interviewee, usually some two hours into the interview itself, did the interviewer ask directly about a policeman's involvement in brutality, torture, and murder. Even then, these subjects had to be handled with great care or the interviewee would stop the interview. Twenty interviews were conducted by the first author in Brazilian Portuguese, and three by the non-Portuguese-speaking authors through a translator. All interviews were tape-recorded. An American anthropological linguist and professional translator then transcribed the twenty-three tapes, translating nineteen of them into English; the remaining four tapes were later translated by a bilingual language specialist. All translations were checked by the Portuguese-speaking author against the original interview text. For each interviewee there were between 25 and 35 double-spaced pages of English-language text, about 600 pages in all.

Violence Worker Demographics

Of the twenty-three police in the final interview sample, fourteen showed solid evidence through their interviews or reliable supporting materials of having been torturers or murderers. Among these direct perpetrators of atrocities, eight were civil police and six were militarized police (Table 3.1). The civil police—with some men holding several operational positions simultaneously or sequentially—included two from the DOPS political police, one of whom had been a prison warden; two others who had been members of special police squads—RONE and Rondas Unificadas de Departamento de Investigações (RUDI); several had worked in intelligence units; and one had been in a death squad. Among the six militarized police, some of whom also held multiple statuses, one had been in the national DOI/CODI; two had been in a death squad; one had worked in Militarized Police Intelligence (P-2); and two had been members of the GOE special operations squad.

Among the nine atrocity facilitator interviewees—used for comparing the training and the organizational and social-psychological factors that may have shaped atrocity—eight were still on their Militarized Police Force; the one civil policeman had retired (Table 3.2). The civil policeman had been jointly attached to the SNI; all but one militarized policeman was rank-and-file.

From a sample of twenty-three police, with fourteen of these being atrocity perpetrators, we recognize that caution must be exercised in making generalizations. Yet, at the same time, as small as our sample is, it represents a larger number of torturers and executioners than most prior studies have located and interviewed. At the very least, therefore, because of its

TABLE 3.1. Violence Worker Sample

Pseudonym	Force	Year Entered	Selected Characteristics		1993 Status
			Other Forces	Position	
Armando	Militarized Police, Metropolitan Police	1964	SWAT, GOE	Officer	Head of his city's Municipal Guard
Bernardo	Militarized Police, Federal Police, Civil Police	1967	Operations, Intelligence	Rank-and-file to officer	Civil Police official
Bruno	Civil Police	1961	DOPS Operations, Warden	Rank-and-file to officer	Civil Police official
Eduardo	Civil Police	1968	Operations, Intelligence	Rank-and-file to officer	Civil Police official
Ernesto	Civil Police	1985	Operations, Intelligence, death squad	Detective	Imprisoned (but still in police)
Fernando	Militarized Police	1963	SWAT, GOE, Intelligence	Officer	Militarized Police official
Ignácio	Civil Police	1959	Operations	Rank-and-file	Rank-and-file
Jacob	Civil Police	1971	Operations	Rank-and-file	Expelled and petitioning for amnesty
Julius	Civil Police	1956	RONE Operations	Officer	Retired
Jorge	Militarized Police	1980	Operations, DOI/CODI	Rank-and-file	Imprisoned
Márcio	Civil Police	1957	RONE Operations police chief	Officer	Retired (heads police consulting firm)
Roberto	Militarized Police	1987	Investigator, death squad	Rank-and-file	Imprisoned
Sérgio	Civil Police	1957	DOPS Intelligence, death squad	Officer	Retired
Vinnie	Militarized Police	1964	SWAT, death squad	Rank-and-file	Imprisoned

TABLE 3.2. Facilitator Sample

| Initial | Selected Characteristics | | | | |
	Force	Year/Entered	Other Forces[a]	Position	1993 Status
A.	Militarized Police	1964	None (R)	Rank-and-file	On force
I.	Militarized Police	1980	None (R)	Rank-and-file	On force, member of FENAPOL
L.O.	Civil Police	1964	Intelligence (SNI)	Investigator	Retired
L.U.	Militarized Police	1968	None (R)	Rank-and-file	On force
L.U.C.	Militarized Police	1967	Militarized Police psychiatrist	Officer	On force
M.	Militarized Police	1963	None (R)	Rank-and-file	On force
M.E.	Militarized Police	1983	None (R)	Rank-and-file	On force, member of FENAPOL
O.	Militarized Police	1964	None (R)	Rank-and-file	On force
P.	Militarized Police	1963	None (R)	Rank-and-file	On force

[a]Other forces: None = no other forces than one assigned; (R) = assigned to routine street policing; (SNI) = Brazil's National Intelligence Service

larger size and more in-depth examination of subjects, our police sample can cast new light on the dynamics associated with carrying out and legitimizing state-linked and -sponsored atrocities. Moreover, when combined with studies from other cultures and historical periods, our research on Brazilian police atrocities gains a more general comparative scope.

This said, however, we must still ask how an interviewed policeman's organizational position—still on the force, retired, expelled, in prison—may have influenced his responses. An easy assumption might be that those no longer in policing talked more openly about their own and others' atrocities and that the manner by which each man left the police—successfully retired or expelled—would make him less or more negative, respectively, about the institution itself. Looking at Table 3.1, we see that among the fourteen atrocity-perpetrating policemen interviewed, eight were no longer in a police force: three had retired; one was in prison but had not been stripped of his police badge; three others were in prison and expelled from their force; and one, having been expelled from his police organization (but not in prison) was petitioning to reenter his police force. The other six atrocity perpetrators were still working policemen.

Among the nine atrocity facilitators, in contrast, eight were still working policemen and one had retired. In addition, two of the working atrocity facilitator policemen were members of the dissident Federação Nacional da Polícia (FENAPOL) Militarized Police movement that was challenging that police force's violence.

The question is how an interviewee's status as a working policeman, a working policeman and a dissident, a successful retiree, or a prisoner might influence his testimony. Will police still on the force be less open and more positive about their pasts? Will they distort or withhold more information to protect their own positions and maintain their institution's code of silence? Are imprisoned police so disgruntled about the "justice" that they received that they will tell everything or even exaggerate the violence of their police organization? In other words, are those who identify personally and positively with policing more likely to have held back information or to have tried to deceive us?

Although we can never fully know the answers to these questions, we did note great reluctance among all interviewees, whether in the police, in prison, or retired and whether direct perpetrators or facilitators, to disclose their secrets as well as those of their organization. Indeed, whether interviewees were positive or negative in their evaluations of policing, they were still very reluctant to talk about the institution's or their own violence. The degree of that reluctance depended on their relationship at the time to policing. For example, the police who talked most consistently and openly about atrocity work tended to have moved farther away from their prior police identities. For example, Jorge, an imprisoned born-again former DOI executioner, wanted to be interviewed about his past because he now saw himself as "a different person under the Lord." Vinnie, expelled from his Militarized Police force and also incarcerated at the time of his interview, was somewhat guarded about his participation in hundreds of death squad executions. Ernesto, an imprisoned policeman who was nevertheless still on his force (and looking forward to returning to active duty), felt betrayed by the police officials who had gotten him arrested but liked the work itself. Ernesto explained bitterly that he wanted to talk about his death squad murders because, even though "the police institution's heads—higher echelons— are generally corrupt themselves, they won't accept a policeman being caught making a mistake," referring here to Ernesto's having kidnapped a suspect, thrown him tied up in his car trunk, and then taken the man out on a dark road and threatened to kill him.

The policemen whose names were on human rights groups' published lists of known torturers and murderers were simply unwilling even to be interviewed. Most of these men, successfully retired, certainly had reason to feel abandoned by a police institution that had failed to come to their defense against human rights groups' and journalists' "persecution" of them. They self-censored their disclosures about violence because, having already experienced public exposure as well as socially and sometimes even professionally negative censure for their actions carried out on behalf of the earlier military state, they did not want to risk the new problems that could emerge if their interview became public. This was so even though they were assured that their real names would not be revealed.

Interestingly, we found that the two members of FENAPOL—the nascent social movement that encouraged open criticism of Militarized Police organizational behavior—were very willing to grant an interview but not necessarily equally willing to talk openly about police violence in general or their particular role in it. One was extremely open about the institution's violence, whereas the other was visibly afraid to talk about it.

Among the direct perpetrators of violence, the largest subset —nine violence workers—still defined themselves within the police institution, even though three of them had long since retired from policing. The violence workers who identified with the police (as well as eight of the nine atrocity facilitators) all cloaked their discourse about violence in subterfuge and metaphor, transforming the information that they pos-

Name	Police Organization	Specialty
Sérgio (São Paulo)	Civil Police	DOPS intelligence official
Bruno (Pôrto Alegre)	Civil Police	Intelligence/warden
Fernando (Rio de Janeiro)	Military Police	Police official/ intelligence

FIGURE 3.1. Known Torturers and Killers

sessed—and that the interviewer wanted to hear—into a commodity of exchange, discussed in detail in Chapter 4.

Discovering Violence

Given the reluctance of interviewees to talk directly about police torture and murder, we developed four associated and alternative indicators of their involvement in such violence—an indirect method for "outing" those who had committed atrocity and therefore for distinguishing direct perpetrators from facilitators.

The first indicator was whether we found a policeman's name on a Brazilian human rights group's list of known torturers (Figure 3.1). An individual's name being on such a list meant that he had been a defendant in an internal military trial against him (see Archdiocese of São Paulo 1998; Weschler 1998), or that he had been identified publicly by former victims or their families. By comparing our list of interviewees' names with human rights groups' lists of known atrocity perpetrators, we discovered that three of the fourteen direct perpetrators whom we interviewed—Bruno, Fernando, and Sergio— were on such lists. However, these lists include only a portion of all torturers and murderers from Brazil's military period.

A second indicator (Figure 3.2) of a policeman's involvement in torture or murder was a statement to that effect by an interviewee's associate, either another interviewee or a police colleague. This usually took the form of one interviewee asserting that his friend—another of the interviewees—had been involved in "political repression"—code in Brazil for having participated in violence. Eight of fourteen interviewees were identified in this way, including two of those already identified as torturers by human rights groups.

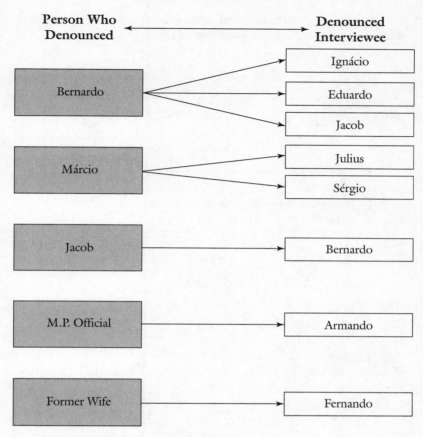

FIGURE 3.2. Denounced by Colleagues or Family

The third indicator was a network analysis of each interviewee's personal and working relationships with denounced torturers, murderers, and murder organizations. In our network diagram (Figure 3.3), an organization that engages in torture and murder is represented by a triangle; an interviewee, by a square; and a previously documented torturer or killer, by an elongated circle. The rationale for linking an interviewee to a denounced torturer or murderer or to a murder organization, in descending order of association, was (1) the interviewee's claim to have worked as a superior, peer, or subordinate of such a person or organization or (2) his calling a known torturer or murderer a "friend" or (3) his expressing respect for such a person as a police agent. Rather than each of

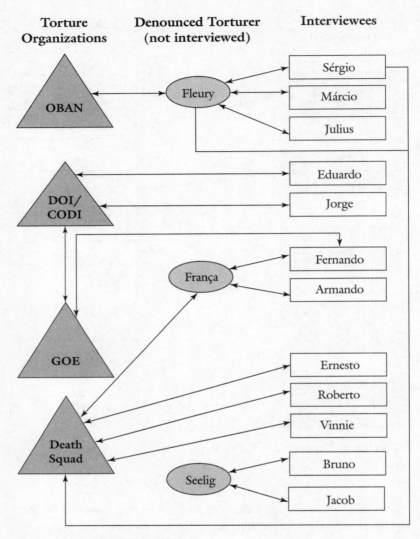

FIGURE 3.3. Network Analysis

these indicators producing a separate set of torture associates, they usually overlapped: an interviewee who had worked with a known torturer (or his organization) usually admired him and considered him a friend. According to our network analysis (Figure 3.4), twelve of the fourteen direct perpetrators had close involvement with torturers or killers or with a violent organization—from supervising them or working for them, to

Violence	Person	% Involved*
1. Torturing	Jacob, Sérgio, Eduardo, Márcio, Ernesto, Roberto, Bruno, Ignácio	57 ($n=8$)
2. Killing	Jorge, Márcio, Jacob, Ernesto, Roberto, Vinnie, Julius	50 ($n=7$)
3. Using excess violence	Sérgio, Fernando, Eduardo, Márcio, Ernesto, Roberto, Bruno, Bernardo, Ignácio	64 ($n=9$)
4. Seeing torture	Jacob, Sérgio, Eduardo, Márcio, Ernesto, Ignácio	43 ($n=6$)
5. In group that tortured or killed	Jorge, Jacob, Fernando, Vinnie, Roberto	29 ($n=5$)
6. Commanded group that tortured or killed	Márcio, Sérgio, Julius, Fernando, Bernardo, Armando, Eduardo	50 ($n=7$)

*Does not total to 100 percent because some interviewees fall into more than one category.

FIGURE 3.4. Violence Committed

being a close friend and associate, to respecting a known torturer or his organization.

The fourth and most direct indicator of involvement in torture or murder was the number of acts and the types of violence that an interviewee himself admitted having carried out (see Figure 3.4). Eight of our fourteen-subject subsample admitted to having tortured; seven said that they had killed; nine indicated that they had used "excess" violence in performance of their duty; six reported being present when torture had taken place; five admitted having been in a group that tortured or killed; and seven said that they had commanded a group that had tortured or killed.

Remembering and Recounting a Painful History

Exploring the rich and varied interviewee testimonies about Brazilian policing in general and about violence in particular, we will examine several themes in subsequent chapters: What is the role of secrecy in securing violence workers' collective memories? How is state-sponsored police violence historically situated in Brazil? Is one kind of police masculinity more associated with atrocities than others? What is the role of training, work, and social environments independently and relatively in shaping Brazilian torturers and murderers? What are the violence workers' socially constructed moralities about their violence? What is the long-term impact on the perpetrators themselves of carrying out sustained atrocity?

We probe these questions from the underlying assumption that state-sponsored torture and murder in Brazil cannot be easily reduced to an act of deviant psychology. The violence that is rooted in state mandates and policies is both the result of and more than the acts of numerically aggregated individual direct perpetrators—whether these actors are sadistic or not. We invite readers to draw their own conclusions about perpetrators and facilitators of violence, beginning in the next chapter with how interviewees managed their secrets about atrocities.

CHAPTER 4

Deposing Atrocity and Managing Secrecy

I am forbid to tell the secrets of my prison house.
Ghost in William Shakespeare, *Hamlet*

Any research on political violence runs into too many skeletons to handle, too many closets to inspect.
A. Robben, "The Politics of Truth and Emotion among Victims and Perpetrators of Violence"

Beginning with Armando's testimony, we examine secrecy as a process that involved researchers and violence workers. Seeing secrecy as an interaction that includes a person who has something that another person wants, we illustrate how shared memory about atrocity was jointly constructed within an economy whose valuable currency was secrets. Recognizing that memory could not be created until the dynamic of silence that controls both researcher and interviewee was penetrated, we became part of a secrecy interaction that contained four elements: initial security measures, espionage, entrusted disclosures, and post hoc security precautions. The interviewees used security strategies throughout the interview to protect sensitive information and personal identity and to guard against our efforts to secure secrets; the interviewers used espionage of a sort to penetrate their defenses. In giving over their secrets, violence workers utilized entrusted disclosures of information to structure the interviewer's understanding of their testimony. Post hoc security precautions were employed to neutralize the researcher's negative impressions of an interviewee. The product of this interview process, a jointly assembled account about state-sponsored violence in Brazil, grew out of a process of "research bargaining," as this chapter illustrates (see Beck 1970; Geer 1970; Habenstein 1970).

Armando's Secrecy Management

Armando, the militarized policeman-turned-municipal guard whom we met in Chapter 1, was a case study in secrecy management. He vacillated during our interview between being guardedly defensive—communicated through body language, voice tone, and the content of his responses—and employing a series of discursive devices that distanced him from atrocity. In most cases, Armando couched answers to our questions about his violence in vague terms that neutralized its impact and meaning: "There was nothing serious...a few slaps on the head." Or he advanced by-the-book legalistic explanations about violence that made police misconduct appear administratively impossible—military policemen "cannot by law conduct interrogations," so they could not possibly have tortured. At other times, Armando resorted to outright prevarication: "It is possible that a member of [my GOE] group had *that type* of [torture] conduct...but I have no record of any such conduct." Armando also engaged in outright denial: "Torture never happened in my group."

In the end, the sheer number of Armando's distancing strategies made it impossible, on the basis of the interview alone, to label him a substantiated torturer or murderer, a situation that frustrated us as interviewers because we had reasonably strong suspicion that this man's career had involved extensive violence. Attempting to elicit more information about Armando's past so that we could probe more indirectly his possible involvement in violence, we explained that violent policing can victimize those who must use it. Armando's angry response was "I can't say I'm a victim of that [repressive police] system," a reaction we thought best handled by not openly challenging it.

Armando's past was more clearly revealed at dinner with the state's commander of militarized police, a man who had been Armando's colleague for decades and who had secured an interview with him for us. He told us that Armando had been deeply involved in repression. The militarized police commander's candor about his colleague's dubious career raised a question: why would one police official tell us that his former colleague, now also a high police official, had carried out extreme violence? The commander's openness turned out to be a lesson in how the sheath of police secrecy can be penetrated. Normally, the police code of silence would have led this commander to shield Armando's past from an outsider's prying eyes. Instead, the politics of police appointments in Brazil opened a window into our interviewee's secrets.

Armando—after almost three decades in his state's Militarized Police—had been appointed as police chief for his city's Municipal Guard, a civil police force but not the Civil Police itself. The Municipal Guard answered to the city's mayor, Armando's friend and boss, who was himself a political rival of the state's governor. The governor had appointed Armando's Militarized Police colleague, the Brazilianist interviewer's dinner partner, to command the state Militarized Police, which is superior jurisdictionally to the Municipal Guard. Note the addition of another layer of secrecy to an already enmeshed system of silences: we cannot disclose the state or city where these men were working without making their identities known. The politically competitive nature of these two men's police positions, within the context of Brazil's fiercely partisan and personalistic politics of loyalty, made breaking the code of silence possible for Armando's rival. However, this informant still remained sufficiently guarded about his colleague's past to make his disclosures seem not to fully violate the police secrecy code, while in fact being incredibly revealing for us.

Excavating Secrecy

As Armando's interview illustrates, personal or social memory cannot be reconstructed until the dynamic of silence that controls both researcher and interviewee has been neutralized. For the researcher, this requires becoming conscious of both interviewee and interviewer identities that can reinforce certain kinds of silences. For example, if a violence worker is to speak truthfully about his career, he must be willing to become public, at least to the interviewer, about his past deeds. This often means squaring past violence with the current sociopolitical climate and the interviewee's own, usually changed, status (Huggins 2000a). At the same time, the interviewer must be conscious of bearing witness to atrocity and recognize the ways that in working to expose atrocity, an interviewer can inadvertently promote an atmosphere of silence and secrecy. As Chapter 2 argued, moral sensitivity to difficult topics can keep researchers from pursuing or probing atrocity testimonies in the first place. The pain of listening to these histories can lead interviewers to distance themselves emotionally from such material. And hierarchies of credibility can make the assertions of violence workers appear illegitimate. Together, these factors can lead interviewers to silence violence workers' stories and censor their atrocities.

Our strategy for breaking the secrecy surrounding state-linked violence, a method we call "deposing atrocity,"[1] involves an intentional play on words. It suggests simultaneously the two meanings of *depose*—in legal terminology, "to testify," and in political terms, "to remove from a position of authority." Accomplishing the first version of deposition leads the interviewer to solicit deponents' explanations, justifications, and accounts of atrocity—getting them to testify about what they have done, how they did it, and why they carried it out. To accomplish this, deposing atrocity also requires overthrowing the authority of secrecy that silences interviewer and interviewee. For the interviewer, this is facilitated by taking the role of an "onlooker witness," a phrase we coin to indicate that the researcher is simultaneously inside and outside the interviewee's account. As Robben (1995: 84; see also Nordstrom and Robben 1995) argues, ethnographers "need to analyze [violence perpetrators'] accounts and be attentive to [ethnographers'] own inhibitions, weaknesses, and biases [in order to] better understand...both victim and victimizer." Using onlooker witnessing to depose atrocity leads a researcher to mediate between two pairs of research conditions—listening without accepting, empathizing without condoning—a process that begins with an interviewee account that raises questions about the interviewer's own identity. One example of such a reaction is that of a young child who for the first time sees her father use physical violence against her mother without them knowing that their daughter is watching. The child feels fear, a loss of innocence, and betrayal. She does not fully understand these feelings and cannot easily and openly communicate them. She recognizes at least subliminally that she cannot speak openly about what she has seen. For her to testify to this event requires breaking a web of externally mediated and self-imposed secrecy that might neutralize her current identity. If the system of identities bound up with her positive relations with others in her family and the world around her is to be maintained and her image of the identities is to be linked with and protected by it, she must remain silent. Once the interactive and reinforcing nature of secrecy has been recognized and its silences penetrated, an onlooker witness can then move from fostering secrecy and silence to conducting an archaeology of memory. But for both interviewer and inter-

---

1. We wish to thank Tom McGee for suggesting this term to explain the process of interviewing perpetrators of extreme violence.

viewee, deposing state-sponsored torture and murder is still likely to elicit painful introspection. The interviewer clearly needs to get interviewees to talk about torture and murder yet may not be ready emotionally for the sheer cumulative negative impact of accounts about such violence. In addition, she may not anticipate her own deep unease or voyeur guilt when a torturer or murderer implicitly or explicitly communicates that the interviewer should not be hearing what is being said.

Nevertheless, as Caruth (1995: 7) points out, traumatic events can be fully witnessed "only at the cost of witnessing oneself." For example, one interviewer in this study was moved to question her own moral position for seeming to accept the policeman's moral claim that he was better than the "real" torturers because he only watched the violence, doing nothing more than snapping pictures of a man being tortured on the "parrot's perch." Should the researcher have challenged this policeman's fictional identity construction? Does listening without objection or comment to a murderer's accounts of violence suggest implicit or even explicit support for those acts? Because deposing atrocity involves, at a minimum, establishing the interviewee's trust, what are the ethical and moral meanings for interviewers of having gained an atrocity perpetrator's confidence and approval? In a process of research bargaining to secure secret information, where an interviewer must successfully demonstrate what Habenstein (1970) calls "harmlessness"—the interviewer's own and the interviewer's assessment of the interview material itself—ample opportunity exists for an interviewer of atrocities to question her own moral stance. Where interview material is about atrocities committed by an interviewee or by a police interviewee's colleagues, does promoting a climate of harmlessness connote acceptance of such behavior? Whatever the correct moral and philosophical answers to these questions, one thing is clear: as an archaeologist of memory, the interviewer must become an onlooker witness to accounts that evoke surprise, disbelief, and revulsion and that encourage silences. The researcher must deal with these realities while faithfully and accurately recording all that is said for later retelling.

Managing Secrets about Violence

For the interviewee whose atrocities are being deposed, the exposed nerve of his violence is best protected by shielding it from public view. Georg Simmel (1950) has thus appropriately pointed out that secrecy is more than something hidden—a product to be concealed—it is a *process* that is set into motion once a secret exists. Implicit in this process is that secrecy involves something that others want, making secrets into a medium of exchange within a secrecy economy. Or, as Simmel puts it, secrets are "inner property": what has been obscured has exchange value (332). Secrecy structures the relationships between participating actors by "mediat[ing]...between the person who has [a secret]...and the person who does not" (345). For example, in this study, as an interviewee manipulated secrecy to protect himself against his violent past, the interviewer sought and used symbolic capital to penetrate and purchase the deponent's valued secrets. Robben (1995) calls one aspect of this give-and-take (or sometimes cat-and-mouse) game "ethnographic seduction"—where an interviewee uses affability to lead the researcher away from the research focus. Such seduction has to be successfully dealt with if the interview is to continue, with identity modifying consequences for both interviewer and interviewee.

In this study, the secrets being hidden, deposed, and seductively guarded were embedded within formal organization. A particular reason that police organizations are so very secretive, according to Harris (1961), is that they are defensive "bureaucracies." Lacking informal, interactive support from the community, police must "psychologically, emotionally, and intellectually seclude themselves from their environment" (24). Police organizations protect their secrets from outsiders through a series of strategies—from oaths to physical punishment. Most commonly, however, group members are socialized into "the art of silence"—they learn the value of "guarding one's tongue" (Simmel 1950: 349). As Jacob, a very violent civil policeman, explained, in his early days on the force he had to learn to "see things and keep quiet" because most of the policemen on his team "were able to kill anybody as easy as 'click, click,'" suggesting that violence within police organizations helps to regulate behavior. In any case, it was Jacob's uncle, a district police official, who had taught him "to avoid working with some...guys," to avoid "seeing something that [he] shouldn't see." Jacob learned to navigate the daily pitfalls of policing by separating his police colleagues into two morally distinct groups: "That guy...is a very dirty one; the other one is a very good guy"—a categorization that violence workers also used to dehumanize victims and maintain a positive self-image.

With this distinction in place—and promoting himself as one of the good guys—Jacob could effectively explain to himself and the interviewer his presence during torture. Even though Jacob "didn't agree with" what was happening during a torture session, he reported that he did not leave the room while his colleagues were torturing a prisoner on the parrot's

Torture victim on a "parrot's perch," police station, Pôrto Alegre, Brazil. This photograph was taken by interviewee Jacob, who says he "only" watched as colleagues tortured their suspect.

perch—a device from which a victim is hung upside down by the knees from a horizontal pole with the wrists bound like the legs of an animal to be slaughtered while water is forced into the mouth and anus and electric shocks are applied to various sensitive parts of the body. Perhaps because Jacob claimed not to have agreed with what was happening, he was able to justify his having snapped photographs of a man tortured to death in this manner without feeling negatively judged by the interviewer. Jacob did not consider himself part of the torture session, and his colleagues apparently were not concerned about his presence there because nobody talks about what they see. Even if "they go to jail and are condemned,... policemen do not talk. It's a kind of secret agreement."

An important reason police do not disclose their organization's secrets is because all secrets, and the relationships that compel them, are embedded in the secret holders' shared self-identifications. Revelations about institutional secrets would wash away the shared exclusivity of their knowledge; this is the social glue that maintains their institutional structure, group solidarity, and associated identities. According to Simmel (1950), secrets are well kept because a group held together by them becomes invalid once the secret is revealed. Thus, when a community's secrets are exposed, there is a loss both of community and of self. Helen

Lynd (1958) would add that shame—which she identifies as visible identity loss—isolates those whose secrets have been discovered and shatters the individuals' trust in the dependability of their immediate social world and the people in it. Such actors then feel "blind-siding shame," realizing that they have "acted on the assumption of being one kind of person, living in one kind of surroundings, and unexpectedly, violently,...discover that these assumptions are false" (35).

Secrecy as Exchange

The interviewer archaeologist of secrets must recognize that the interview process includes real and fictional identities on the part of both participants. For example, interviewers cannot be all that they are and expect interviewees to give them what they want; interviewees cannot disclose everything that they were and are and still maintain their coveted hidden identity. Recognizing this, the interviewers became conscious of the interview process itself. By studying its dynamic, we discovered four elements that made up the interview's secrecy exchange, a set of processes that have in fact been identified by others working in similar domains. The first of these is the security measures used by an interviewee to protect his secrets. For example, the secret holder may refuse to interact with anyone who wants access to secrets or may delay giving them over until the other's bona fides have been established. In response, the person in search of a secret uses espionage, the second element, including finding what the secret holder wants to exchange for partial or complete revelation. This, in turn, encourages the secret holder to use the third element, entrusted disclosure, to structure how a secret is disclosed, understood, and distributed. Finally, the secret holder uses the fourth element, post hoc security measures, to soften the effects of disclosure—as in using discourse that neutralizes shame, guilt, or punishment or that incorporates the other person into the secrecy process. For example, one torturer trainee-turned-murderer in our study, after telling about the killings he had committed in a notorious DOI/CODI murder squad, suddenly began looking for some poetry he had written. After presenting it as a gift to two of the interviewers, he continued to explain the violence he had committed. He had briefly deflected attention from his bad side and used gift-giving and the social reciprocity associated with it to incorporate the interviewers into his more positive side, an illustration of ethnographic seduction.

Because perpetrators of violence have a personal and political stake in making the researcher adopt their interpretations, seduction is particularly prevalent in research about violence, as the following narrative demonstrates.

INITIAL SECURITY MEASURES

Because secrets are social resources, secret holders have some power over those who want their information. This was illustrated in various ways during our interview process. For example, some prospective interviewees—most commonly the publicly denounced torturers—protected their secrets by outright refusal to be interviewed. Although these men do not appear in the final sample, they illustrate how those with dangerous secrets attempt to protect their pasts and hide in the present. One common security strategy employed by police denounced by human rights groups as torturers and executioners was to deflect attention from themselves by pointing to their colleagues' supposedly more important evil deeds. For example, one known murderer from Goiás, in Brazil's west-central region near the federal capital of Brasília, refused to be interviewed about his own past. Instead, he offered the names of other police to interview, claiming that unlike him, they had engaged in "political repression"—that is, they had carried out gross human rights violations. Although pressed by the interviewer and her Brazilian colleague to grant an interview, this former Militarized Police death squad leader continued to refuse. As his family observed these negotiations from behind the counter of his luncheonette shack, the man's wife walked over to his side, next joined by the couple's two teenage daughters and finally by the man's adult son. In the end, this former policeman's family was standing around him like an encircling wagon train in an effort to keep out dangerous outsiders and to offer him tangible support for maintaining secrecy.

Frustrated, on the return trip to Brasília the researcher asked her university colleague, a former journalist, how Brazilian print and television media have so successfully secured testimony from several high-profile torturers and murderers. The woman responded that TV reporters employ methods that social scientists cannot ethically use. Arriving with cameras running, they inform a prospective interviewee that they already have, and are ready to use, the full story of his violence. They offer the interviewee an opportunity to tell his own side of the story—off camera—or they will tell his story their way, using the man's name and photograph. If he cooperates, the man can present an image of an honest and repentant man, with his anonymity perhaps guaranteed.

Another well-known denounced torturer who would not grant an interview, a former DOPS policeman, is on at least two Brazilian human rights groups' lists. From Recife in the northeastern state of Pernambuco, this man had been known by the Brazilianist interviewer in the mid-1970s when she had conducted research at the prison where he was warden. When the interviewer contacted him in 1993 to set up an interview, the former prison warden claimed initially to be "too busy." He promised to call the interviewer the following week and make an appointment—literally, "Don't call me, I'll call you." When no call had arrived several days into the following week, the interviewer called the prospective interviewee again. He then asked when the interviewer was leaving town. When she said at six on the following Sunday morning, he set his interview for nine on the Saturday evening just before her departure. The policeman never showed up: outfoxed by the reluctant interviewee, the interviewer would be gone early the next day, and his secret would remain vaulted.

A denounced torturer from Pôrto Alegre in Rio Grande do Sul State agreed initially on the telephone to be interviewed but claimed that he needed his wife's permission because his family had "suffered a great deal" from human rights groups' denunciations. After giving the prospective interviewee the requested time, the interviewer again telephoned over several days at the times this man himself had proposed. A different family member answered each call and indicated that the policeman was not at home. After a week of trying to locate the former civil policeman by phone, the interviewer abandoned hope of an interview. The wife and adult children of this infamously brutal torturer had skillfully managed to secure his silence.

Julius, a former civil policeman who had headed a police team infamous for murder, actually granted an interview, albeit one very much mediated by his family's presence. In this case, the interviewer was met at the door to his apartment by his wife, a lawyer who had herself worked for the Civil Police. Julius's wife took charge by introducing her husband—even though he had already talked with the interviewer over the telephone—and the couple's twenty-year-old daughter. The family and the interviewer chatted socially in the living room for thirty minutes until the interviewer, with a cab waiting outside, urged that they begin. Julius's wife directed everyone to the dining room, where each family member took a seat at a different side of the large rectangular table. Not long into the interview, the interviewee's oldest daughter—a professional psychologist—arrived and took a seat next to her father. The family never answered questions for Julius, but his wife leaned forward or made eye contact with her husband when questions moved toward police violence. She seemed to be silently policing this former policeman's admissions.

Just the same, each time that Julius requested the tape be turned off, he revealed a good deal about his violent work. In addition, much additional information about Julius's violence in the RUDI operations squad was given by his former Civil Police colleague, Márcio, who had been interviewed a week earlier and had referred Julius. Urged to give additional information about his own violent past, Márcio had employed the security measure of offering up the history of Julius, whom he maintained had committed much more violence than Márcio during his police career.

ESPIONAGE

Even to merely secure accounts about a policeman's violence, and especially to go beyond them into his more deeply held secrets, the interviewers had to engage in espionage. Therefore, while a violence worker searched for security mechanisms to manage the interview and maximize his control over revelations that could cast him in a negative light, the interviewer tried to discover something to exchange for part or all of a secret (see Tefft 1980a, 1980b). Within this secrecy-espionage dynamic, both interviewee and interviewer implicitly negotiated for what the violence worker knew and the interviewer suspected was being hidden. This fostered the interviewer's search for ethical ways of securing what a violence worker was reluctant to disclose. Because money or other material goods would not be exchanged for information, the interviewer had to come up with ethical forms of what Pierre Bourdieu (1977) has termed "symbolic capital." Such capital, which could be exchanged for an interviewee's secrets, included continually reminding interviewees about the importance of their insider knowledge of policing, this rare opportunity to contribute to an understanding of Brazilian police, their chance to provide information into the role of violence work in its agents' own victimization, and the importance of their personal history to the history of Brazil.

Another, more subtle, form of symbolic capital was for the interviewer to acquiesce in interviewees' digressions, including listening to long autobiographies and unfocused self-analyses: by allowing an interviewee to adorn some part of his answer—usually to questions about violence—in a way that was seemingly off the subject, the interviewer could purchase the trust necessary for securing other secrets later on. Or as Robben might explain, by allowing an interviewee to use seduction—that is, employing "personal defenses and social strategies...[that lead] astray from an intended course" (1995: 83)—we set the stage for securing secret information in the future.

However, at first it seemed that allowing long digressions would never take us back to the person's hidden stories. Indeed, Simmel (1950) argues that the function of symbolic adornment is to distract from the hidden. Yet, rather than an interviewee's adornments wasting the interviewer's time, they signaled that she had come close to the most precious secrets. It therefore became clear that interviewees' digressions were really a form of entrusted disclosure that allowed the interviewee time to structure a response that would diffuse responsibility for the violence being acknowledged. In other words, an unexpected consequence of interviewee seductions was to give the interviewee time to regroup, not simply to lead the interviewer away from a threatening subject. In turn, as we have said, these digressions were transformed by the interviewer into symbolic capital.

For example, Márcio was initially asked if he could have tortured a captive or if he had seen others torture, rather than being directly asked about his own involvement in this violence. The good faith earned through these indirect questions became symbolic capital for asking more direct questions at a later point. However, an exchange with Márcio illustrates that even when an interviewer finally tackled questions about violence, it was still necessary to deal with the subject of torture more or less indirectly. For example, when the interviewer asked, "Could you torture someone?" Márcio responded:

M: As a rule, anyone who works in a police station [could]...

MH: But could you?

M: When his boss doesn't keep an eye on things, he is able to torture.

MH: I don't understand, "When his boss...?"

M: If his hierarchical superior says, "I don't want any torture here,"...and his boss leaves but every once in a while goes in early in the morning or late at night to see how the prisoners are, that makes it hard.... Anybody torturing there is going to have a serious problem.

MH: And couldn't you torture?

M: I didn't understand you.

MH: Speaking of yourself, could you torture someone?

From this point, Márcio went on unhindered for one-and-one-half more pages of transcribed text, talking around the subject and avoiding answering questions about his own involvement in torture, never talking about it in the first person. His disclosures indicated, at most, that torture was something that just happened or that other people did. Yet after Márcio's trust had been more firmly established by giving him permission to digress for several more minutes, the interviewer began asking more direct questions about his involvement in torture, finally asking point-blank, "You haven't answered my question: Have *you* used torture?" Márcio's response was "I think at the beginning of my career I did some torture. Let me remember...only at the beginning." Even then, Márcio continued to distance himself from this violence by turning the process (a verb) into a noun (torture) rather than stating that he had directly tortured someone. The object—victim—of torture was almost completely omitted from Márcio's discourse.

For Márcio, talking even indirectly about torture removed some of his prior reluctance to deal with the subject. In fact, as Simmel (1950) has noted, every secret contains a tension that is dissolved at the moment of its revelation. Thus, once Márcio had admitted—albeit indirectly and conditionally—that he had done "some torture" at the beginning of his career, he began speaking much more freely about this violence while continuing to refer to torturers categorically—"they," "he," "we"—instead of assuming direct personal responsibility ("I") for torture. Such discourse helped foster the invisibility of his violence by placing responsibility for it on a large group of nameless and faceless others, apparently allowing Márcio enough security to admit having carried out violence himself as a member of that group.

ENTRUSTED DISCLOSURE

While evident throughout an interview, entrusted disclosure usually manifested itself right at the beginning. Interviewees would routinely engage in up to thirty minutes of general discussion about their personal life in general. We in fact encouraged this through questions about childhood, schooling, and family. In turn, an interviewee usually asked extensively about the study's purposes and outcomes, even though these had already been explained. The subtext for these extensive preliminaries was for the interviewee to establish an appropriate meaning context within which interviewers were to interpret the interviewee's accounts. The anthropologist B. L. Bellman (1984: 68) identifies this initial stage of secrecy interactions as "pretalk"—a "preface to formal discourse" during which the secret holder establishes the ground rules for interpreting secrets. This is akin in linguistic exchange to establishing common ground.

Violence workers often used their pretalk to size up the interviewer and set the terms for an interview. In one case, the interviewer was asked to promise not to publish anything in Brazil for three years and never in any case to mention the interviewee's name. In another case, two interviewees actually requested (but did not receive) monetary payment for an interview. One said that he needed a thousand dollars to produce an art exhibit about police and military repression. The other claimed that his information was so potentially threatening that he would not be able to remain in Brazil after the study's publication. Although this man, Jacob, finally agreed to be interviewed without payment, he still claimed that he could not discuss the most inflammatory facts about his police service unless he was given an airline ticket to the United States. Because he never received a ticket for having participated, some information presumably remained inaccessible, although much pertinent information was ultimately disclosed anyway.

With their ground rules in place, interviewees disclosed their secrets in a way that maintained the secrets' exchange value—giving each one over only indirectly or disclosing it in bits and pieces, not as an explicitly articulated whole. Such indirect disclosures, presented as "deep talk," take the form, according to Bellman, of "talking in a roundabout way about something." Deep talk, which "allud[es to] but never directly discuss[es the] event in question" (Piot 1993: 357), uses the language of metaphor to communicate things that are hidden. This involves "analogical description that refer[s] to meanings other than those contained in the [verbal] narrative" (Bellman 1984: 60).

Among our interviewees, entrusted disclosure's metaphorical phrases were most common in accounts about torture itself. For example, violence workers seldom used the word *torture,* selecting instead such indirect vague language as "that type of conduct," "doing these things," "committing unnecessary excesses," "that conversation with our prisoners," "committing mistakes," and "conducting research...and looking for data." Or they would admit to having carried out what they considered lesser and more acceptable forms of violence such as "slapping... and punching him around a little" and "hanging him up there." Besides these common rhetorical distancing mechanisms, interviewees' narrative deep talk commonly used subjunctive clauses: "If I were to..."; generalized indications: "It sometimes happened that..."; passive tense: "violence was committed;" and other such linguistic devices to deflect attention from their own involvement in violence (see Cohen 1993).

We discovered that the violence workers' metaphorical narratives about torture and murder took one or more of five forms: (1) diffusing responsibility into organizational, social, or cultural contexts: "In Brazil they are used to this kind of behavior—like torture. The Catholic Church tortured people for years and years"; (2) portraying perpetrators as *uniquely* bad apples: "The police who are more identified with [torture are] very cold by nature,...very aggressive"; (3) demonizing victims: "They were tortured because they were stupid," "thieves and assailants...deny things so cynically that if a policeman...doesn't have a certain balance, he'll slap him around a little"; (4) advancing a just cause to explain their violence: "We worked as if at war. We were patriots... defending our country.... We were a religious people, a Christian people"; and (5) cloaking violence in professional and organizational mandates: "To kill [properly], you can't [just] react...you have to act with reason." Decoding this metaphorical deep talk meant examining omissions, contradictions, characterizations, legitimations for violence, and ascriptions of responsibility—with any personal responsibility on the violence worker's part usually denied.

Indeed, even when a violence worker occasionally assumed personal responsibility for his actions, they were often presented as if carried out by a separate and distinct professional self—what Robert J. Lifton (1986: 419) calls "doubling" the self—a "division of the self into two functioning wholes" such that one side is violent and the other is not. Lifton's work focuses on Nazi doctors who attempted to neutralize personal culpability for their violence by allocating authorship to a separate professional self that had seemingly exclusively carried it out. In a modification of Lifton's idea for our interviewees, we argue that they were compartmentalizing their actions by linguistically dividing themselves into a personal and business side. There was nothing personal about torture: "I was only doing the business of policing." As one violence worker put it, "I don't use...violence outside the standard of my conscience.... I'm a conscientious professional. I know what to do and when to do it."

Some interviewees used this discursively created compartmentalization of the self to diffuse responsibility for torture to a generalized group of professional personas: "There's torture in the specialized Division of Crimes against Patrimony [the DEIC]," but it was only used there "when there was certainty that a person had committed the crime and he was refusing to say where he'd hidden or sold the articles involved in the crime." A violence worker who made a moral distinction among different police professional selves, Jorge—the former DOI/CODI murder team operative—argued that as a murderer he had been "softer...very sentimental," very different from his colleagues in torture teams who were "objective, cold people." Likewise, Roberto made a distinction between his controlled professional self and the irrational older police who also carried out violence: "Even though new [to the death squad], I was controlling myself; the other men [in the death squad] were very nervous and agitated, ready to kill the individual right then and there."

Sounding like pure and simple prevarication, such discourse in fact illustrates how interviewees shaped entrusted disclosure to try to influence an outsider's view of the professional who appropriately carries out torture and murder. Violence workers used such explanations to neutralize the possible negative image of their past conduct, a post hoc security measure. In the process, we as interviewers learned something about what violence workers considered a culturally acceptable explanation for atrocity.

POST HOC SECURITY

All people need to sustain a sense of integrity and self-worth. When that image is threatened or lost, post hoc security measures are enacted. This involves devising ways of correcting or neutralizing information that could damage an interviewee's (and others') positive image of himself. For example, one violence worker allocated responsibility for torture to a policeman's immaturity or to a policeman's having followed orders. This helped him dilute the publicly identity-shattering effects of disclosing information about his own involvement in torture. Another police official, after reporting on the torture that he had carried out, claimed that he had not been alone in committing such violence; it was the act of a group, "the machine" to which he had been attached. Presenting himself as one among many nameless young policemen, this man advanced an account of his violence that portrayed it as having been controlled by a few "immoral" police officials.

Sociologist Irving Goffman (1961) might point out that such post hoc security will become more prevalent when a person is unable to effectively sustain his line during an interview. For example, two different policemen—after each had revealed his part in repression—started to cry, temporarily interrupting their narrative and the interview itself. Their post hoc security measure involved reestablishing face by placing the interviewer in the helper role: Bernardo, a Civil Police official who now heads a police amnesty organization, thanked the interviewer, explaining that the interview had been like "a strange catharsis" in which he felt torn between wanting to talk about his former work and feeling "strangely forbidden" to do so. Ernesto, an imprisoned civil policeman who had been in a death squad, stated emotionally that no one had ever been interested in his life and work; our interest made him feel better—while also fearful about his past. We had in fact designed the three-hour interview to explore a host of personal issues besides violence work in order to manifest our interest and curiosity in the policemen's lives and careers.

The unexpected outcome of this interview strategy was the power dynamic that it established. By sharing his discomfort with the interviewer, Ernesto incorporated her into his narrative. And by encouraging Ernesto to continue, the interviewer was validating her incorporation into Roberto's "face maintenance." With this dynamic in place, the interview moved forward toward discovering more of Bernardo's memory through a new collaborative synthesis between interviewer and interviewee, a form of research bargaining. A much more dramatic example of a disruption requiring post hoc security and resulting interviewer-interviewee collaboration in narrative construction came during an interview with the former prison warden, Bruno. At the time of his interview, Bruno was subdirector of Civil Police for an important southern Brazilian state. This man, on a Brazilian human rights group's list of known torturers, stated numerous times during the interview that he had never been involved with torture or any other such violence. Bruno alleged that he could not have been because he had been warden of a prison outside the urban area. (This was an unlikely alibi because many facilities for political prisoners were in just such regions precisely because of their isolation and relative security. Bruno may have assumed that the interviewer did not know this.)

In any case, the day after Bruno's interview, he arrived midmorning, two hours late, to drive the interviewer to the Civil Police Academy. In a sweat on a cool day, highly agitated, smelling of alcohol, and on the verge of tears, Bruno stated that the interview had left him nervous, upset, and depressed. He said that his life was falling apart: his marriage was failing, his job was boring, and he had no reason to live. When the interviewer asked what had happened, Bruno said that looking at his present life through the eyes of the past had made him wonder who he is today. This created an ethical dilemma: Bruno needed help, but the researcher could not tell his colleagues at the Police Academy what he had shared with her. The problem was resolved when one of Bruno's colleagues confided that Bruno had "been very upset and troubled" for some time. Bruno's colleague had already intervened to get his friend psychological help. It was not the interview disclosure that had precipitated the emotional turmoil; it had merely refocused it.

Goffman (1961: 18) might argue that Bruno—having been "caught out of face" by the interview—where "strong feelings...[had] disrupted [his] expressive mask"—had been left "in a state of ritual disequilibrium or disgrace." By sharing this distress with the interviewer, Bruno was making "an attempt to reestablish a satisfactory ritual state," in part accomplished by explaining that "the interview both upset [me] [interviewer's fault] and made [me] feel better [interviewee's gain]." This disclosure implicitly invited the interviewer to facilitate in Bruno's face maintenance, with the outcome that Bruno's image of himself as a good policeman would be anchored in a process that at least implicitly required the interviewer's participation in Bruno's social construction of reality. Naturally, reinforcing Bruno's view of himself produced several interrelated problems for the interviewer: Was it proper for her, even if only implicitly, to support a torturer's construction of a persona that hid, underplayed, or neutralized his atrocities? Was this torturer's testimony sufficiently important to warrant the researcher's becoming part of, and therefore promoting, his fictional identity? Was the researcher likely to compromise research ethics by her awareness that a failure to support Bruno's identity narrative could suspend the interview itself?

Whatever the answers to these questions, it was quite clear that once the interview equilibrium had been reestablished—with this troubled torturer's identity implicitly validated by the interviewer—he was able to talk more openly about his past, without feeling such an immediate threat of losing face. By inviting the interviewer to validate his grief about his soiled identity, Bruno was able to reassert control over the interview and his narrative. In other words, the disruption—caused by Bruno's temporary loss of dignity and its restoration by the interviewer's lending credibility to Bruno's narrative persona—had been used by Bruno to strengthen his control over himself, the interviewer, and the narrative.

Through a depositional dynamic of ethnographic seduction and research bargaining that involved interviewees' initial security precautions, our espionage measures, interviewees' entrusted disclosures, and post hoc security measures, interviewers and interviewees created a jointly constructed memory about state-sponsored atrocities in Brazil. It is our hope that the moral costs of this process may be outweighed by the prophylactic, preventive information and insights gained from our research. Ironically, however, this is one of the same arguments used by the torturers and murderers to legitimize their violence as being for a just cause, as Chapter 11 will illustrate.

CHAPTER 5

Biography Intersects History

Neither the life of an individual nor the history of a society can be understood without understanding both.

C. Wright Mills, *The Sociological Imagination*

The authoritarian history of Brazil that the interviewed police helped to create and sustain began officially with the Brazilian military's overthrow of President João Goulart on March 31, 1964—promoted and supported by the United States (Black 1977; Parker 1979) and bolstered over time by generous U.S. support for Brazil's military and police (Huggins 1998). Even though some interviewees had entered police work several years before and others did not join their force until after military rule, most of the twenty-three interviewed police spent the better part of their careers in that cold war political system.

In this chapter, we recreate that historical period by weaving the biographies of several violence workers into it. Through this process, demonstrating C. Wright Mills's premise that neither personal nor social history can be understood without comprehending the relationship of each to the other, we begin to place Brazilian atrocity within the political and social dynamics that nurtured, supported, and excused it.

Policing Brazil's Coup

Promulgated just nine days after Brazil's military coup, the new military government's first repressive Institutional Act (April 9, 1964) included a

63

number of authoritarian features. It rescheduled for later Brazil's November 1965 military-run presidential elections, drastically reduced congressional powers and transferred Congress's legislative responsibilities to the military executive, abolished a long list of civil rights, and set conditions for canceling individuals' political rights for ten years—the *cassação*. Government repression widened between mid-1964 and late 1966 as General Castelo Branco—Brazil's military-appointed president—launched the countrywide Operação Limpeza (Cleanup Campaign) to eliminate "subversives" from federal, state, and local political, military, administrative, police, and judicial systems (Dulles 1978). This "moral rehabilitation," aimed at removing supporters of ousted President Goulart from elected office and public service, involved scores of arrests and dismissals of politicians and government personnel. Up to 10,000 civil servants were banished from office, 122 military officers were forced to retire, and 378 political and intellectual leaders were stripped of citizenship rights, prohibiting them from holding electoral office or even voting for ten years (Black 1977; BNM 1986).

In the streets, where police and military dragnets carried out the cleanup, there were broad searches and seizures and mass arrests. By the end of the first week after the military coup, more than 7,000 people had been taken into custody in Brazil (Black 1977). After another three months, as many as 50,000 people had been arrested (Alves 1985). *Time* magazine (Brazil: Toward profound change 1964) estimated conservatively that during a single week in early April 1964, at least 10,000 people had been taken into custody—4,000 just in the city of Rio de Janeiro itself.

Jorge, a murder team operative who joined Rio de Janeiro State's Militarized Police in 1979, remembers that at the age of six or seven his own family became the victim of such a *limpeza*—ironically the same kind of repression that Jorge himself would one day carry out as a murder operative for Brazil's military government. Jorge recalls the raid on his family's house in Rio de Janeiro's Tijuca neighborhood:

We were sleeping when the door [was pushed open].... They didn't knock on the door.... It was that traditional Brazilian raid: kick in the door with everybody armed; invade the house. They turned everything upside down, looking for papers and books. They handcuffed my father in front of us and beat him.

Jorge's mother, raped by the soldiers, was in terror that she would be murdered then or later. She assumed that her husband, who had been taken away, was killed.

Jorge's father, a French national and alleged subversive, in fact ended up in Rio's infamous Barão de Mesquita torture facility; he remained there for six months of torture until his deportation to France as an "undesirable." Jorge never saw his father again. His mother, unable to bear the trauma of her own rape and her husband's abduction, suffered an incapacitating stroke; the last straw had apparently been when she found out that her husband was going to be deported. The military government's child welfare officials ruled that Jorge's mother "no longer had the psychological capacity to raise [her children]." Without family to care for them, in 1965, Jorge and his three siblings were placed in one of his state's Federação Estadual do Bem-Estar Social do Menor (FEBEM) orphanages—the overpopulated and physically brutalizing facilities where youth are treated more like convicts than children. Each sibling went to a different orphanage, with their names changed and their paternity erased from official documents. Jorge's mother was issued a new "birth certificate [that erased] her marriage, [making her] a single woman" without children. The military's *limpeza* had completely eliminated Jorge's family and set the stage for institutional socialization of the orphaned children.

In FEBEM, Jorge was violently shaped into conformity by the institution's repressive military regime. Its youthful inmates wore uniforms, participated in drill exercises, and followed a strict daily timetable. Children who transgressed FEBEM rules were beaten with clubs, whips, belts, or sticks. Jorge remembers "torture [as] the method they used for punishment...you got the shit beat out of you. They forgot that we were simply kids." At sixteen, Jorge ran away from FEBEM: "revolted" by the treatment he was receiving, he traded the routinizing violence of the orphanage for a freer but even more precarious life on the streets. Jorge returned to FEBEM after two years on his own because, according to this violence worker, FEBEM graduates were offered a choice in their compulsory military service: Jorge wanted to go into the army— ironically, the same organization that had erased his family's existence just over a decade earlier.

After his two years of army service, in 1979 Jorge joined Rio de Janeiro's Militarized Police, moving very quickly into DOI/CODI, the infamous police/military torture and murder organization that had been established in 1970 by the military to centralize, coordinate, and carry out the regime's war against subversion. As a DOI/CODI murder operative, Jorge would take many of his captives to the Barão de Mesquita torture facility for interrogation, the same place where his father had been detained and tortured. As the philosopher George Santayana has warned, "Those who do not remember the past are condemned to repeat it." Yet, in fact, as we shall see in later chapters, when Jorge and other violence workers remembered the past and tried to slow its progress into the present, the system of repression's speeding engine threatened them and their families with death for even questioning its course.

Protest and Violence

In the mid-1960s, as FEBEM was shaping Jorge into a predictable and loyal violence worker, Brazil's military government was expanding and deepening its control over the wider society. The Second Institutional Act (IA-2), announced on October 26, 1965, declared the military executive's right to rule without congressional consent. Direct presidential elections were replaced by military-controlled indirect ones. The Third Institutional Act (IA-3) of 1966 replaced scheduled direct gubernatorial elections in eleven states with indirect ones overseen by government-controlled state assemblies. If state assemblies did not act as Brazil's military president desired, recalcitrant legislators faced *cassação*, the loss of political rights for ten years.

Protests in Brazil's Congress and in the streets spread as Brazil's military continued eliminating civil and political freedoms. The military responded to civil disobedience by closing Congress. This, in turn, spawned a citizens' movement urging the withholding of votes for candidates of the military-controlled political parties. Most channels for legitimate citizen dissent had been blocked by Institutional Acts and the new authoritarian constitution, which gave the president ultimate jurisdiction over "national security affairs." Law 317 of March 1967—popularly known as the Police Organic Law—placed each state's regional and municipal police forces under the state's secretary of public security. By then, he had become a military appointee, although not necessarily from the military himself.

Under Law 317, each state's secretary of public security would clarify and tighten the jurisdictions of the two main state police forces. The Militarized Police were to be responsible for all uniformed "ostensive" (first-response) street policing—their traditional role—and the nonuniformed Civil Police were in complete charge of post facto investigations of crime. The Militarized Police still had units for interrogating prisoners, and the Civil Police got new militarized squads and SWAT teams. Among the latter were São Paulo's violent RUDI and RONE, from which several death squads were spawned. Among the fourteen interviewed direct perpetrators of violence, two former Civil Police officials, Julius and Márcio, had commanded RUDI and RONE. Márcio—who, like Julius, had entered the Civil Police before the military coup—became a RONE policeman, then its commander, and then a district-wide police official. Julius, a RONE official, was Márcio's subordinate.

The RONE night patrols—whose emblem was an owl on a tree branch with a machine gun under its wing—carried out violence with impunity. Under cover of darkness and headed by a *delegado*—a police chief with a law degree—any RONE violence that became publicly visible would be quickly legitimized as falling within the unit's legitimate line of duty. RONE, defined by its operational autonomy and savagery, had police who "never thought twice about drawing their guns or beating a suspect" (Rudi não moudou na volta 1969).

Ironically, however, São Paulo state officials apparently found RONE's operational autonomy insufficient because it was not long before RONE was allowed to create its own informal death squad. As former RONE Commander Márcio recalls, state politicians believed that society needed cleaning up but that the courts were very slow about deciding things. They believed that the law was tying the hands of the police, so RONE and its associated death squad had to untie those hands and put them to work. Márcio remembers that "everyone in the death squad [under his jurisdiction] worked [also] as an investigator in RONE." RONE's chief—who was directly subordinate to Márcio—got his future victims' names from the state secretary of public security; RONE would then be sent to pick up the alleged criminals and take them to jail. After "wait[ing] a few days, [the RONE-linked death squad would] take the prisoners out of jail and kill them." Thus, even as one part of Brazil's police system was being militarized and becoming more centrally controlled, through the creation of specialized police patrols like RONE, another part was being privatized into autonomous death squads that were nevertheless closely integrated into the formal system of repression. A seamless symbiosis was emerging between the action of RONE and its affiliated death squad.

Protest and Repression Spread

In Brazil by the late 1960s, there was rising citizen protest against deepening political repression. Military rulers saw unrest as a subversive challenge to their regime and mobilized police into riot control squads and SWAT teams. Fernando, a Militarized Police official who participated in street violence against dissenters, remembers with pride an incident that occurred between March 28 and April 4, 1968. Protests erupted across Brazil after Militarized Police shot and killed Edson Luís, a working-class secondary school student who was taking part in a student demonstration near Rio's majestic Candelária Cathedral. Protestors were denouncing the governor's withholding of subsidies for student meals. Violence escalated at Catholic masses held for the fallen student. It particularly inflamed crowds that Edson had been killed when Militarized Police fired indiscriminately into a group of student demonstrators.

At the public Seventh-Day Mass in Rio de Janeiro for Edson, almost 20,000 police and military were mobilized to control the mourners. In one account of what happened that day, the Militarized Police cavalry "wait[ed] for the end of the memorial mass...[to] attack...the unarmed population as it left the church, [using] clubs and even swords...against those who attended the mass" (Alves 1985: 84–85). At another memorial mass later that same day, the police beat and arrested so many that clergy and citizens had to form a circle around the outside of the cathedral to protect those inside from further attacks. After the mass, as clergy escorted mourners away from the cathedral, a cavalry unit of Militarized Police charged: nearly a thousand people were beaten by police, who used "swords and tear gas" against the mourners (Alves 1985: 84–85).

Fernando, later implicated by Brazilian human rights groups for involvement in torture and murder, remembers this incident proudly, explaining that as commander of the Shock Battalion's Second Company, he was

in the middle of all that confusion, [yet it] was the happiest period in my life in professional terms. We had a group of determined people there, well-trained and friends with one another because we suffered together.

Fernando recollects thinking that his group was not "going to lose this war;...the thirty-six of us [in the battalion were] going to win this one." Fernando regretted that just one day after police bullets had killed Edson Luís, the Militarized Police were ordered "not to go out armed anymore; only officers and noncommissioned officers were [allowed to be] armed." From Fernando's perspective, fortunately, this order did not last long. Armed with a familiar justification for violence, Fernando recalls that "[our] enemies were using weapons," so the Militarized Police shock troops had to do the same.

Fernando had entered Rio de Janeiro State's Militarized Police in 1963, just before Brazil's military coup and after completing an Army Reserve Officers training course. Fernando's uncle's glamorous police life (he had served under President Getulio Vargas [1930–1945; 1950–1954] in the notorious Special [political] Police [S-2]) had shaped his desire to become a policeman. Fernando had been "totally fascinated" by his uncle's charisma—he arrived at Fernando's house on one "of those shiny motorcycles"—and stories of police life.

After several years commanding a Militarized Police Shock Battalion, Fernando—already a cut above the rest because he had a high school degree and specialized military training—began studying law at night. Yet Fernando's rapid advancement within the Militarized Police seemed as much a function of his aggressive leadership against strikes, riots, and subversives as his educational and technical preparation. Fernando's fast track was also nurtured by his strict belief in the military government's national security doctrine. It divided Brazil's population into good citizens and dangerous subversives, with the police assuming a central role in protecting Brazil against the latter. At midcareer, Fernando was promoted to Rio de Janeiro's Militarized Police P-2 intelligence division, where he would develop and refine his infiltration and interrogation skills—important and valued as Brazil's dirty war developed.

Political Crisis and Peak Repression

After 1968, especially in Brazil's biggest cities, government repression escalated. Thousands of suspected subversives were rounded up and jailed. Seeking a more effective means of internal control, military-controlled state governments began creating new Militarized and Civil Police joint operations squads. Emblematic of such militarization against subversion was the formation in Rio de Janeiro of the GOE, made up of men handpicked from the Militarized Police, DOPS police, army, and firefighters. Fernando, one of the GOE's first members, explains that the primary criterion for recruitment "was courage already demonstrated during [the candidate's] professional life." The ideal candidate, however, was "a man intimately linked to moral principles and the [military's] national constitution." Fernando recalls that the ten men who were finally chosen for Rio's GOE were, above all, "trustworthy," in other words, men with unquestioned loyalty to Rio State's military-appointed secretary of public security.

GOE recruits received a military commando course taught by the Brazilian Air Force Paratrooper Brigade. They were also trained in urban guerrilla warfare by the Brazilian Army, assisted by American, Arab, and Algerian instructors. GOE members—seeing themselves in a war with 'subversives' and common criminals—were taught the use of explosives and how to conduct chemical warfare. According to Fernando, GOE training "wasn't only for combat—[for] destroying, arresting, [and] seizing—we trained for everything," with the militarized political system granting carte blanche for repression, especially after 1969.

State of Emergency

In the midst of the full-scale parliamentary crisis of 1969, with Brazilian military hard-liners demanding that dissident members of congress be stripped of political rights, junta-appointed President Arthur da Costa e Silva promulgated the Fifth Institutional Act (IA-5). Described as "the most far-reaching and most repressive" of the government's internal security measures up to that time (Flynn 1978: 420), IA-5 gave the military executive unilateral power to declare a state of siege, close Congress, expand press censorship, and suspend all constitutional and individual guarantees for those found guilty by a military tribunal of "political crimes." The private property of such "criminals" was to be confiscated by the government.

Julius, a Civil Police official from São Paulo state, remembers the value of IA-5 permitting arrests without formal charges or warrants: "You sometimes found a guy you wanted out of circulation because of the threat he represented to society; you didn't have any proof [against him],...[but] the law allowed you to arrest him." The military's war against subversion placed no limits on the police, whose violence was in any case ideologically legitimated by a pervasive national security doctrine that legalized violence against ever-wider segments of the Brazilian population.

Brazil's National Security Law of March 31, 1969, a product of national security ideology, stripped away any remaining civilian controls on Brazil's military government. Secrecy for government repression was guaranteed by media censorship: newspapers were forbidden to "publish news or fact [that was] slanted in such a way as to dispose the population against the constituted authorities" (Alves 1985: 118). All strikes were forbidden in essential services, and only the two government-approved political parties were permitted to operate (Alves 1985). The International Association of Jurists declared Brazil's National Security Law "a formidable weapon of repression" (Flynn 1978: 424). However, despite all this, Brazil's internal security apparatus was still not considered by the military to be an effectively functioning system of internal control. In the words of one Brazilian military analyst, "When terrorist actions began [in Brazil], the [country's repressive] system did not have the capacity to put out the fires" (Lago and Lagoa 1979: 6). There was apparently poor coordination among Brazil's various police forces and between these and the military, even though states such as Rio de Janeiro already had the beginnings of such coordination in its GOE. Law 317, enacted in 1967 to better coordinate Brazilian police and subordinate them to central government officials, was still falling short of its expectations. Law 667, enacted in 1969—which more specifically subordinated all police to the military—was still being implemented.

In a step toward more centrally (e.g., militarily) coordinated policing, on July 2, 1969, OBAN was secretly established in São Paulo at the encouragement and assistance of the United States (Huggins 1998). OBAN's general purpose was to coordinate São Paulo State's police and military forces and facilitate rapid collection of intelligence information. OBAN's more political goal was to "identify, locate, and capture subversive groups that operate in the Second Army Region, especially in São Paulo, with the objective of destroying or at least neutralizing [them]" (Departamento de Ordem Político e Social 1974: 3).

Because of the way OBAN was structured and operated, it has been described as a Vietnam-style Phoenix Program for Latin America (Saxe-Fernandez 1972). The United States had established Phoenix in South Vietnam just two years earlier as a countrywide intelligence network consisting of CIA, Vietnamese, and U.S. Army operatives. It had been designed to unify South Vietnam's fragmented intelligence apparatus and to "neutralize" the National Liberation Front's political infrastructure (25). The Phoenix Program carried out its mission through interrogation, intimidation, torture, disappearances, and murder. It has been estimated that between 1968 and 1972, while Phoenix was under direct U.S. administration, 26,369 Vietnamese civilians were killed and another 33,358 were imprisoned under brutalizing conditions (Klare and Arnson 1981: 25). Two important differences between Vietnam's Phoenix and São Paulo's OBAN were that first, Phoenix was national in scope whereas OBAN was to operate only in São Paulo State, and second, Phoenix—while very secretive—was formally constituted and funded by the United States. In contrast, São Paulo's OBAN was extra-official and privatized, financed through local business owners and national and multinational corporations, among them Ford and General Motors (Flynn 1978; Langguth 1978; Weschler 1987). Threatened by the prospect of socialism "winning" South America's largest economy, such corporations were enthusiastic about promoting and improving the Brazilian government's war against subversion.

Sérgio, a civil policeman who had connections with OBAN, began his police career in São Paulo in the late 1950s. His first post was as a *delegado* in rural São Paulo State. Sérgio recalls positively police *delegados* being "highly respected" there: the rural poor "feared the *delegado,* [and this] restrained these men's aggressive impulses." Sérgio did not remain there long, largely due to his close connections with the state's powerful governor; transferred back to the state capital, he became the governor's special assistant for internal security affairs. On a career fast track, Sérgio was assigned to São Paulo State's prestigious DOPS organization, first as an intelligence operative and than as an official. Sérgio spent most of his career in intelligence, even receiving training midcareer from the CIA.

Although Sérgio claims that he did not himself work in OBAN, he says that he commanded men who did. On a human rights list of documented torturers, Sérgio recalls the kind of men recruited into OBAN as a specially selected group of "hard-nosed" police. These men had cut their teeth in the semi-official death squad that Sérgio had set up to accomplish what the more legalistic police were reluctant to do. According to Sérgio, because of the violence his men had already carried out— some in the death squad and some in regular police units—these police who were recruited into OBAN were already "very bestialized." Sérgio's theory is that these men then became even more brutal from carrying out violence for OBAN and DOI/CODI, the national-level extension of OBAN.

Torture

During the short year or so of OBAN's operation, this internal security organization was perhaps at that time the most violent of Brazil's various repressive forces. Tortured for two hours by OBAN operatives who all called themselves "'Guimarães' to avoid anyone knowing their identities," one OBAN victim contrasted the anonymity of his torturers with the striking and painful reality of their brutalizing techniques and technologies. He reported that field radios were hooked up to his anus, lips, tongue, or nose, with "the shocks provoking...muscle contractions so strong that if the torturer [didn't] put something in [the victim's] mouth...[he] would eat his tongue" (Departamento de Ordem Político e Social 1969).

A widely publicized case of OBAN torture involved Frei Tito Alencar, a twenty-seven-year-old Dominican friar from the northeastern state of Ceará and an activist in the Catholic Church's Young Christian Students group (JEC). Arrested in São Paulo by OBAN on November 4, 1969, for allegedly being in contact with the Aliança Libertação Nacional (ALN) guerrilla group, Tito underwent several weeks of brutalities at the hands of police and military in an OBAN facility. In one interrogation session, Frei Tito was kicked and beaten with rods and fists, followed by an extended round of electric shocks. One of the friar's accusers forced him to "receive the Eucharist" by putting a live electric wire to his mouth; it became so swollen that the priest could not speak. After hours of such brutality in a room two by two meters in size, with no furniture except a stand holding the implements of torture (Departamento de Ordem Político e Social 1969), Frei Tito had to be carried back to his cell, where he lay all night on the cold cement floor. The following day, OBAN security forces kicked Tito and then struck him with "hard little boards" (*palmatòria*), alternating this with electric shocks and cigarette burns. At one point during this five-hour torture session, Tito was forced to walk what Brazilian security personnel call the "Polish Corridor"—a gauntlet of soldiers who beat Tito until he couldn't walk. Following this, his interrogators wanted to attach the Dominican friar to the parrot's perch—where Tito was to be suspended upside down with his wrists and ankles tied to a rod while he was given electric shocks. But, instead, the OBAN team decided that the friar would be more valuable in the next day's interrogation session after a good night's sleep. Before returning to his cell, an OBAN security officer warned Tito that if he did not talk in the next day's session, the interrogator would "bust [his] insides." It was well known among victims of the parrot's perch that this transformed the victim's "body...into a mass that no longer obeys the brain" (Departamento de Ordem Político e Social 1969; see also Departamento de Ordem Político e Social 1977).

That night, Frei Tito resolved that the "only...way out [was] to kill [him]self" (Alencar 1969: 2). Thus, after four months of persistent torture by OBAN, the friar was rushed to the University of São Paulo Hôspital das Clínicas—he had slashed his wrists. For Frei Tito, even death by suicide—a mortal sin in the Catholic religion, especially difficult therefore for a priest—was preferable to another torture session. Tito survived his suicide attempt, and in his hospital bed he wrote the deeply disturbing letter about his treatment by OBAN—portions of which were quoted previously. The letter was smuggled out and distributed to religious groups inside and outside Brazil and was used as evidence in human rights workers' campaigns against the Brazilian military regime's violent practices.

Waging Internal War

By late 1969, with the final building blocks of Brazil's authoritarian state cemented into place and given an aura of legality by the 1967 constitution, the military government had almost total control over economic, social, cultural, and political life. Yet all was far from calm within the military junta itself. Its rule was undermined just three days after installation by the kidnapping in Rio de Janeiro of U.S. Ambassador C. Burke Elbrick. A climate of civil war spread as police and military moved across Brazil in search of the ambassador's captors. Dragnets were carried out in Brazil's major cities, with OBAN leading the search in São Paulo State (Departamento de Ordem Político e Social 1969). Following Elbrick's release seven days after his kidnapping, dragnets intensified: Up to 5,000 people were arrested and imprisoned in Brazil, almost 2,000 in Rio alone (Cava 1970: 136).

In the wake of these widespread arrests, in late 1969 Brazil's military government issued two additional Institutional Acts, which struck down citizens' remaining constitutional guarantees against banishment, life imprisonment, and capital punishment. The military government waged its internal war in the streets—using aggressive interrogation and torture in police precinct basements, secluded houses, and military barracks. Ironically, the government's violent actions were documented in its own military tribunals. The records—*processos*—of these proceedings were secretly xeroxed by human rights activists and smuggled out of Brazil (Weschler 1998). The impunity granted to security forces apparently made the military government unconcerned about documenting its own violence; in any case, the bureaucratic legalities of military justice required such documentation. The result is an impressive archive of military government atrocities that covers twelve volumes and 6,946 pages. This public memory, the *Tortura Nunca Mais* (TNM) collection (n.d.), redresses the tendency of officials of torture regimes to deny the brutality of their own agents and discredit as exaggerations the voices and stories of victims. These official files of what some atrocity workers did offer a correction to this misattribution.

From the *Tortura Nunca Mais* archive, a picture emerges of Brazil's dirty war as a mix of superficial legality, visible violence, and willful illegality. National security ideology, which provided the mechanism for smoothing over these paradoxes, saw Brazil as fighting a special kind of war against internal subversion—"a war without uniforms, situated in the streets, where the enemy was mixed within the general population, [where] the police cannot distinguish by sight the terrorists from good citizens." Proclaiming this view, Army General Carlos Brilhante Ustra (1987: 71) has explained that in such situations police could easily pull away from central control and begin to "fight each other, thinking that they are taking action against terrorists."

In one strategy to ensure that this would not occur, national security ideology was aggressively promoted in police and military training academies. Civil Police Investigator Ignácio remembers with disdain that during his Civil Police training program, military instructors told new recruits that "there were two Brazils, the Brazil of the Revolutionary Government—which was an honest, pure Brazil that we should follow—and a different Brazil that belonged to criminals—dreamers who were trying to lead Brazil into chaos." Ignácio, a beat cop well known for his liberal use of violence—including beatings and torture—and who considers policing "a vocation...[my] *'cachaca* and soccer'" (i.e., life blood), was scornful of the ideologically motivated bureaucrats conducting police training. He particularly resented the military's "infiltrating people into the police academy courses.... They planted people from the revolution, military people, to work on your head [to accept the national security doctrine]." Ignácio was also indignant that military officials were at the academy to spy on and weed out potential dissidents and to shape police loyalty to the military.

In contrast, Fernando—a Militarized Police official—fully embraced the military's national security doctrine. Fernando believed that Brazil was in "such a bloody war, so violent, it was...just like World War II, [yet in Brazil] no one respected anything." Bernardo, a Civil Police official who now heads an organization to consider amnesty for police who had carried out the military's political violence, shares Fernando's viewpoint: "There was internal conflict.... In that climate of disorder, there were enemies...of the current regime," and the police had to combat them. National security ideology justified the government's taking extraordinary measures against its internal enemy.

Authoritarian Consolidation

By the early 1970s, military hard-liners controlled Brazil's government, with General Emílio Garastazu Médici newly installed as president. Médici, who had headed the SNI and commanded the important Third Army Region, would stick to tough policies and use violent measures to ensure their implementation. To prevent and protect against internal strife, Médici created a special executive-level "commission...of top Militar[ized] Police and security officials to coordinate all security matters... [concerning] subversion and...dealing with internal security problems in [Brazil]" (TOAID 1969: 4). The timing and composition of this commission clearly suggest its parentage to the DOI/CODI—a national network of both police and military security forces, all under direct military control. Although only a small part of Brazil's overall internal security apparatus, DOI/CODI—because of its direct subordination to the federal military executive—had higher status than any other element of it.

DOI/CODI began in 1970 as a countrywide extension of São Paulo State's OBAN. The CODI branch in each military district conducted research and analysis to identify a region's internal security priorities, to plan DOI "combat" missions (in its military-style terminology), and to coordinate DOI operations. DOI detachments, on the other hand, were "combat-ready force[s to] combat subversive organizations, directly... dismantle their personnel and material structure, and block their reestablishment," according to one DOI/CODI commander, General Ustra (1987: 126).

DOPS official Sérgio, whose own police often interfaced with OBAN and DOI/CODI, recalls the first men recruited into the São Paulo region's DOI/CODI: "No one intellectualized about their work.... They just killed a bunch of people—Boom! Boom!" Sérgio explains recruitment into the DOI/CODI was based on personality traits: those men most "identified with torture were very cold,...very aggressive. They had to be." But he goes on to state that the policemen who demonstrated these characteristics had been "recognized" for these useful characteristics and then "classified for [funneled into]...torture work." Sérgio makes it clear that being *initially* aggressive—without elaborating how this manifested itself behaviorally—was *qualitatively different* from what these men *became* in the process of carrying out DOI/CODI work. The brutalizing work of cruelty to others turned DOI/CODI operatives into finely tuned instruments of terror who, in Sérgio's words, became "more bestialized" than could have resulted from decades of normal police work.

Institutionalizing and Devolving Terror State

By the 1970s in Brazil, torture and murder by security forces had not only increased markedly but had also become fully institutionalized as government policy. Institutional violence had become so prevalent, and stories about it so much a part of everyday life, that "it was difficult to meet a Brazilian who had not come into direct or indirect contact with a torture victim or [witnessed]...a [violent] search-and-arrest operation," particularly in the more industrialized adjacent south-central states of Rio, São Paulo, and Minas Gerais (Alves 1985: 125). Brazil's security forces had become specialized tools in a system kept humming by the constant, rapid flow of suspects and information. Its victims were grist for the torture mills.

By the end of the 1970s, quite aside from frightening everyone into submission and murdering "malefactors," internal security operatives had displaced their official goals of social control to repressively eliminate subversion for its own sake. Once such violence had been institutionalized, it eventually began turning against itself. The combination of pressure on security forces to make arrests, get confessions, collect intelligence, and eliminate dangerous elements—all carried out in a climate of total war—exacerbated competition among them. The stakes were high, time was precious, and operatives knew that the system's rewards went to the units that most successfully—and quickly—found, captured, extracted information from, and neutralized undesirables.

This dynamic contributed to a decentralization of social control. As we have seen, many informal death squads evolved out of formal police organizations, as with RONE in São Paulo. They then partially split off from such specialized units, entering into a mutually supportive relationship between the formal and informal systems of social control (see Huggins 2000b). Sérgio, the former DOPS intelligence official, recalls how the agency he headed for a time, the São Paulo State DEIC, devolved into a semi-official death squad. According to Sérgio, he assembled a "secret team within his directorate" to take care of "very big, very important cases...that other specialized police branches were reluctant to deal with." Pointing to this squad's utility in tough situations, Sérgio knew that one day a police chief would come to him with an impossible social control problem and say, "I can't do anything because my investigators...seem to be a little reluctant [to take tough, violent action]. They're not used to dealing with that kind of people." Sérgio could then guarantee the other police chief that his death squad would do what was necessary.

A significant organizational outcome of this devolution of social control was that different parts of the internal security system began turning against one another. For example, L.O., a former intelligence operative for the SNI—Brazil's National Intelligence Service—revealed that by the end of the 1970s, "the regular police, even the Civil Police, were targets of the military revolution; there must have been thirty spies just like me in my city, who watched me, too. Nobody knew [trusted] anybody else." Although working for the military's important national intelligence system, L.O.'s life was threatened by other Brazilian security forces. In a similar case, Sérgio, the DOPS official from São Paulo, was investigating "high-level smuggling, including guns and drugs." In the process, Sérgio had gotten "close to the aorta" of illegality—even the state's governor and secretary of public security were suspected of being involved. In the middle of Sérgio's investigation, he learned that a friend was investigating him. Then his and his daughter's lives were threatened. The net effect was that Sérgio began not even trusting friends in the intelligence services—a sure sign that devolution was well under way.

An associated outcome, as well as a reflection of such devolution, was a range of systemic illegalities. Brazilian journalist Hélio Gaspari (in Weschler 1987: 86) argues that the violence and illegal money-making activities of the military's internal security system poisoned the whole social system. "A sort of gangrene set...in. [There was] an accumulation of peripheral debts contracted in clandestin[e work] which [could] only be rewarded illegally." As Weschler (1987: 86) notes, Brazil's internal security agencies, working outside of the law, "inevitably start[ed] behaving illegally as well. The torturers became smugglers and blackmailers and extortionists, and no one dared to stop them." Márcio, the former São Paulo Civil Police official, remembers that the men in one of his police divisions who were also in a death squad

got hooked on drugs [and] no longer had the courage to cleanly execute a guy, so they'd do drugs whenever they'd go to kill someone. In time, they became friends with a gang of drug traffickers and [before long] they became bandits—more crooked than any other bandit in the world.

It is clear that police violence and illegality were not a mere deviant exception to an otherwise legal and rational system of internal control. These were part of the authoritarian system's operating logic. In Brazil, the devolution toward widespread competitive, uncoordinated, and mutually destructive violence and terror was clearly rooted in the military's goal of spreading the national security doctrine throughout the internal security system. An example of this occurred when the military infiltrated Brasília's police academy to shape the consciousness of its graduates. Yet the system that had been restructured to coordinate and eliminate competition and conflict among security forces ended in exacerbating old conflicts and creating new ones. In the process, such friction contributed to a disintegration of centralized control as well as fostering and justifying violence. As Brazil's social control system moved into the 1980s, its operational foundation of illegality and impunity was generously interwoven with paranoia: The system was turning against itself.

Political Decompression and Democratic Opening

Brazil's authoritarian political system began a slow liberalization as the last two military presidents took steps to deescalate state-sponsored repression. Simultaneously, however, informal death squads that were seemingly not linked to the state proliferated. Entering a death squad very early in his police career, Roberto joined Rio de Janeiro's Militarized Police in 1987. Hoping to capture the people who robbed his brother's house and avenge the rape of his sister-in-law, Roberto worked day and night, alternating between formal police work and being a driver for the death squad that he had solicited to help him in his crusade for justice. Moonlighting as a death squad chauffeur, Roberto was able to augment his income: "If we caught a criminal, [the amount paid to us]—$250.00, $550.00, $850.00—would be divided among the five death squad members in equal shares, giving each man between $50.00 and $170.00 per killing." Among the guns that Roberto's death squad confiscated from victims, the death squad kept the best; the cheaper ones were sold to purchase better guns.

Of course, there was nothing completely new about this privatization of social control associated with death squads. Yet it seems to have become more marked as Brazil's redemocratization progressed. Perhaps, because death squads seem fully privatized rather than formally attached to government or business, both military and civilian governments in Brazil have been able to take a contradictory approach to such murder teams. The formal social control system can shift between secretly working with and protecting death squads, to generally ignoring their existence, to once in a while trying them for crimes. Vinnie, one of the rare police in prison for alleged death squad involvement, just the same denies having committed hundreds of murders when he was associated with Rio's notorious White Hand death squad. Vinnie admits having murdered his wife in the late 1960s, in a fit of passion during a fight. And he recalls also murdering "a few" poor people in the legitimate line of duty while he was moonlighting in Rio as a rent-a-cop for propane companies.

Perhaps because many Brazilian death squads, especially after the mid-1980s, operated as private security for businesses and residences—just what Vinnie was doing with his White Hand squad—their violence was easily explained as a private response to crime. In fact, the police who were working off-duty in death squads most often had the blessing of their superiors. Roberto, the militarized policeman serving time in 1993 for murders, explained that his death squad was made up of colleagues from the Militarized Police. The murder team got its lists of victims from a "justice official" who would only "kill people while they were sitting down." The funds to pay his death squad for killing alleged miscreants came from public officials—judges, attorneys, and politicians, according to Roberto. Militarized police officials knew the death squad system operated within its police organization, but they "[did not] do anything about it."

The porous moral and physical boundaries between formal and informal social control and its associated informal death squads became increasingly obscure as Brazil's redemocratization progressed. Such murders continued along with torture, with the support of violence workers and associated facilitators. Looking more deeply into the social, political, and personal makeup of Brazilian torturers and murderers, the next three chapters examine the varieties of men who carried out such extreme violence for the state—whether military or democratizing. Suspecting that not one kind of man or masculinity commits or is responsible for such atrocities, we discovered in fact three modal masculinities—personalistic, bureaucratizing, and blended—among the atrocity perpetrators. The following chapter begins our examination of these.

CHAPTER 6

Personalistic Masculinity

Man is not the creature of circumstances. Circumstances are the creature of men.

Benjamin Disraeli, *Vivian Grey*

The terms *torturer* and *executioner* suggest an extreme version of normal male aggressiveness, characterized by coldness, brute force, and pleasure in carrying out such activities. The labels "torturer" and "killer" are less likely to evoke an image of a professionally competent, formally trained, and "rational" person or of an empathetic, feeling man. In fact, these labels are so gender specific that they almost never conjure up a female image, although some research has suggested that women have been involved in torture complexes, albeit much less often than men. Cohen (1954), for example, argues that female guards in Nazi concentration camps were as violent as male guards. Conroy (2000: 104) reports a Uruguayan torturer's recollection that his *compania* had two female torturers: one made sure that the male torturers did not "go soft when the victim was female," and the other would "tell the men to go harder" in general. A torture denunciation published in Brazil's *Jornal do Brasil* (Jovem photografado em "pau-de-arara" confirma tortura 1985) disclosed that a policewoman from Brazil's drug police had tortured a suspected drug dealer. Stanley Milgram's landmark experiments (1974) on obedience reported no differences between his female and male subjects when they were prodded by a person in authority to administer pain to a victim. Moreover, Lee, Zimbardo, and Bertholf's research (1977) found that 70 percent of men imprisoned for having committed murder suddenly and for the first time described themselves as more feminine than masculine. In light of these facts, it makes sense to examine the assumption that only one kind of masculinity invariably carries out violence, including torture and murder.

First, let us set the stage for our analysis of torturers' and murderers' masculinities with a closer view of a man who might be thought to represent the quintessential violence worker, Ignácio. From a struggling working-class family, Ignácio's father was a typesetter, and his mother was a housewife. Ignácio remembers his father not wanting him to join the police, having always hoped that Ignácio would be a typesetter like himself. But Ignácio knew that his calling was to "discover" and "inspect," so in 1959 he signed on with Rio de Janeiro's Civil Police, working almost a year there as an investigator. When Brazil's federal capital was moved in 1961 from Rio to Brasília—the newly constructed futuristic city in Brazil's deserted west-central region—Ignácio elected to relocate to the federal capital's new Civil Police DOPS organization.

Recalling his first important assignment as a young Rio de Janeiro policeman—an experience Ignácio now dubs "picaresque"—this violence worker had to carry out secret surveillance and set the stage for a police invasion of a heavily fortified gambling house. With little more than a theoretical introduction to policing—only Ignácio's youth had made him eligible for this tricky operation—he was thrown into a potentially very dangerous mission. Being young and new to the police, he would not be recognized by the gambling house enforcers, a fact not shared by older police who were frequent customers of illegal gambling. Ignácio had to "hold the place" from the inside as a police team broke down the door. As his mission began to unfold at the appointed time— a moment Ignácio could not predict accurately because he could not afford a watch—Ignácio was supposed to create a diversion by tackling the gambling house bouncer; police outside would then begin their assault. Ignácio remembers rolling around on the floor, exchanging blows with the bouncer as his colleagues axed down the door. Ignácio dubs his first big mission successful: the team made its arrests, and Ignácio had "a good fight." But he was disappointed that the gambling house employees had managed to avoid jail, complaining, "Just like always happens in Brazil, they were released and the policeman ended up looking like the bad guy."

Ignácio, a tall, stocky man with strong features and an imposing presence, carries the nickname "Dirty Harry" for a working style that resembles the no-nonsense, shoot-first policeman portrayed by Clint East-wood in films. In many ways a quintessential macho policeman, he ab-hors physical and mental weakness, demands respect, and likes to demonstrate personal power through hand-to-hand combat. At the same time, Ignácio's masculinity has a softer, more feminine side, high-lighted by his explaining that if a policeman has "affection" for poor slum dwellers and they "respect" him, he doesn't need "to beat anyone to find things out." "When you see someone poor who is stealing, you have to tell him that it's wrong, that he has to be arrested.... But inside you don't have to be that tough. You have to be tough on the outside and humble on the inside." Ignácio even remembers a crook who moved him so much that he cried along with him. Reverting quickly to a more typically masculine presentation of self, Ignácio explains that he was al-ways very severe with the criminal who stole out of greed: "I don't cry with someone who pulls a gun to steal your [valuable] tennis shoes, your bicycle, your watch.... I'm hard on them, rich or poor." Ignácio re-calls positively that he once beat up the robber son of an appellate court judge: "I overpowered him and slugged him; I was even proud of it. " Ignácio believes that violence is necessary when the thieves or assassins use "crocodile tears and the evidence is so obvious and they deny things cynically": such criminals deserve a beating. Ignácio would even torture criminals who wanted to make a fool out of him, arguing that under such circumstances—where his own intelligence and authority have been challenged—"we're going to spin him" on the parrot's perch, rotat-ing him "as if he were a pig on a barbecue spit, turning him while giving him electric shocks."

Pointing to the intellectual side of his masculine police persona, Igná-cio maintains that his satisfaction as a policeman "is greatest... discover-ing things by investigating; you overpower someone with your intelli-gence..., [and then the] person folds in front of you." For Ignácio, calculated torture is not effective; he prefers "beating" a suspect or using psychological "cunning" (that is, psychological terror) to secure evi-dence. Ignácio maintains that a suspect who is fearful of physical assault will confess to anything, resulting in a worthless confession.

Apparently a mix of masculine contradictions, Ignácio presents him-self as violent and tough, caring and soft, and rational and professional. He has beaten suspects, seen torture and carried it out, watched murder and murdered. At the same time, Ignácio claims to have empathized and cried with victims, loaned them money, taken food to their families, been godfather to their children. The complicated mix of images that

Ignácio discloses about himself suggests a number of questions about the nature of masculinity. What does it consist of? Does it change according to situation and social conditions? Does it change historically? Is Western patriarchal masculinity inevitably associated with violence? Our three-chapter analysis attempts to answer some of these fundamental questions.

Masculinities as Scarce Resources

Much social science scholarship on masculinity demonstrates its complexity both within Western and non-Western cultures (see MacCormack and Strathern 1980; Ortner and Whitehead 1981). Yet despite the differences among culturally constructed masculinities, a common thread is that each society "differentiates between genders, specifies the spheres of masculinity and femininity, and assigns to each gender specific attributes, characteristics, and expectations" (Ramirez 1999: 27). Such designated gender spheres and their affiliated behavioral expectations are encapsulated within and serve to promote gender-based hierarchies of power and domination. Recent research and theorizing highlights the powerful, pervasive, and insidious role that gender-based social dominance hierarchies play in societies throughout the world (see Pratto 1999; Sidanius and Pratto 1999). Such hierarchies result in power and resource allocation disparities that contribute to discrimination and stereotyping of the weak by the strong. These inequalities, in turn, are legitimized by sociopolitical ideologies that justify and normalize gender-, race-, ethnic-, and wealth-based structures of domination. This elaborated ideological rhetoric influences both individual thinking and sociopolitical structures.

Our analysis of Brazilian violence workers simultaneously attempts to interrelate societal-level ideology and personal rhetoric with the behavioral and mental processes of dominance structures. Central to this analysis is the functioning of masculinity as an important social dominance category that is performed and validated (or not) in interpersonal interaction.

In Western industrialized societies, successful masculinity performances are expected to have patriarchal characteristics, with *patriarchy* defined as an institutionalized all-embracing system of male domination that shapes men's views of themselves, their prerogatives, their relationships to one another and to women, and their relationships to physical force (Jefferson 1996). "Real men," according to the expectations of Western patriarchal masculinity, must be able to dominate some men and all women. A paradigmatic test for masculine dominance is confrontations involving danger—whether physical, social, or intellectual. In these competitive interactions, masculinity is elusive: "There are always men who fail the test" (Ramirez, 1999: 33).

Speaking specifically about Puerto Rican machismo, a dimension of Western patriarchal masculinity present in Brazil as well, Ramirez argues that machismo is not qualitatively different from non-Latin Western masculinity performances: Latin American masculinity expectations merely emphasize machismo to a greater extent. With competitive sexuality accorded great importance in successful macho performances, there is an assumption that "the male is an essentially sexual being, or at least...should look and act like one." The man is expected to "enjoy his sexuality, declare it, boast about it, feel proud of it, and, above all, show it" (Ramirez 1999: 44–45). Western patriarchal masculinity—like Latin American machismo in particular—gains its power from asymmetry in social relationships, whether among males or between males and females. One important way that such asymmetry is manifested is through men's sexual domination of women.

Social interactions based on power, competition, and possible conflict have winners and losers. In these interactions, getting and having respect is central to demonstrating successful masculinity. The "real" man who wants respect from other men must suppress any feelings that might suggest weakness. "Being strong, courageous, and in control... are...requirements of masculinity," according to Ramirez (1999: 63).

Within a gender system of competition for scarce masculinity resources—whether for respect or for women or for power—men must constantly demonstrate that they possess the required attributes of masculinity. Although such validation may be pursued in the presence of women, it is mainly directed at other men. In these masculinity performances, one man demonstrates that he has more masculinity than another one (Ramirez 1999). For example, Jacob, who will be discussed later in this chapter, is proving his masculinity when he pits his fighting skills against those of prisoners and uses these fights to entertain and impress police colleagues. Jacob promotes himself, and by extension his masculinity, by minimizing other policemen's and suspects' credibility— they were "dirty" police, "bad" criminals—with the implicit assumption that Jacob, as a man and a "professional" policeman, is just the opposite. Within Jacob's world, there is zero-sum availability of successful masculinity resources. Ramirez, who argues this from an academic stand-point as well, adds that aggression and violence are common strategies for promoting one masculinity over and against another.

Differentiating aggression from violence, Ramirez defines the former as "coercion, imposition, limitation, domination, or cancellation of the other person's will." Violence, in contrast, is specifically "action that causes physical or emotional harm and is geared toward destruction or punishment" (75). In masculinity contests that include competition, degradation of other men, and demand for respect, the thin line between normal masculine aggression and physical violence is easily transgressed. Ramirez, in fact, argues that "living according to the requirements of masculinity means assuming a self-destructive behavior of high-risk vio-lence" (77). Because few men are able to successfully demonstrate their masculinity constantly within a system of pervasive competition over scarce and elusive masculinity resources, aggression turns easily into vio-lence. As we shall argue in Chapter 10, when the structural realities of masculinity itself are combined with a larger political war against subver-sion or other crime, police violence becomes even more likely.

Masculinity and Violence

Much theorizing about the relationship of masculinity to violence as-sumes that masculine gender role socialization intrinsically fosters ag-gression and violence. According to one argument, masculinism—"an ideology that justifies and naturalizes male domination" (Brittan 1989: 4)—shapes aggressive, controlling, competitive, power-oriented, and instrumental behaviors in men. As we have seen, Ramirez essentially ar-gues that the struggle for masculinity generally creates social pressures to use violence. Of course, such an argument acknowledges neither masculinity differences within Western cultures nor the abundant non-Western masculinities that diverge from this style and are not associated with aggression or violence. We know, for example, that not all mas-culinities demonstrate the same types and degrees of competitiveness, aggressiveness, control, and domination. Western societies themselves contain a range of masculinity variations, with no single one represent-ing all Western male gender role behavior. Yet, at the same time, within Western patriarchal masculinity not all masculinity presentations are ad-judged equivalently socially successful. Some are more positively evalu-ated than others, as, for example, the Western preference for nonfeminine masculinities over the more female-identified ones. A culture's dominant patriarchal masculinity type is most commonly used as the measuring rod for establishing the limits to acceptable variations from dominant masculinity.

In any case, even the culturally most dominant and socially acceptable Western masculinity forms are not frozen and static. As masculinity is performed, it is modified by situational pressures; class, racial or ethnic, and age hierarchies; and organizational structures and processes. Masculinities may also shift with wide-sweeping historical changes. According to a growing body of research, the masculinity performances that result from each of these factors have different relationships to violence. For example, Messerschmidt (1993) believes that certain kinds of male violence are in fact a public representation of masculinities that place a premium on respect and situational control. Where male control is directly or indirectly challenged—as, for example, where an alleged or possible perpetrator fails to demonstrate sufficient respect for a policeman—violence may be expected to follow. Accordingly, Adler and Polk (1996: 409) argue that where there is a perceived affront to a man's "personal integrity, [to] pride, and [to] mastery of the social environment," male violence may result from "righteous fury" (399). This response to a suspect's lack of respect was frequently enunciated by the interviewees we label "personalistic" police.

Although patriarchal masculinity involves domination through control of the weaker by the stronger, the possibilities for accomplishing this can vary according to social class (Kersten 1996: 383). For example, in most corporate business structures, poorer subordinate men cannot freely exercise aggressive masculinity against powerful superordinates of either gender. They can more acceptably assert it against those of their own or a lower social class. However, interestingly, police in general and police torturers in national security states in particular frequently assert official and extrajudicial force against political subversives of higher social status. In other words, masculinity's relationship to violence can vary according to a man's social class position within an occupational or social structure.

Masculinity performances can also change historically. Arguing that masculinities vary according to changes in the structure of a state, Liddle (1996) explains that the shift in the English state from feudalism to capitalism saw the creation of a more defined division of labor between men and women and a change from "aristocratic warrior" to "bourgeois-rational/calculative" masculinities. The feudal aristocratic warrior masculinity placed a premium on a man's relationship to family and blood-line, on his duty to honor appropriate others and to gain honor through praiseworthy acts. In contrast, bourgeois rational/calculative masculinity performances place a premium on individualism, scientific rationality, control, and a subdivision of the psyche into public and private spheres, with a separate persona required for each sphere. Thus, with England's transition to capitalism, the dominant masculinity changed from one em-phasizing connectedness to collectivity and community—a characteristic we found among the personalistic police—to one that was segmented, privatized, and rationalized—a characteristic that was most evident among the "institutional functionary" violence workers (see Chapter 7).

A Trio of Violence Workers' Masculinities

With the previous theoretical background in mind, in this and the next two chapters we take a fresh look at the lives and careers of eleven of the fourteen direct perpetrators of violence. Setting aside the three whose tes-timonies gave insufficient information for our purposes, we will examine masculinity's relationship to assertions about police work, violence, and explanations of police atrocities. The important issue for this and the next two chapters is not whether the interviewed violence workers were con-structing false images of themselves for interviewers—to cover up, excuse, or make themselves look better—but that, for whatever reasons, their tes-timonies ended up inadvertently producing three distinct masculinity groupings. We do not use these masculinity constructions to claim either that masculinity itself caused violence or to assert that it structured certain kinds of atrocities. Our goals at this point are to illustrate that the violence workers were not of a single masculinity type and that masculinity has a place in examinations of police atrocities—something that many special-ists of routine police violence have failed to systematically consider.

We begin in this chapter with three personalistic violence workers—one was a civil police official, and two were civil police investigators. The personalistic police masculinity can be seen in the beat cop who presents himself as a passionate true believer in the cause of bettering society and protecting it from criminals. Driven by an internal commit-ment to "their" civilian communities, these police are like Hollywood's "Dirty Harry," as with Ignácio. When the personalistic violence worker talks about his own or police colleagues' violence, he commonly assigns responsibility for it to bad individuals (whether victims or perpetrators) or else diffuses the causes of violence among vague social or cultural phenomena, rather than consistently relegating it to organizational conditions or pressures.

At the opposite end of our theoretical masculinity continuum are the violence workers we can label "institutional functionaries." These men presented their masculinity as an extension of, and subordinated to, the needs and prerogatives of the internal security organization. They considered themselves dispassionate and rational extensions of the police organization and the state. The institutional functionary is represented in Chapter 7 by five interviewees—three spent most of their careers in civil policing, whereas the other two were militarized police. Only one of the institutional functionaries was from the rank and file—a militarized policeman from an elite execution squad.

The third set of violence perpetrators, discussed in Chapter Eight, are characterized by what we label "blended masculinities." Falling between the other two masculinity types, these violence workers identified fully neither with the communities they policed nor with the police force and the state. They simultaneously carried out violence within, for, and outside the police organization, with their loyalty shifting according to who was purchasing their services. They vacillated, on the one hand, between demonstrating personalistic and physical masculinity when talking about violence outside police organization and, on the other, trying to justify that violence through institutional functionary discourse that linked it to rational-legal police bureaucracy; that is, they subordinated their masculinity to police bureaucracy when discussing violence for and within the police organization. Among the three blended masculinities in our violence worker subsample, one is a Civil Police detective, and the other two are Militarized Police rank-and-file members.

Having discovered three modal combinations of characteristics that defined each masculinity set and distinguished it from the other two, we then explore in this and the following two chapters how each modal masculinity type talks about the police—themselves and others—who had carried out atrocities in Brazil. Yet as theoretically valuable as this analysis was for communicating hidden patterns in violence workers' testimonies, a word of caution is necessary. As real actors, these men do not always fit neatly into specific masculinity compartments. Most violence workers are more multidimensional than any analytical categories can communicate. For example, in our research, they constantly presented some exceptions to our sociologically constructed ideal-type masculinity groupings. This was especially true, of course, for the blended masculinity violence workers, as their label suggests. That each masculinity type, in fact, included a margin of variation around its primary defining features and that there were still differences in how those who carried out atrocities presented themselves, suggests nonetheless that no one masculinity type was consistently associated in Brazil with atrocity—the central research premise of this and the next two chapters.

The Personalistic Cop

Ignácio and Jacob, along with Sérgio, present a personalistic violence worker masculinity. Returning again to Ignácio, the clearest example of this type, in 1993—after thirty-four years in the Civil Police—he was still only a rank-and-file investigator, working the slums as his beat. Even though passed over consistently for promotions, he still considers police work "a calling" to be carried out with passion and commitment twenty-four hours a day. Ideally, Ignácio wanted a "good" partner to work with, but even in the old days before the military regime, he could not find such a man. Police associates often let him down in an emergency. In one particularly painful example, a partner abandoned Ignácio in the middle of a violent arrest operation. As Ignácio explains it, he and his partner had gone together to a poor neighborhood to capture a man who had entered a police station and "confronted the police with guns." Describing the perpetrator as "absolutely surly, with a . . . totally Lombrosian physique"—implying that he was what nineteenth-century Italian criminologist Cesare Lombroso would label an "atavistic throwback," a born criminal—Ignácio had to single-handedly restrain the man. After the perpetrator had attacked Ignácio with a screwdriver and a fight broke out between Ignácio and the perpetrator, Ignácio's partner split. Left all alone at the scene, Ignácio had to struggle for his life: He threw a punch and forced the man onto the ground, rubbing his captive's face in the dirt and squeezing the man's neck until he passed out. After subduing his captive, Ignácio shoved the guy into his car and drove him to the police station.

Knowing that police there "would want to beat the perpetrator," Ignácio took the key to the man's cell to ensure his captive's safety. As a result of what Ignácio calls his own "fair play" with this criminal—including beating the man in a fair-and-square fight—the perpetrator became "really humble," saying to Ignácio, "'You were decent to me, you fought me, you beat me in the fight, and you didn't let [your police colleagues] knock me around'" at the station. Out of gratitude, the man asked Ignácio to be his four-year-old son's godfather. Ignácio accepted, recognizing "the respect he had for me: it wasn't because of the violence; it was because I didn't let anybody beat him, even through he had a long rap sheet." Although Ignácio remembers positively the patron-client relationships that he developed in the communities he policed, he recalls his partners only negatively for their betrayal.

Looking back over the years of disappointment by different partners and by the police system itself, Ignácio laments that he still cannot find a good partner—a man who will dedicate his life to policing and demonstrate unflagging loyalty to Ignácio. He is particularly disillusioned that "younger police work by the clock"; they are just in police work for the salary. "They do not want to go into a slum to arrest someone who is dangerous; they don't want to search anybody because they're afraid of being attacked." Never having found a good partner, Ignácio has been a loner for most of his police career.

Perhaps because of his old-fashioned values, Ignácio has constantly run afoul of police administrators. Ignácio dates his problems with administrators to the military period, when he got "revolted" at the military's bringing men into the Civil Police who "weren't policemen by calling; they were 'just policemen'" doing the military's work. In part because of attitudes like this one but more likely because of Ignácio's attempting during the military period to organize a Civil Police union, the military government subjected Ignácio to *cassação*. In the last five years, with his rights and his police job restored, Ignácio has been transferred from police station to police station. His brand of policing, his belief that police work is a calling, and his populist policing style all seem to violate modern ideas about "professional" police work. Ignácio, who entered police service in the afterglow of Brazil's corporatist and populist Getulio Vargas government, has become increasingly marginalized in the police system. The institutional functionary police officials who came increasingly to dominate Civil Police administration see Ignácio's policing style as irrational and unprofessional, labels that make his values the antithesis of "good policing."

As a personalistic policeman, Ignácio now finds himself more connected to poor, sometimes even criminal, communities than to his police system. Explaining the necessity of his having connections with the communities he polices, Ignácio discloses that on Saturday and Sunday, like other men in the *favelas* (slums), he still

puts on Bermuda shorts and a T-shirt to go into [the slums] to drink a beer, because that's where you get information. You're not going to find it in your office.

You go to the streets. Somebody comes along and asks you for money; you buy milk for his kid. He comes back and says, "I want to tell you something."

Administrative pressure against police socializing in poor neighborhoods—at a time when "community policing" philosophies were still not in vogue in Brazil—subjected Ignácio's working style to censure and criticism. Ignácio complains that "the administration still sees something wrong with that kind of behavior." Thus, Ignácio—who ideally prefers collective approaches to policing and defines himself through personal connections with other like-minded police and with poor communities—ironically has ended up a loner within his Civil Police organization.

How does Ignácio's personalistic masculinity presentation—as a man who is simultaneously tough and soft—correspond to his assertions about violence? Ignácio's "ideal of working, investigating, . . . [was to use] a process of reasoning: the person folds in front of you, and you wind up discovering things." He prefers "beating" information out of a suspect to what he considers "torturing them." For Ignácio, beating is not torture because beating involves what Ignácio dubs "fair play," contrasting it with a military torture session that he observed: "The floor was wetted down so that you could use wires, poles, in order to make a closed circuit. The military torturers would put the victim on the floor and put . . . water on it; the barefooted victim would close the electric circuit and. . . . receive a terrible shock." Ignácio, who claims to have "only" stood by as captives were brutally tortured, distances himself from such "impersonal" violence by claiming that these forms of torture were "brought to police stations by [the governing] military." In his opinion, the military used "much more physical force than diligence in interrogations because they thought that the person was not going to withstand a beating."

Ignácio—although known for having liberally employed torture— claims to have only seen it extensively but not to have used it himself. He freely admits to have been present during torture sessions but always speaks of torture as something that someone else did. Quick to denounce the military's use of torture, Ignácio describes one of these sessions that he observed:

[The military torturer would] put the victim in a large bathtub, electrify the edges, and leave him with water up to his neck. The guy's in there for an hour, two hours, three hours. At some point he's going to get tired [and talk] because if he lies down, he'll drown. If he puts his hands on the edge, he'll receive an electric shock and die.

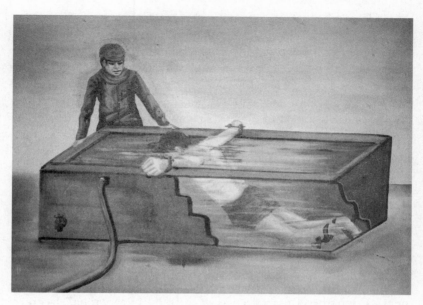

Cambodian version of the full-body water torture known in Brazil as "the submarine." S-2 Tuol Sleng Prison Museum, Phnom Penh, Cambodia. Van Nath, artist.

Ignácio grudgingly admits that police in Brazil use the infamous parrot's perch. It cannot be explained away as a special military invention. But he blames its "inappropriate" use on either temporarily out-of-control policeman or recalcitrant victims. For example, Ignácio explains that the parrot's perch is employed primarily on manipulative victims who use "crocodile tears...even when the evidence is so obvious and they deny things so cynically." In such a case, a "policeman who doesn't have a certain balance will slap the victim around a little." By recasting torture as little more than a slap fight, Ignácio disguises and denies the brutality against the person who is hung powerless from a rod as blood concentrates in rope-bound wrists and ankles. He pushes into the background the fact that this victim has water from a crude garden hose forced into his or her mouth and anus while being spun and electrically shocked in the genitals and mouth. Turning the interviewer's attention to what Ignácio calls his "softer side"—a discursive strategy that Robben (1995) labels "ethnographic seduction"—Ignácio concludes his superficial overview of brutality by explaining that he "got tired of seeing" parrot's perch torture in Brazilian police stations.

Jacob, another personalistic policeman, entered his state's Civil Police in 1971, a period of intense political repression in Brazil. Jacob recalls that he joined the police to "fill the blanks in [his] life." Police work was natural for Jacob because it was a family career; two of Jacob's brothers and an older cousin were in the Civil Police. Jacob had actually been doing police work informally with his favorite cousin for several years before he officially joined the ranks. He would accompany the operations team on its violent night rounds, a period in Jacob's life that he dubs "very, very exciting because some nights we had three shootings." Jacob's cousin—a personalistic cop who had entered the force in the early 1950s—was a powerful influence in Jacob's life.

Socialized into police work by his cousin, Jacob remembers this older policeman teaching him who were "good" and who were "rotten" cops. Considering himself morally and professionally better than the dirty cops, Jacob, like Ignácio, takes pride in having made a reputation for himself as a fighter. A black belt in karate, Jacob credits this martial art with giving him focus, discipline, and control: "It very much trains the mind. I don't become ineffective when [things go] wrong." Jacob remembers his police colleagues encouraging him to use his fighting skill: "My companions knew that I [would not] hurt [criminals] too much, and I was not going to shoot them, so they wanted to see a fight [between me and them]."

Like Ignácio, Jacob frequently duked it out with suspects. Employing a standard of what Jacob labels "fair play," this violence worker explains that he only used fighting to "demobilize a suspect." This was not violence, he says, because fighting "is…a skill," proven by Jacob's never "overdominat[ing]" a suspect, even though he frequently "beat them up." In Jacob's mind, he always gave criminals a fair fight. Jacob forgets that in such fights he had the weight of the state behind him, a police team looking on, and a gun at his side. Preferring to focus on what he sees as the consensual side of his policing style, Jacob recalls one criminal telling him, "I fought [guards] many times in prison,…but never with both hands and both feet free. You choked me in a way that I couldn't lift my hands." According to Jacob, such moves earned him criminals' respect: "All the [criminals] called me 'sir.'" Respect is very important in Jacob's relationships with criminals and in the presentation of his masculine self.

Jacob claims to have felt very little camaraderie with other police, apart from his cousin, who died of cancer early in his police career. In fact, he describes most police very negatively: they are "stupid guys," "corrupt," "cruel," and "dirty." According to Jacob, "Policemen are insecure, very insecure; when they are alone they are...cowards. [Only when] they are in the company of a guy who fights well, who knows how to fight, do they feel brave." During our five-hour interview, Jacob only once mentioned "a few very good workers" among the police, always promoting his own masculinity at the expense of most of his other colleagues. The good cops could be found in the DOPS and the robbery and homicide divisions—known in Brazil for liberal use of violence. Jacob, who describes himself as a "good policeman"—different in his mind from the police who worked in "political repression," exactly what the DOPS did—claims to have completely rejected the military government's national security ideology, which he saw as "an invention to allow [stupid people to use] cruelty against people." To the extent that Jacob actually felt this way, he was an outsider to a police system that was bound by the military to uphold national security policy in the streets.

In spite of his frequent proclamations to the contrary, Jacob has been identified by Bernardo—an interviewed violence perpetrator and the head of his state's organization to consider amnesty applications for police who committed atrocities during Brazil's military period—as having engaged in a good deal of political repression. Jacob's current petition for amnesty, which would allow him to return to Civil Police work, asks that the executions he committed on-duty in the early 1980s be adjudged part of his legitimate police role.

Jacob denies having killed or tortured anyone. Freely admitting to having been in shoot-outs with suspects—which he found "exciting"—Jacob maintains staunchly that he did not kill anybody in such operations. The closest that Jacob comes to talking about police violence—his and others'—is to diffuse responsibility for it into vague social or cultural situations:

Some guys died, but I don't know who killed them. There were many guys shooting and I...don't know who hit the guy.... I just knew that people died. Fortunately it was on the other side.

Or he blames it on deviant individuals—"bad" and "stupid" police or their recalcitrant victims. For example, pointing to the police who committed torture, Jacob maintains that they were "stupid guys doing stupid things."

Jacob argues that he "never agreed with torturing people," preferring *mano-a-mano* karate fighting because it "is different than torturing—tying someone's hands up [and torturing them]—I never liked it." Yet, although Jacob thought torture was terrible, he did not leave the room when it was going on. When asked how he could remain where torture was taking place—and even snap pictures of it—Jacob explained that police torturers did not find his presence troubling because "nobody talks" about such violence. Acknowledging only the possible negative outcome of others' finding out about torture, Jacob instrumentalized and therefore disguised his own complicity in this violence. It was not harmful if no one talked about it.

As with Ignácio, Jacob's discourse presents traditional Brazilian personalistic machismo. He demands the behavioral respect of suspected criminals and uses physical force—describing it as if little more than a fair-minded physical fight between equals—to get the respect he deserves from suspects. To garner respect from police colleagues, Jacob fights criminals and prisoners, verbally belittles them, and boasts about his black belt status. If, as he maintains, other police are cowards, stupid, and bad, then, by implication, Jacob is courageous, smart, and honest. Jacob, whose masculinity is organized primarily around being physically tough and controlled, just the same manifests a passionate emotionality when explaining his need for excitement—shootings are "exciting" and fights are "entertaining."

Sérgio, who will be discussed at greater length in Chapter 11, entered Civil Police service in 1957, serving initially as a rural police chief in São Paulo State—a time that Sérgio remembers positively. In those days "the *delegado* was highly respected, . . . even more so than the judge or district attorney." Sérgio believes that respect for police authority was especially necessary in the rural backlands because the "cowboy" had to fear the *delegado*. Sérgio remembers exploiting that fear "because it restrained certain men's aggressive impulses." Placing a heavy emphasis on respect for his authority, especially from "impulse-driven" crude backlanders, Sérgio laments that today the police receive very little respect.

Indeed, this fact seems to have begun to disclose itself to Sérgio after he was transferred to his state's DOPS. Coming to this very important political policing position just before the military came to power in 1964, Sérgio quickly became the governor's trusted operative—a position that would sometimes require Sérgio's supporting his powerful boss against the military's expanding power in his state. Sérgio's work in the political police apparently initially gave him great satisfaction:

[It was] interesting, provocative—everything . . . had to be kept secret. I . . . thought it was very absorbing; I slept four hours a night—Saturdays, Sundays and holidays included. The man in the secret service is very important to the state. We kept in touch with…[American] consuls—[particularly] those who were CIA agents.

Sérgio is proud that during his tenure with the DOPS intelligence service, he was his own boss, answerable only to the governor: "I didn't [even] go through the governor's secretary; I went directly to the governor." But Sérgio now believes that this work took a big toll on his life. Being so "totally absorbed" by the work "was stupid [because] there has to be a limit." Sérgio tried to leave the intelligence service several times, but the governor would not let him resign. As head of the state's DOPS, Sérgio was "more trusted than any other state official." This honor weighed heavily on Sérgio and placed him under a great deal of pressure. He felt set up for failure: as the Governor's personal confidant, Sérgio could not develop working or personal relations with other internal security professionals (many of whom were linked directly to the military), and the intensity of his work severely restricted Sérgio's social life outside the police.

Sérgio's real and perceived isolation from work associates is especially reflected in the way he talks about intelligence assignments and operations. His extensive use of the personal pronouns *I* and *me* suggests Sérgio's perception that he alone made things happen: "You couldn't transfer the work to someone else. The final decision belonged to only one man—me. Everything came back to one man."

Sérgio's intense sense of personal responsibility for his state's internal security is also reflected in his mistrust of subordinates' ability to carry out his orders effectively. In Sérgio's words, when labor and student strikes were illegal, "there was only one man [himself] who would know whether there was going to be a strike or not." If Sérgio's own intelligence indicated that a strike was not in the offing, then he would not send police to the site. However, if a strike did in fact occur and if there was damage, Sérgio alone would be held accountable. According to Sérgio, there were times when "there was a strike every two, three days. It was crazy. I'd say that I had infiltrated literally everywhere. I had to pick up on everything." Sérgio maintains that "you couldn't delegate this kind of work. The final decision [to act] belonged to only one man," Sérgio himself.

Reflecting on how his life in intelligence contributed to his use of force, Sérgio explains that violence was a function of the pace and intensity of his work. He cites time constraints on police work: "If I arrest someone who has kidnapped a little girl who might be killed in four hours, I'm not going to waste time by questioning the suspect for two or three days. I'll hang that guy up [on the parrot's perch], work him over, and he'll tell me in five minutes." Sérgio remembers that when he was in the thick of intelligence work, he became "very aggressive" against subversives in "national security" emergencies. However, at most Sérgio admits to having ordered operatives to torture and murder. Appealing to his rational side to explain why his aggression never resulted in torture, Sérgio argues that a good policeman does not have to use extreme violence to get what he wants: psychology and rational planning can be just as effective as brute force.

Sérgio argues that "good" police authorities can influence whether subordinates' violence reaches beyond normal bounds. For example, in the informal death squad that Sérgio assembled and directed, there were men "who were dangerous to control." But he resisted challenges to his authority by saying, "Okay, slow down." Sérgio believes that without such control, his special police would have "killed people as coldly as you'd kill a chicken." Demonstrating the appropriateness of his leadership over the death squad, Sérgio explains how one of the murder team's killings was acceptably carried out: His men were "trained, skillful, and had the courage to go in under fire." As a good administrator, Sérgio would first "find out where the criminal was and set a place for an ambush [so that] even if the criminal didn't resist arrest, his men...were going to kill him." Sérgio argues that he "wouldn't be sad about this, either"; he'd even say that it was "a good thing, better than maintaining the criminal in jail." Besides, Sérgio believed that his special murder team wasn't really a death squad because it "didn't go out just to kill." In fact, however, because of the violence that Sérgio is known to have perpetrated during Brazil's military period, he has been condemned by Brazilian human rights groups for torture and summary executions. Today, after a heart attack and a stroke, Sérgio is still committed to and very positive about the Civil Police system that he admits is responsible for his stress-related illnesses.

Like other personalistic police, Sérgio sees some police violence as caused by outrage against "subversives" and "bad criminals." For example—contradicting his own claim that he never used extreme violence—Sérgio owns up to having committed violence against "bad perpetrators" who brought it on themselves: These "uppity" victims, he explains, "can keep [torture] from happening" if they just talk.

Sérgio in fact straddles the line between a personalistic policeman and an institutional functionary. As an important Civil Police official, Sérgio was structurally integrated into his organization's national security bureaucracy. Yet because of the secrecy of his work, his unflagging personal loyalty to the governor, and his belief that he alone could accomplish important intelligence work, Sérgio was ironically marginal to the larger social control system and its web of bureaucratically structured relationships. Moreover, besides being isolated from subordinate police and suspected by, or invisible to, most other police officials, Sérgio was socially divorced from nonpolice friends and family.

On balance, therefore, Sérgio manifests much more of a personalistic police masculinity than an "institutional functionary" one. He describes his work in personalistic terms and does not consider himself part of a bureaucratic work team. Micromanaging every aspect of his statewide police organization, Sérgio believes that personal control, rather than organizational structures and relationships, was essential to effectively accomplishing his intelligence work. Indeed, Sérgio held himself so personally responsible for his state's internal security that he rarely even delegated work to others. Therefore, most of the time—unlike the institutional functionary—Sérgio does not diffuse personal responsibility for violence into police bureaucracy.

Interpersonal Connections

Looking more closely at the personalistic masculinity performances, they clearly manifest several characteristics stereotypically associated with some kinds of Western patriarchal masculinity. The personalistic police placed a premium on interpersonal physical rather than structural control, on an inner-directed reciprocal (although not always equal) responsibility to others—whether an imaginary idealized other (the perfect partner) or just one other person (the state governor, a police relative) or to a larger community of acceptable and reciprocal others (the relationship of patron to client). The personalistic policeman demanded respect and was not reluctant to liberally employ bodily force to obtain it from others.

At the same time, the personalistic policeman's masculinity presentation sometimes diverged from a purely patriarchal norm. Although Jacob and Sérgio were controlling, aggressive, silent, emotionally frozen, and socially alienated from others, Ignácio sought—although infrequently had—connections with other police and took pride in maintaining connections with the poor he policed. Ignácio liked spending time *passeando* in slums—hanging out, drinking, and talking with people for hours. Rather than keeping his feelings frozen and hiding them from others, Ignácio openly communicated them—even claiming to have cried with criminals—for which he was chided by his more traditionally masculine or bureaucratically rigid colleagues.

All three personalistic police made abundant use of violence when their masculine honor was violated. Their most common explanation for it blamed bad people, whether perpetrators or victims. In their discourse about violence—in conjunction with their brand of personalistic connectedness—they embodied violence as a visible physical act carried out by one person against another one. Compared with the institutional functionary, the personalistic policeman is relatively embarrassed and morally outraged by what he labels "torture" because it involves an unfair balance of power within an inhuman (i.e., technocratic rather than physical) social control interaction. Seeing torture as somewhat unseemly and definitely unmanly, the personalistic policeman discursively distances himself from it as a violation of fair play. However, in fact, all three personalistic policemen carried out some of the very acts that they themselves would define as torture.

As students of masculinity have aptly demonstrated, no gender construction can be understood in isolation from other ones. Not only is masculinity constructed in relation to female gender presentations as well as in opposition to them, but masculinities are also created, reinforced, and maintained in relation to other idealized and existing masculinities. Among the violence workers in this study, the modal masculine distinctiveness of the personalistic police can best be seen when compared with the institutional functionary police, the focus of Chapter 7.

CHAPTER 7

Bureaucratizing Masculinity

It is not that the Englishman cannot feel — it is that he is afraid to feel. He has been taught at his public school that feeling is bad form. He must not express great joy or sorrow, or even open his mouth too wide when he talks.

E. M. Forster, "Notes on English Character," *Abinger Harvest*

This chapter examines the bureaucratically controlled Brazilian institutional functionary. He is represented primarily, although not exclusively, by the men who entered policing after Brazil's military coup — all but one of the five men whom we examine in this chapter are part of the second generation among our violence workers. Yet the defining feature of this policeman is not when he joined the force but rather, and much more central to his masculinity construction, that the vast majority of his discourse about self and violence is phrased in bureaucratic organizational terms. For example, the institutional functionary masculinities were more likely than the other two modal types to consistently link themselves professionally to a broad internal security structure and the state and much less likely to routinely define themselves as independent policemen. In other words, rather than communicating a persona distinct from a bureaucratized internal security structure, the institutional functionary's self — and especially the physically passionate aspects of his masculinity — are subordinated rhetorically to, and presumably muted by, organizational processes and structures. In compartmentalizing work and self, the institutional functionary masculinity rhetorically isolates his affect and cognition from action. Seeing themselves as dispassionate and rational internal security functionaries, these police present violence as if it instrumentally achieves the most appropriate and efficient social control ends, as Márcio clearly illustrates.

Márcio entered his state's Civil Police in 1956, eight years before the military coup. During Brazil's military period, he became a supportive functionary of the authoritarian state. Márcio's definition of respect is rooted in and derives from bureaucracy: it is structurally relational and hierarchical; transgressions are redressed by the structure itself, and not—as the personalistic policeman would assert—by interpersonal brute force. Respect is presumably achieved within, and rewarded meritoriously by, an organizational structure. It does not derive, as for the personalistic masculinity, from one-on-one interactions or from acceptably fulfilling mutual obligations. For the institutional functionary, respect is structurally mediated, not personalized.

Márcio's explanations for police "corruption" reflect his belief that social structure rightfully controls police behavior. According to Márcio, in the "old days"—when police acted outside the law—"they did so within a relatively narrow margin":

You'd only make an arrest when you'd reached the conclusion that there was a reasonable suspicion for detaining the suspect. The...*delegados* would call for his arrest record, look it over, see if the suspect was or wasn't employed. There were criteria for acting outside the law [because] there was some proportionality between resources and the job.

In contrast, today "there is no [longer] proportionality," defined by Márcio as a lack of symmetry between the number of criminals and the number of police chiefs to process them. This imbalance leads police to commit violence, Márcio points out. Today, there are so many criminals that a police official cannot effectively do his job because

a patrol car arrives [at the police station] with three policemen and three prisoners, [and then] another arrives with three [police] bringing in three more criminals, [and then] another three [police] bring in six [more prisoners].... If the police chief were to do what he should in each of those cases, he could not get anything accomplished on any one of them, so he starts resolving them with his eyes and through violence without first getting their records.

But, Márcio maintains that as "we get older, we start reaching...[the conclusion that] the law prohibits torture and law is the product of the popular will. So if I torture, I'm doing something that people don't want done." It concerns Márcio that today, in the public's estimation, the "faster [the police chiefs] act, the better [and] the more highly they are valued." Public pressure on the police to solve crimes quickly and at the lowest possible cost results in police chiefs having to cut corners and allowing their police to be "unprofessional." Therefore, rather than "doing an operation against one man [that might require] five men to catch and interrogate [him]," a police chief under pressure will allow his men to use two hours of torture and get what he needs.

For Márcio, the only criterion for establishing the acceptability of torture is proportionality, explaining that in the past the social climate provided an opportunity for police to appropriately apply it:

If the police caught a thief who had stolen 200 watches, and 20 were in his possession, [they would ask], "Where are the other 180?" If the robber said, "I'm not going to tell you where the other 180 are," then he [was] tortured.

However, according to Márcio, in more recent times the marginal proportion for acceptably using torture "has expanded," although his example implies that it has in fact contracted: the police now "torture whoever had twenty, or whoever didn't have any [watches at all], on the supposition that he had some." In any case, Márcio believes that such violations of proportionality cause police chiefs to lose control of their subordinates, and when that happens, they torture.

From this logic, Márcio comes up with two kinds of torturers—the rational, moral ones and the irrational, immoral ones. Speaking like an institutional functionary, Márcio explains that scientific rationality should guide torture: the rational torturer has "a view of the common good" and believes that "torturing will gather more evidence so there are greater possibilities of indemnifying the victim, as well as convicting the thief or murderer." The irrational, immoral torturer only "wants to find out...evidence and extort [gain from others]." Márcio believes that moral and rational police, who only use torture to discover evidence, are "apparently normal [and] controlled in their torture [because they] have limits." Such normal police respect the philosophy behind torture, that it "must cause suffering but must not cause injuries," adding at this point yet another criterion for making torture acceptable. According to Márcio, legitimate torture has "to...make the suffering compatible with a lack of injuries." This can be accomplished if "the policeman who is... torturing [is]...completely aware of what he is doing so [that] he'll know [his] limits." The policeman needs to make sure that torture causes

The "rational" torturer interrogates as water drips for hours on his victim's head, leaving no visible marks. The victim feels the weight of each drop like a blow to his brain. Vietnam War Remnants Museum, Ho Chi Minh City, Vietnam. Unidentified artist.

just the right amount of suffering to achieve the most optimal ends, a formula that apparently each rational torturer establishes in the process of coercing a confession, albeit often with the assistance of facilitator physicians.

In a corollary premise that indeed recognizes the role of facilitators in fostering atrocity, Márcio argues that rational police authorities should influence subordinates' use of violence. In fact, he excuses young police for inappropriate torture because they "have no choice" about their actions: they "belong to a machine [and] ... may or may not [torture] according to who is materially or morally directing [them]." When the highest police official "doesn't keep his eye on things, ... [ir-rational] torture" by young police can result. But as the *delegado*'s work load increased, his control over subordinate police disappeared—an indirect reference to the proportionality mandate that implicitly excuses police chief Márcio for his men's violence. Developing this argument further, he explains that within a climate in which police chiefs are under pressure to solve political, social, or criminal problems quickly, in deciding whether to lock people up or just torture them right then and there and then let them go, officials were no longer able to use "detailed criteria in each case" to establish the legitimacy of using violence to get information. As a result, Márcio argues, "improper things began to happen—physical violence, torture." Police apparently reasoned in such cases that "violence is faster [and] cheaper" than using sluggish legal procedures.

But Márcio still believes that torture can appropriately be carried out by police who manifest certain professionally mediated masculine characteristics as rationality and who hold certain kinds of organizational offices—for example, police chiefs, detectives, and investigators. Such "good" police know how to employ torture within proper bounds because they are "professionals," an institutional status that encapsulates the policeman, shapes his behavior, and grants legitimacy to anything that he does in the performance of his job. Given the legitimate authority that Márcio ascribes to the police system and its hierarchy, whatever a professional policeman does—if acting within the parameters and rules of his jurisdiction and institution—is ipso facto legitimate. For Márcio, inappropriate torture occurs because the otherwise rational professional structure has been *inadvertently* compromised.

Through such an argument, Márcio skillfully inserts violence workers and their violence into the kind of idealized rule-based bureaucratic context that sociologist Max Weber (2001) would label "legal-rational." Within such a structure, social control activity is presumably appropriately regulated and constrained by a system of written or consensually agreed-upon rules that are applied consistently. Therefore, as we have noted, for Márcio, torture is legal-rational if it is based on two criteria: guided by proportionality so as to cause suffering but not injuries and overseen by a rational superior. As a quintessential institutional functionary, Márcio sees these torture criteria and the police who embrace them (or not) within a larger structural whole that necessarily shapes police choices and guides their behavior.

Indeed, in further justifying police violence, Márcio would undoubtedly embrace functionalist sociologist Emile Durkheim (1933) in thinking that the moral core of a professionally regulated social control system is its "organic solidarity," where a system's component parts are functionally integrated and hierarchically organized and each part plays an important role in maintaining the health of the system itself. Within Durkheim's scheme, such an organic system becomes a moral regulator for the behavior of its constituent parts so long as each part operates generally within the jurisdictionally defined scope of its established hierarchical position and function. In an inadvertent application of this conservative functionalist perspective to his own work, Márcio argues that his position within the Civil Police system bestowed authority on his actions.

Within such an organizational framework, there was no place for emotionality. The rational violence worker could not have positive feelings for a victim, and he even had to modulate his extreme negative feelings so as not to go "too far" with a victim. By seeing himself as a functional component of a larger system—rather than a human actor with mutually supportive links to other such actors—he subordinated his feelings and emotions rhetorically to the organization itself. Márcio, a "good police *professional*" (a designation common to an institutional functionary's description of himself, compared with the personalistic masculinity's person-centered view of police work), believes that a policeman must push his own identity, self, personality, and needs backstage. The internal security organization's rational rules, hierarchy, and procedures must dictate his occupational behavior. To achieve such an outcome, Márcio even limited his own collegial interactions to a few other men whose professional needs (not mutual personal obligations) provided the glue for their rationally instrumentalized relationship.

Difficult as it is to locate traditional masculinity in the discourse of an institutional functionary, this violence worker's masculinity is implicitly defined by what it is not: passionate and expressive or visibly aggressive. As a conscientious professional, the institutional functionary defines his masculinity through, and in terms of, internal security organization: the hierarchy's rules, procedures, and structure replace his physically embodied persona, as Bernardo's narrative also points out.

Bernardo entered his state's Militarized Police in 1967, three years after the military coup. His first assignment was to an operations unit and next to an intelligence squad. Then, Bernardo made a career change, transferring to the Federal Police, where he became a censor of books, films, and magazines. Finally, he transferred into the Civil Police and became a *delegado*. He now also presides over a state organization to evaluate petitions from police seeking amnesty from their past atrocities. Bernardo reasons that if the successful applicant carried out violence under "legitimate orders" to protect Brazil's national security, then he is ready to help such police reenter their police organizations.

It is within such a national security framework that Bernardo frames his own conduct and career in internal security. As a young policeman in Militarized Police operations, Bernardo spent long periods away from home. Remembering up to twenty of his missions as "dangerous," he declares that he "wasn't afraid [or] concerned, because when you're young, it seems that you have more courage." Besides, Bernardo "believed in what [he] was doing.... [He was] a soldier fighting for his country, for internal control of that [subversive] movement...agitating the country." He considered himself "part of an institution whose mission it was to maintain law and order." Taken together, Bernardo's assertions suggest that he sees his police force as an extension of the larger national security system that enveloped the Militarized Police.

Declaring his loyalty to the police and military government greater than his own religious identification, Bernardo explains that he had no problem "entering a Catholic church and arresting everyone there." Bernardo could carry out such a mission because he "was very disciplined for militarized actions" and because the people in the church were "violating a principle of God by having a meeting that had nothing to do with religion" and everything to do with subversive politics. After seemingly fully justifying this arrest operation with a professionalism argument that diffused responsibility into the internal security organization, Bernardo distanced himself further from the consequences of that operation by explaining that he did not "know what happened" after his team arrested someone because he was just "part of the troops. [He] had to obey orders." Much more than a simple "I was just following orders" explanation for having carried out a violent arrest operation, Bernardo's assertions point to his segmentation of police action, a central characteristic of institutional functionary discourse about violence.

Elaborating his argument that diffuses responsibility for violence into professional structures and mandates, Bernardo claims that he never used "excess violence" in police operations. In fact, he "never tortured anyone," even though he admits to having headed police units that were well known for torture and murder. Bernardo, in fact, believes that "there are certain situations where [torture] is needed" as long as officials appropriately regulated it. However, if unprofessional "higher-ups"—presumably people other than Bernardo—"want the job done quickly, and don't do anything to prohibit torture and even let [policemen] do it," then all kinds of violence will occur.

Pointing to what he sees as a complicated causal relationship between torture, individual responsibility, and organizational mandates, Bernardo asserts that torturers are quite likely to come from the ranks of "very aggressive" policemen: "If anyone analyzed their psychological profile, it would be obvious that they have a higher tendency for aggressiveness—a very high degree." However, these men, he claims, are soon identified by their less-professional superiors who earmark them for the most violent police units. Police officials know that the more brutal police are easily found "in the judicial [i.e., civil] police area" and especially in units pursuing grand larceny and large-scale drug trafficking. In other words, initial tendencies are not sufficient for Bernardo to explain how men become torturers. He maintains that such already belligerent policemen become even more so because they constantly "deal with a certain type of delinquent," an explanation that in part blames victims for the policemen's violent behavior. Nevertheless, according to Bernardo, the aggressive police are "really exploited by their bosses, by those who [just] want to get the job over quickly," a rhetorical construction that also places the blame on some police administrators.

Like the other institutional functionary police, Bernardo's self-definition and professional identity were presented as resulting from the requirements of police work:

[As] a militar[ized] policeman, I really defined myself as a soldier who was fighting for his country.... As a federal policeman, I felt like a functionary of the intelligence service,... in the area more linked to national security. [As a Civil Police official], I felt like someone serving the nation with the mission to enforce the law within technical-juridical parameters.

Of course, many people define themselves in terms of their occupations. But most do not have occupations that shape them to carry out murder and torture or to order others to commit such acts.

As an institutional functionary, Bernardo was part of a larger social control structure that divided the work process into seemingly isolated segments, with each carrying out increasing levels of violence along a continuum of physical repression. Each set of actors within this hierar-

chical division of labor participates in only part of the violence, allegedly, in each case, at only those points where either less or no "real"
violence is carried out. And each set within this hierarchy is assigned
such a formally narrow role in carrying out the final violence, that—as
the institutional functionary sees it—inappropriate torture and murder
can result only either from a violent actor's being caught in the middle
and thus unfortunately vulnerable to an irresponsible authority above
him or from the policeman's being a bad apple. It is up to the system to
make sure that operatives serve the larger moral and social goal of regulating their violence toward acceptable means and ends. With discourse
about torture and murder framed in such a manner, the agent of violence is almost erased as a person, along with—in the case of institutional functionary Bernardo—his passions, humanity, and self, as Fernando illustrates as well.

Fernando entered the rank and file of his state's Militarized Police in
1963, one year before the military coup. His decision to become a policeman was influenced by his charismatic uncle, who would arrive at
Fernando's house on a shiny police motorcycle and regale the entire
family for hours with stories about his dangerous police operations. Fernando remembers always wanting to be a part of his uncle's glamorous
world. Under the military regime, Fernando moved up fairly quickly
through the ranks, first commanding a Militarized Police Shock Battalion and then heading a GOE elite SWAT team. By the end of his career
in 1993, Fernando had become a Militarized Police intelligence (P-2)
official.

Fernando regrets that his professional commitment to Militarized
Police service ruined his first marriage. Seeing the trouble that his work
was causing at home, Fernando tried to hold his marriage together by
resigning from the GOE: the "work...was never ending," and Fernando was away from home much of the time. His wife usually did not
know where he was or when he would return. Believing in the importance of keeping work and family separate, Fernando kept her in the
dark about much of his work. However, he later learned that his wife in
fact "knew some things," because in the democratizing 1980s she began
denouncing Fernando's violent policing to news media and human
rights groups. Although deeply depressed by the failure of his first marriage and the negative publicity about his work, Fernando is proud that
he was a good father who "was always very affectionate" with his children. This illustration of ethnographic seduction is often in fact part of
the mix of rhetorical ingredients in the violence worker's profile—he

presents himself as a good dad, able to show affection to his wife, the kids, or the dog.

In fact, Fernando has been denounced for his involvement in official violence during the military period. Denying these charges, Fernando points out that his street units engaged only in riot and strike control, street-sweep dragnets, and other forms of legitimate "population control." This did not include interrogation and torture, he declares: "We didn't work in the intelligence area [where torture occurred]; we were an operations group." In another example of Fernando's bureaucratically compartmentalized view of his own and others' police behavior, he contends that he could not have tortured because he was always "operational," apparently forgetting his career in Militarized Police intelligence where he was, by his own definition, in a position to torture. As an institutional functionary, Fernando asserts respect for jurisdictional boundaries, which allows him to claim that what occurred within one professionally defined jurisdiction was appropriate as long as boundaries were maintained.

But although Fernando believes that the professional policeman must submit to control by the formal organizational hierarchy, with his actions necessarily guided by organizational mandates, Fernando himself remembers his time in the violent riot control squad as the happiest time of his life. Behaving in those years more like a personalistic policeman than a bureaucratized institutional functionary, Fernando recalls engaging in physical fights to save Brazil from political subversion. He recalls one or two fist fights with criminals and subversives: he was in the middle of a large demonstration in Rio de Janeiro in the late 1960s when he resolved that his team "[wasn't] going to lose this war." Supporting the dignity of his men's struggle against subversion, Fernando "took off [alone], cleaning up the street." He "jumped [and]...kicked [some] guy in the chest with both feet." Fernando, describing himself as a "professional fighter," says that he properly dominated his opponents with skill. Having been prepared to confront danger, Fernando would not "do things...that aren't compatible with [his] professional reality."

For the most part, however, Fernando asserts his masculinity like an institutional functionary, arguing that through training, a man's passions and fragility are shaped into "courage," which he defines as dispassionately exercising professional control in violent situations. Describing his Shock Battalion, Fernando explains that he admired his men because they "had backbone": They were "determined people, well-trained and friends with each other." Fernando believes that the Shock Battalion was strong because "we suffered [together]." Yet although Fernando respected his men's determined commitment to the goal of ridding Rio's streets of political protesters, he maintains that "it doesn't do any good to have systems [or]...plans if the man is fragile.... There's no use in giving orders if [men] don't know how to follow them."

The only way to break that fragility is through "professional training," including using violent hazing to promote "value building" and "humility." The result is a militarized policeman who knows that if [he] is a professional, he will be successful. An unprofessional policeman will end up "the victim of his very own stupidity." Believing that professionalism moderates a man's basest impulses, Fernando argues that "when a man does not feel like a professional, he's vulnerable to corruption,...to deserting his post,...to getting killed." If a man is "frightened and... doesn't want to die, during the first gun battle, he'll take off shooting and kill someone who doesn't have anything to do with anything."

Embodied physical discourse was relatively infrequent in Fernando's explanations about himself and violence. Fernando included such physicality only in discussions of his early years in policing. The vast majority of violence during Fernando's police career was framed in discourse that disembodied physicality into a dispassionate and rational professionalism, which appropriately absorbed Fernando's nonprofessional persona into the internal security organization's hierarchy—a rhetorical process that institutional functionary Eduardo communicates as well.

In describing his early DOPS missions, Eduardo almost always situates himself within a police team, who, as that term implies, are vertically or horizontally attached to a larger bureaucracy: "We'd be given the job." "Our mission was to arrest him." "We'd submit our reports to superiors." This rhetorical pattern makes Eduardo different from the personalistic police. For example, personalistic policeman Sérgio (Chapter 6) almost always used the personal pronoun when talking about his intelligence work; all three personalistic masculinities inserted their policing—either ideally or in fact—within personalized mutual reciprocity networks. In contrast, the institutional functionary, even more than describing himself as working within a team, positions himself squarely within the internal security bureaucracy and then uses, as we have seen, this segmentation to his moral advantage. For example, institutional functionary Eduardo maintains that as a DOPS policeman, he could not have tortured or murdered because his police team—appropriately subordinated to the national security bureaucracy—could only "investigate [and] write a report" about subversive activity. On those supposedly rare occasions when Eduardo's unit actually made an arrest—as with a group of dissident priests—the team merely tape-recorded a religious ceremony and turned its report over to its boss. Eduardo does not know what happened to the priests after that, although it is likely that they suffered the same kinds of brutalities as Frei Tito, whose case was described in Chapter 5. Nevertheless, the jurisdictional framework that Eduardo presents as constraining his group's behavior makes it possible for him to assert—like Fernando—that he "never participated in torture because [he] never carried out interrogations," where most of the torture occurred. Applying the rhetoric commonly used by other institutional functionaries, Eduardo divides violence work into so many distinct parts that no one person need assume full responsibility for it. As just one element in the assembly line of Brazil's segmented system of social control, Eduardo instrumentalizes security-force violence. He need not admit to having seen or take responsibility for the consequences of his having facilitated extreme violence, because his actions were merely to accomplish a single narrowly defined social control task.

From the point of view of the institutional functionary police professional, when internal security bureaucracy is in excellent working order, it guides a policeman toward the correct conduct as Márcio has asserted so frequently. Speaking about his own violence, Eduardo advances an ideological justification that absolves him of personal responsibility and explains his violence as politically necessary: "We were patriots...defending our country." Eduardo's team had done what was necessary because he was a "patriot...ridding the country of a threat." Under such a national security climate, according to Eduardo, some torture is likely to grow out of "zealousness in trying to discover [and] unravel a crime." Just the same, he believes that the police who tortured "with good intentions...to protect society" were engaging in legitimate violence. If they went too far, it was because they had to "handle a lot of work and did not have the resources to work on an investigation, on all of the investigations. So the shortest route is by torturing." Alluding to what Márcio labeled "proportionality," Eduardo explains inappropriate police violence as rooted in an excess of external demands over resources: there are too many problems and insufficient time and technology to address them, so individual police are pressured into exceeding professional limits.

The residual inappropriate violence that Eduardo admits to having committed as an intelligence operative was attributed to his excessive drinking. Eduardo recalls getting into fights and shooting at people while intoxicated. But with his life neatly divided between professional service—where Eduardo claims he did not murder or torture—and his drunken carousing on- and off-duty—where he beat people, shot at them, and sometimes killed them—Eduardo could successfully claim that he had not committed excess violence when acting as a professional policeman on duty. When his drinking got so out of control that he was drunk on duty as well, he could write this off as a deviant *exception* to professionalism and thus not professional conduct at all.

Although depicting himself as a Damon Runyon figure in his colorful private life, Eduardo's picaresque narrative was in fact very much subordinated to what he described as the necessities of bureaucracy. Even the seemingly personal—like romance and marriage—was explained by Eduardo in terms of its relationship to DOPS national security work. The prostitute that Eduardo married knew about his secret life, did not ask questions about it, and accepted and mostly supported his work. Ever the pragmatist, Eduardo knew that this relationship would very likely work out, but even if it did not, it would not get in the way of his commitment to internal security service while it lasted.

Jorge joined his state's Militarized Police in 1980, relatively late in Brazil's military period. The kind of violent, aggressive policeman that police officials are claimed to have selected for their torture and murder squads, Jorge spent eight years of his youth in FEBEM—the state-run orphanage for poor, parentless children. Jorge remembers FEBEM with a mixture of anger and pain: "unruly" children were subjected to "the needle"—having to "lean against the wall, holding yourself up with your fingers until your fingers couldn't take the weight any more. If someone fell, they'd put a heavy weight around his neck" and make him assume the needle position again. Jorge maintains that this treatment revolted him and contributed to his aggressiveness.

Jorge was funneled very early into violent police work, when a few years after entering Militarized Police service he began working undercover in a DOI/CODI "bust" (execution) squad. Explaining that police training contributed to his capacity to carry out violence, Jorge remembers, "They taught us terrible things—how to torture, how to kill." The DOI/CODI internal security organization wanted only "objective, cold people" with the capacity to obey orders. Jorge maintains that his background abundantly prepared him to be a murderer for Brazil's military state.

As the only violence worker who openly confessed to having tortured or murdered, Jorge claimed that he never really believed that national security justified police violence. Just the same, like the other institutional functionaries, Jorge still depersonalized his violence by linking it to the national security system's organizational structures and imperatives. However, he believes himself to be fundamentally different from the system's other DOI/CODI operatives. He is "softer, really softer, very sentimental," and he "cr[ied] more than the cold, objective killers." Yet Jorge still believes that he "never had the chance to have...all of the emotions that [other] humans have" and claims to have "never loved anyone"—not even his wife. Labeling himself "cold-blooded" for ulti- mately abandoning his wife and daughter, Jorge argues that he had to leave them or risk putting their lives in jeopardy.

Jorge maintains that his long stint in repression stripped him of "am- bition." "I didn't want a house because I didn't want whereabouts so I couldn't be found." Although claiming no stable sense of place, it still troubles Jorge that he could so easily break off with his wife and daugh- ter—he says it was "as if [he'd] gone to work and not come home."

Speaking about his own murderous past, Jorge discloses that he "ac- counted for eighty deaths" annually just in the two years between 1980 and 1982, although he may be deliberately underreporting, as is often done by violence workers, and may actually have murdered hundreds of people. Jorge explains that his violent career began one night when he and his buddy were standing guard in a cemetery. Looking up, they saw a group of "ghostlike creatures" dressed in white walking nearby. Jorge's buddy panicked and shot at the people, wounding some of them. Jorge ran for help and got his superiors to return to the scene with him. Realiz- ing that the injured victims had been conducting a Candomblé religious ceremony and that there could be serious criticism of the shooting, the Militarized Police superior ordered the religious group killed. As Jorge and his buddy loaded the fifteen people onto the back of a truck—with their captives "screaming [and] asking for help"—Jorge's police captain passed his gun down the line of subordinates, first to the squad's sergeant, who then passed it to the corporal, who then passed it to Jorge. Ordered to shoot the prisoners, Jorge—who claims to have "never shot anybody in [his] life" up to that point—was "obliged to hold the heads of the people and kill them." But when the captain ordered Jorge to put the victims' bodies in a nearby garbage truck," Jorge refused, enjoining his superior "to do [his] own dirty work." Apparently, in the compartmentalized world of execution, some tasks are just too menial for the professional.

Jorge was promoted after that operation to the Militarized Police Re- served Service. Jorge explains that Reserved Service would detect a per- son who was involved in a certain crime and then "go in, pick him up, and waste the criminal, whether he was a civilian or policeman." Jorge remembers with some disdain that the Reserved Service even "used their own men to kill [a policeman who was] out of line." For Jorge, that was "crooked." He also believes that shooting people in an ambush is wrong because such murders have no objective; for murder to be legitimate, there has to be a plan.

Comparing himself to the torturers, Jorge believes that murderers are professionally and morally superior. First, a professional executioner "perfect[s] ways to kill hand-to-hand; he learns to exploit vital pressure points." (In fact, of course, Jorge usually killed his victims with a gun.) Second, according to Jorge, it is "much easier to kill because the torturer [by contrast] has to have a commitment to his victim. The killer has no commitment to his victim." Finally, therefore, murder is quicker, more impersonal, and more humane than torture. Bringing these moral criteria together, Jorge tells about one of his DOI team's "death flights" (see also Verbitsky 1996; Feitlowitz 1998) to Brazil's Amazon region. The group's objective was to return from the mission "with no one [of the prisoners] on board." Jorge recounts his story about this horrible incident, as if watching it from outside the scene itself: the DOI team's prisoners were being subjected to "all kinds of torture;...women [were being] raped... and [then] thrown out of the helicopter [alive]." Jorge, still speaking in passive voice, remembered feeling "so badly" at seeing his colleagues torture and rape a female prisoner that he simply "had to kill [her]." Jorge's partners "were torturing [the woman]...too much—she was screaming." Having discursively reentered the scene of the violence, Jorge—now speaking in active voice—justifies his violence as having been the morally most appropriate course. Although his colleagues had ruthlessly thrown their victims out of the helicopter alive, Jorge had "at least" killed his victim before her lifeless body had been tossed into the rain forest below.

After almost five years of being what Jorge himself labels a "murderer for the state," he began asking himself, "What am I going to do with my life if I only know how [to kill]? I wanted to be myself a little, to know, to think, to have all of the emotions that humans have and I never had a chance to have." Now in prison for committing a postmilitary period murder for which Jorge says he was "framed," he maintains that he has spent his entire life controlled by one government bureaucracy or another. Jorge laments having given the government "almost [his] entire life," adding

I've never had anything. I've never known civilian life. I was put in FEBEM [as a child]—[then] the army, the Militarized Police, and now I'm in jail. I don't know what it's like to put a labor registration card in my pocket and work and have a profession.

As a subordinate murder functionary, Jorge was literally just one element in a functionally organized atrocity hierarchy. At the rank-and-file operational level, in Jorge's words, "[violent police] groups...are united. [When engaging in] support and assault, they can even work together like brothers." But overall, in fact, the internal security system that controlled Jorge was directed by nameless public safety officials—the secretary of public security, judges, notaries—who sent lists of faceless victims targeted for murder to nameless senior Military Police officers, who passed these lists to Jorge's murder team. Replicating the anonymity of this system, Jorge's execution team would go out—usually hooded and working at night—to round up the listed subversives so that his team—acting as one—could execute them. The victims of Jorge's assassination squad were little more than depersonalized projects to be crossed off a list.

As an exception among institutional functionaries in a bureaucratized system of what Arendt (1951: 40) calls "rule-by-nobody," Jorge openly admits to much of the violence he committed—although not without some contradictions. Reflecting discourse common to the other institutional functionaries, Jorge presents himself as one of many police within a violent chain of command, as enmeshed within an internal security hierarchy that had been subdivided into so many distinct segments that no one violence worker needed to consider himself fully responsible for any particular outcome.

Contrasting Masculinities

Comparing the institutional functionaries' masculinity presentations with those of the personalistic violence workers, we see that—in marked contrast to the latter's physically embodied and visibly present masculinity—the institutional functionaries' physically passionate masculinity was subordinated to internal security bureaucracy: "The demands of authority [were] paramount; the thoughts and feelings of individuals disregarded" (Skovholt, Moore, and Haritos-Fatouros, n.d.: 7). Within the institutional functionaries' occupational world, there was apparently no place for either masculine brute force or feminine emotionality—potentially unprofessional manifestations of personalism.

In his analysis of 1920s German protofascist Freikorps writing about the perfect soldier, Theweleit (1989) has discovered a similar subordination of this soldier's self and emotions to the larger whole. According to Freikorps ideological expectations, "feminized men

[were] as repellent...as masculine women. [The] quintessentially negative 'Other' lurking inside the male body of the good fighting man was the 'liquid female body.' By contrast, the Freikorps soldier ideal was a body devoid of all internal viscera which finds its apotheosis in the machine,...the acknowledged utopia of the fascist warrior' " (Benjamin and Rabinbach 1989: xix). The Freikorps soldier had to be "a physical type devoid of drives and of psyche; he ha[d] no need of either since all his instinctual energies ha[d] been smoothly and frictionlessly transformed [through training] into functions of his steel body" (Theweleit, 1989: 159). The most urgent task for Freikorps trainers, and as chapters 9 and 10 demonstrate, for Brazilian violence workers as well, was to "damn in, and to subdue any force that threaten[ed] to transform [the violence worker] back into the horribly disorganized jumble of flesh, hair, skin, bones, intestines, and feelings that [suggest he is] human." The new man "owes allegiance only to the [military] machine that bore him" (160).

The narratives of Brazilian institutional functionaries make clear that they saw themselves first and foremost as members of a police organization—in Theweleit's words, a "machine" that was subordinated to a larger social control system and state. Given this bureaucratized perspective, to the extent that the institutional functionary violence workers manifested any rhetorical masculinity at all, its most visible features were dispassionate rationality and operational instrumentalism. Talking about himself and police colleagues as if they were little more than positional categories whose existence was only in relation to other such categories—"the police team," "our unit," "operatives' jurisdictions"—the institutional functionary's police operations were presented as an extension of the organization itself. As Theweleit (1989: 155) has found for German Freikorps soldiers, the "troop machine...place[d] the individual soldier in a new set of relations to other bodies,...[these were] a combination of innumerable identically polished components" that had "become...a miniature of the machine" (159).

Given the Brazilian institutional functionaries' view of themselves and their work, they rhetorically decoupled their atrocities from human physicality and erased from visibility both their violence and their victims' sufferings. Within such a sanitized organizational perspective, police brutality could then be an acceptable outcome of a professional process, a feature that these violence workers share with the "blended masculinity" police—albeit without the latter's being able to use national security ideology to justify their violence, as the next chapter demonstrates.

CHAPTER 8

Blended Masculinity

*O conspiracy! Sham'st thou to show thy dangerous brow by night,
when evils are most free?*

William Shakespeare, *Julius Caesar*

This chapter introduces the policemen who manifested what we label "blended masculinity," which features traits of both the institutional functionary and personalistic masculinities. However, unlike the other two types of police, the central structural characteristic of those with blended masculinity is their ease of movement between formal and informal social control systems: they routinely carried out atrocity on duty as working cops and off duty as paid rent-a-cops for businesses and as private vigilantes—whether as lone wolves or as part of a death squad. These interviewees maneuvered smoothly between institutional functionary and personalistic justifications for violence while mingling those two masculinity presentations to produce a distinct third one.

Looking first at Roberto and Vinnie and recalling Ernesto from Chapter 1, in this chapter we present the ways that our interviewees with blended masculinity talked about themselves and their police work, about police violence, and about its victims. We then address the larger theoretical implications of the three modal masculinity patterns: How does each masculinity's disclosures about violence contribute to the political visibility or invisibility of atrocity? How does each masculinity set differently structure an image of perpetrators as legitimate professional actors, intentional sadists, or hapless victims of the system? Do such discursive images point to differing degrees of each masculinity's absorption into police bureaucracy—with consequences for the public visibility and acceptance of their violence? Is the multiplicity of masculinities within Brazil's atrocity system in fact functional for legitimizing state violence? We complete our foundation for addressing these theoretical questions by developing the third police modal masculinity, that of the blended masculinity violence workers.

Blending Masculinities

Two of the three violence workers who presented a blended masculinity—Militarized Policeman Roberto, in this chapter, and Civil Policeman Ernesto, from Chapter 1—grew up under Brazilian military dictatorship but did not begin policing until after it was over. The third policeman of this type, Vinnie, was primarily in Militarized Police service during Brazil's military period. All three were in prison for murder or attempted murder at the time of their interview, in contrast to all but one (Jorge, also in for murder) of the other interviewees. Yet, as we explained in Chapter 3, the incarcerated police were hardly more open about their and the police system's violence than their working or successfully retired colleagues. And although they were somewhat more critical overall of the police institution, they were still very guarded in their critiques of it.

When interviewed, all three blended masculinity policemen presented themselves as simultaneously part of and separate from the police bureaucracy. In fact, they frequently described their violence for police objectives as if carried out both from within and outside of police organizations—producing a complex set of strategic orientations and self-definitions that contributed to their blended masculinity. Off-duty police violence was often portrayed as if it had occurred on duty, with professional legalisms used to explain off-duty death squad activities. Such a confusion of roles may have increased the likelihood of public disclosure about their ambiguous position and perhaps helps explain the higher chance of their ending up in prison to be interviewed by us. It also helped shape the official characterization by the system as a rotten cop who had, supposedly atypically, gone too far, a designation that absolved both the police institution and the state of responsibility for the blended masculinity policemen's conduct.

Although in some ways they resemble personalistic violence workers, the blended masculinity interviewees did not identify positively with the communities they policed, and their murders of citizens reflect this attitude. But unlike the institutional functionaries, the blended masculinity police also did not identify very closely with formal police bureaucracy either. Although any of the police interviewees might be expected to call up the formal police system's rules if these could be used to defend their actions, the blended masculinity policemen's relationship to them was often problematic. Nevertheless, these interviewees were still willing to use the rules when these served their needs—even when acting as off-duty police-for-hire or as members of death squads or as lone-wolf citizen vigilantes—but their mixing of roles often militated against their legitimately using the formal rules to judge their informal behavior.

Even though the blended masculinity violence workers were not exclusively found in postmilitary Brazil, this period's move toward democracy and privatization clearly has provided particularly fertile soil for them to thrive and multiply. Within a seemingly free market of potential victims and of businesses willing to hire violence workers, such men flow easily into and out of formal policing and informal rent-a-cop and death squad work, as Roberto illustrates.

Roberto, who was from a police family, entered the Militarized Police at the age of twenty-one in 1987, two years after Brazil formally began its political redemocratization; he had grown up under the military dictatorship. Yet even though Roberto's father and two uncles were militarized policemen, his family was reluctant for him to join. Roberto's father warned him that "it's very risky: a tough, limiting life." But proud of his father, "a policeman twenty-four hours a day" who loved his work and was totally committed to it, Roberto wanted to be like him.

Despite his ambitions, Roberto's career was marked by betrayal and disappointments, the first of which actually stemmed from his father's tough life in the police. The pay was so low and his family so large that Roberto's father could not make ends meet on his salary. Roberto remembers his father being too honest to accept bribes, so he had to sell his blood and carry heavy sacks of sand from a lagoon to a construction site to supplement his paltry police wages. It pained Roberto that his father, who loved policing and worked all the time, still could not provide adequately for his family.

Nevertheless, wanting to make his father "proud of having a son who was a policeman," Roberto joined the force. An added incentive was that Roberto had been having trouble getting work that paid more than the minimum wage. A job in the Militarized Police rank and file would at least provide a living income, albeit a poor one. But more than for money, Roberto says that he joined the Militarized Police "to maintain lawfulness in society [and] to work...honestly," as his father had done. But shortly after he started, Roberto faced another severe crisis.

After his brother's house was robbed in his absence and his wife was raped in front of their children, Roberto asked his battalion commander to detail some men to help him and his brother—also a militarized policeman—locate the perpetrators. Frustrated by his commander's refusal to assign men to the case, Roberto approached him with another proposal. Because a policeman had to be on the force for two years before he could carry a gun, Roberto needed his commander's permission to purchase and carry one. He had resolved that he and his brother would simply arrest and interrogate the culprits themselves. But Roberto's commander refused this request as well. Feeling he had no place else to turn, Roberto asked one of the death squads in his Militarized Police organization to help him: "All of us on the force knew that every battalion had its killers."

But before the death squad could even begin its search for the assailants, Roberto and his brother had located them. Questioning the criminals for forty minutes in the back room of his brother's house, with the men still unwilling to confess to their crime, Roberto says that he had no option but to "to slap [one of the perpetrators] and punch him around a little." Believing that "a criminal is a liar," Roberto knew that if "you give him a slap,...he [will] break down completely." Roberto justifies this action because he carried it out with "great emotional control, a calm." As a result, Roberto could "ask questions [and] explain things" rationally to the suspect. Interestingly, even though Roberto was acting as a citizen vigilante when he interrogated and beat the alleged perpetrator, he still refers to himself in that situation as "a policeman." Such rhetorical juxtapositions were, as we have argued, common among blended masculinity police interviewees. They easily mixed formal policing and citizen vigilantism, as if equivalent in some respects and completely different in others. This discursive blending perhaps mirrors the interstitial structural position of the blended masculinity policeman himself.

Once Roberto and his brother had themselves located his brother's wife's assailants, he informed the original death squad that he did not need them any more. But the death squad stepped into the case anyway, eventually torturing and murdering the suspects that Roberto and his brother had found. Analyzing the death squad's behavior in this case, Roberto compares his own inner control with the lack of self-control manifested by the "older police" in the death squad. Having been present when the death squad violence took place, Roberto explained that they were totally "self-enraged. They wanted to hit the guy, scream at him, kill him." Roberto recalls even trying to convince these older policemen to "go easy," but they "were very nervous and agitated, ready to kill the individual right then and there." According to Roberto, the older policemen had "inner hostility" developed from years of killing and because they were "neurotic, mentally disturbed." Roberto believes that as "a policeman, [he had] to stay in control," even though at that time he was acting as a vigilante rather than a policeman on duty. But such fluidity was common among the blended masculinity police.

Although Roberto did not want to continue working with the death squad, he was told that because the death squad had done Roberto and his brother a favor by agreeing to help them locate the culprits and then killing them, the two policemen were obliged to support the murder team or it would kill them, too. Roberto recalls that "whenever they needed us, we would have to go with them on any pretext." As a member of that death squad, Roberto claims that he "observed" forty-five murders but didn't kill anyone himself. As the death squad's driver, Roberto would park the car in "dark and deserted locations...[and] put the...lights on for [the killers] to see." Roberto says that he would hear "bang, bang" and the victims would "fall down"; his job was then to "pick up dead bodies." But because Roberto did not pull the trigger and just stayed in the car watching the killings, he doesn't consider himself a murderer. In fact, he maintains that he even played a positive role in the death squad's activities, sometimes restraining his older colleagues' behavior by "interfer[ing] with their [base] impulses." Roberto "wouldn't let them act unjustly...[and] kill...a completely innocent person."

Roberto later formed and headed a death squad on his own, a vigilante murder team composed of other off-duty militarized police, while still working on the force. Roberto spent many years as a "twenty-four-seven enforcer"—executing people twenty-four hours a day, seven days a week. Although the boundaries between his formal police and vigilante roles blended into one another, at the same time, Roberto was very clear about the moral justifications for his violence in each setting. Contrasting his own murder rationale with that of the older killers in the first death squad, Roberto explains that his own death squad selected its victims by "wait[ing] for the statistics—facts—so we [knew] who was and who wasn't [innocent]." By approaching his potential victims in such a reasonable manner, Roberto was able to "see who is a worker or a student. You see who is a good person, who is a bandit. You zero in on the right person." In the institutional functionary side of his persona, Roberto does not recognize the possibility of his group's executing the wrong person.

Roberto argues that he organized his own death squad only to protect himself from the one he had finally left. Feeling in constant danger of being murdered by the one that had helped with his brother's case— "[I knew] too much.... They were against me.... They wanted to kill me"—the "only thing" that Roberto could do was to assemble one of his own. Of course, economics also motivated Roberto: by working seven days a week, twenty-four hours a day—as an on-duty Militarized Policeman and also off duty in a death squad—Roberto was always earning [the] money that he very much needed, a legal-rational justification for being a death squad leader.

Yet, as we have just seen, Roberto also refers to qualities of his own emotionally positive nature to explain his appropriately selected executions. Because Roberto feels that he is a "good person [who does not] like injustice," he believes his murderous self is different in essential ways from that of the irrational, out-of-control murderers who killed in an overemotional fury. In other words, Roberto believes that some of his killings were carried out by an emotionally balanced and affectively humane self and some by a rational and professional self that murder objectively. Like a personalistic policeman, therefore, he explains some of his violent actions in terms of personal qualities that distinguish him from the heartless police in death squads. Yet like an institutional functionary, he claims that rational thinking sets him apart from the irrational violence workers all around him. Roberto's interesting fusion of two masculine personas produces something more than either of the former two alone produced. And as we have seen, in the process of balancing these two essentially inconsistent behavioral and attitudinal repertoires, Roberto smooths the contradictions into a blended masculinity.

Roberto seems to mediate the contradictions through a moral geography that separates his work domains without making the accompanying assumption that one of them (police work) is pragmatically violent and the other one (his personal side) is nonviolent. Ultimately, as we shall show, a common theme among blended masculinities is to use exceptionalist arguments to explain contradictory behaviors that cannot be handled by a moral geography alone.

Finally, after working for years simultaneously in the Militarized Police and off duty in a death squad, Roberto's greatest betrayal came when he was in uniform and taking a break from policing. Having lunch with his brother and an acquaintance at an outdoor lunch stand outside his police jurisdiction, Roberto spotted five suspected criminals—among them "two [alleged] drug dealers and two drug addicts." At seeing the two uniformed policemen, the suspects fled. When Roberto shouted, "Stop, police!" one of the men allegedly turned and fired his gun at Roberto. At that point, the only thing he remembers is discharging his gun rapidly; he says he want "totally blank... [and] only saw a reflection" of what was happening. When Roberto regained full consciousness, he realized that he had killed all of them. Explaining that the murders had resulted from a blackout, he says that he "lost all [his] emotional self-control.... My head was fuzzy. I couldn't see [the people he shot]."

Yet it was not these murders that Roberto considered a betrayal of his values but rather his brother's abandoning him at the murder scene. Roberto's brother and the acquaintance "came running up, saw everyone fallen on the ground, got nervous, and left," he says. His brother even took the patrol car, abandoning Roberto to deal with the wounded and to explain his way out of the violence. After a failed attempt to give first aid to one of the critically injured suspects, Roberto ran from the scene and hid for several days, leaving those of his victims who were still alive to bleed to death. Returning several days later to his police barracks—with the city's newspapers declaring the murders a death squad killing and without his brother's testimony that he had shot the five people in self-defense, Roberto was arrested and later convicted of murder. As a policeman who had killed suspects outside his jurisdiction and who had for years been suspected of leading a death squad—although with no hard-and-fast evidence against him for its crimes—and with a state government newly committed to eliminating such organized atrocity, Roberto was sentenced to seventy-two years in prison.

Roberto had been trapped in the centrifugal vortex of his institutional marginality: a uniformed policeman out of jurisdiction, behaving as if in a death squad, he had killed people in a society under pressure to replace vigilantism with democratically controlled policing to cut down crime. In place of centralized military authoritarianism—where almost any police violence that fell under at least indirect control of the military was covered up or excused—a free market of murder-for-hire agents had emerged within and alongside a strong Militarized Police system. Together they would combat the democratizing society's crime problem.

This privatized devolution from centralized control over policing can be seen in Vinnie's story as well. Although Vinnie joined his state's Militarized Police on April 23, 1964, just a little over three weeks after Brazil's military coup, his masculinity presentation mirrors that of the postmilitary period's blended masculinity policemen. Raised in rural Espírito Santo, Rio's neighboring state up the northeast coast, Vinnie entered the Air Force at seventeen. After almost three years in this service, he left the military for a construction job. Finding himself laid off from construction, without "anything to do, and…having trouble finding a job," Vinnie was drawn to and then joined the Militarized Police because his cousin was an officer in the force. Vinnie considered the Militarized Police "a…force with integrity that people could count on; the officers, soldiers, all of us were very united." He thus began policing with an outlook that could have placed him solidly within the larger Militarized Police organization; this might have anchored him to an institutional functionary masculinity. However, a series of events in Vinnie's career increasingly distanced him from the organization.

With a background in Air Force intelligence, Vinnie's first Militarized Police assignment was to the Reserved Service intelligence section. While there, Vinnie was imprisoned in 1969 for homicide: six years for killing his wife. Vinnie explains this murder by semantically distancing himself from his wife's violent death, arguing that he had killed his wife during a heated fight: his gun "discharged and [his] wife died," as if her murder had just occurred without his carrying it out.

Released from prison after six years, apparently without credentials being soiled, Vinnie was hired as private chauffeur for the governor of his state. Vinnie was proud of that position because "to work in the [Governor's] Palace, you had to have integrity." Vinnie could have obtained such a position only through family, friends, or political connections. Besides, Vinnie's criminal record would guarantee his loyalty to the governor, who had hired him knowing of his murder conviction.

By benefit of having worked for several years with the governor, his previous dismissal from the Militarized Police was expunged, and he returned to the Militarized Police Reserved Service. Between 1975 and 1982, Vinnie investigated irregularities and crimes committed by his colleagues while himself illegally moonlighting by running a death squad as a bill collector for propane gas companies. In that capacity, Vinnie and his associates strong-armed slum merchants into paying their bills and in the process committed scores of homicides: Vinnie and his squad got a bonus for killing those who could not or would not pay on time.

A physically heavy man of imposing height for Brazil, "Big Vinnie," as he was commonly known, was denounced in 1981 as the shadowy police-

man behind about 300 notorious White Hand death squad murders in
the slums. Vinnie discredits his accuser as a "criminal prostitute," maintaining that he and his squad had never murdered outside the "legitimate
line of duty"—including presumably both their on-duty killings and the
executions he admits to having committed as a rent-a-cop for propane
companies. Justifying the latter murders, Vinnie sounds like a mere employee carrying out an assigned task: "It was a job with a lot of responsibility and very risky because I had to pick up very large sums." According
to Vinnie, "some" murders were necessary because of the danger of his
work—a fact he could "prove by witnesses or by...his police partners."
In the end, charged with only 11 of the hundreds of homicides committed by the death squad that he was assumed to have headed, Vinnie was
acquitted of 10 and convicted of only 1, for which he was incarcerated at
the time of his interview.

Vinnie—who swears that he had not even been in the region when
those executions occurred—admitted in passing that he had indeed
been part of a death squad for pay. But he claims that he had to join it
because of unrelenting peer pressure and because low police pay did not
leave him enough money to purchase a car for collecting the gas company's fees. As a result, Vinnie got "involved in that extermination-
group business," a rhetorically vague way to describe his role in murder
as merely a by-product of uncontrollable external conditions. He defines
his on-duty violence as legal "acts of bravery" and therefore not illegal
vigilantism at all; he feels misunderstood and victimized as regards his
off-duty executions. The political system made him take the fall for a lot
of other people's crimes. As we have seen with Roberto in this chapter
and with Ernesto in Chapter 1, Vinnie mixes institutional functionary
discourse with assertions that could also point to his being a personalistic policeman.

Shifting Identity Designations

As we have pointed out, one of the defining features of blended masculinity police is, as their label suggests, their alternating between two
very different masculinity presentations, showing much more variation
in this regard than the other two types, which were fairly consistent.
Moreover, these police manifested no recognition during their interview that they were presenting a series of difficult-to-square assertions
about themselves. For example, like the personalistic police, the blended

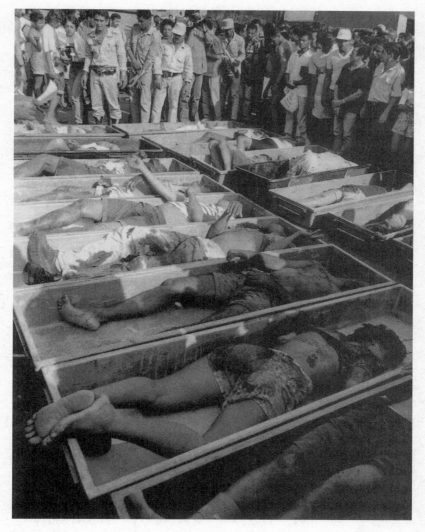

Poor people slaughtered in 1993 in their Vigário Geral slum by police-linked death squads. Zeca Guimarães, *Folha de São Paulo,* August 30, 1993.

masculinity policemen tended to make frequent references to masculine physicality in their descriptions of police atrocities—"I became very violent, very aggressive on the job." At the same time, like the institutional functionary police, the blended masculinity interviewees prided themselves in subordinating aspects of their personalistic masculinity to occupational structures and processes—apparently even the good vigilante had "to act rationally" sometimes, as Ernesto states (Chapter 1) and Roberto declares (this chapter). The blended masculinity police, in other words, often allowed their passion and feelings to shape discourse about themselves and violence: "I felt enraged"; "I got so nervous.... It was the first time...that I was shot [at]." Just the same, these police had no apparent problem appealing to formal bureaucratic norms and requirements, as an institutional functionary would do, even to justify their off-duty violence.

We would argue that these mixed assertions reflect the blended masculinity policeman's position as attached (in reality or by desire) to one person or group (personalistic) yet inserted into police bureaucracy itself (institutional functionary), combined by his own reshaping of these incongruent statuses. In the process of carrying out this samba of clashing identity performances, the blended masculinity policeman presented explanations for violence that deviated from a neatly compartmentalized division of his identity into a self that commits violence as part of a work role and a personal and positive self—husband, father, family man—that is nonviolent (see Lifton 1986). The blended masculinity policeman allowed that he had sometimes been a good vigilante and a rational on-duty murderer and even a momentarily irrational cop, with all of these statuses morally equal to his private self.

Violent Visibilities

It can be seen that each of the three masculinity presentations—personalistic, institutional functionary, and blended—confers a different degree of rhetorical visibility on a policeman's violence and its relationship to the national state. For example, the personalistic policeman's violence is quite obvious: he presents it himself as physically aggressive, expressive, and overtly interactive through colorful discourse about "fair" fights, "deserved" beatings, and explicit descriptions of torture and killing. However, because the personalistic cop presents himself as operating independently of his police institution—a "Dirty Harry" who takes the law into his own hands—he excludes the police organization and, by extension, the state from the atrocity system.

By contrast, the institutional functionary's discourse about violence renders both his violence and his police organization's relationship to it relatively invisible. By discursively embedding his violence within a complicated bureaucracy, the institutional functionary erases the personal role of official perpetrators in state-sponsored atrocities. As Armando explained, "A police professional knows when and how to use violence," an assertion that explained his actions as falling within his legitimate duties. In other words, any violence that is carried out by professionals is merely a necessary component of official social control requirements and role expectations. This renders the state and its agents legitimate actors in police repression while disguising their violence.

Likewise, the individual violence of blended masculinity police was discursively rendered politically legitimate and thus invisible on both counts—as personal and as institutionally legitimate. Alternately masking his violence as private and interpersonal or as formal and legal, this policeman's own atrocities were doubly defined out of the political sphere. For example, when the blended masculinity policeman used on-duty violence in his formal role—even though acting like a vigilante in most cases—he described himself (and was almost always seen by the police organization) as carrying out legitimate crime control. When he was moonlighting off duty—as a private rent-a-cop or citizen vigilante in a death squad—the torture and murder that he committed was sometimes presented as private or personal—not even police violence at all—and sometimes described as official police action, even though it was not. In the former case, the blended masculinity policeman's violence could not possibly be related to illegitimate state action because he was supposedly acting privately, whereas in the case of official action, his violence is defined as a legitimate extension of his state-mandated police role, even though it is not.

Within the framework of the three types' presentations of themselves and their violence, it is difficult to point to the masculinity that best exemplifies the coldest torturer or most brutal executioner. Because the personalistic and blended masculinity violence workers are more visually graphic about their own and others' violence, it would be easiest to claim that these two masculinity sets came closest to the stereotype of a heartless and sadistic torturer or killer. Yet we would argue that the more "rational" institutional functionary police, who did not need to be troubled with questions about whether they enjoyed violence because they cloaked their and others' brutality in discourse that dispassionately erased victims and perpetrators, might be candidates for that dubious distinction. By presenting themselves as the professional alternative to cold or hot sadism and by designating their own violence as rational and appropriately dispassionate, they established the standard for carrying

out acceptable torture and murder and for judging as illegitimate the violence of other police masculinities, a measurement standard that served
to maintain the atrocity system.

Masculinities and Atrocity System Functioning

Seemingly innocent facilitators make up a necessary ingredient in the
volatile chemistry of an atrocity system, and so, too, does the variety
among the actual perpetrators. We have seen that Brazil's atrocity system
(and, by extension, presumably other systems as well) was served by a
number of self-defined masculinity types that supported and shaped personal, group, institutional, and public definitions of one another, of
each others' violence, and of the system itself. For example, some masculinities—by presenting themselves as legitimately pursuing the system's official objectives—could be used to make the violence perpetrated
by other masculinities appear fundamentally and uniquely illegitimate.
The conduct of a policeman who went too far could then be explained
as merely the result of a deviant masculinity performance.

Theweleit (1989) describes this within the German Freikorps system,
in which the professionally ideal soldier was used as the measuring rod
for identifying deviations from this standard. However, as organizationally desirable as the perfect "machine-soldier" was, Theweleit points out
that few had "reached th[is] level of 'polished artwork'; most remained
fragments of the ideal well-socialized soldier. In the first place, some soldiers' "body armor" was "fragmentary... [and would thus] break apart
much sooner [in battle] and reveal human feelings and emotions," even
after rigorous training. Second, such emotionally driven, individualist
soldiers were also the product of the intense battles they fought: in the
heat of conflict, where groups of men might become separated from the
larger troop, the "armor of the... troops dissolved to form tiny, isolated,
uncontrolled groups." Within small battle groups or teams, each having
its own murderous dynamic, "the soldiers... beat and shot to death
whatever [emphasis in original] they met in their vicinity, enemy and
non-enemy" (206–207).

Theweleit goes on to suggest that such deviations from the soldier-
as-machine ideal were not wholly dysfunctional for Freikorps operations. Indeed, Freikorps officers often encouraged soldiers' violent, autonomous behavior, even though the contrary model—the emotionless,
bureaucratically controlled soldier of steel—was officially desired and

formally promoted. In fact, emotional explosions by imperfect Freikorps soldiers were very likely even explicitly fostered by officer facilitators: "If the [man-as-machine] does not drink blood from time to time, it creaks, grinds, and becomes defective" (1989: 209)—a way of thinking that suggests the deliberate norm-breaking intentions of the Freikorps officer facilitators who, even if they might not have "drunk enemy blood" themselves, at least could be expected to ignore and protect their subordinates who did.

Yet those who deviated from the formal ideal of the Freikorps were quickly sacrificed to serve the larger 'cause' of protecting the official hierarchy and the system itself. This dynamic was illustrated in the U.S. military trial of Lt. Calley for his unit's Mỹ Lai atrocities. Calley's murderous passion was implicitly and explicitly compared to the assumed rationality of U.S. operations against the Viet Cong and North Vietnamese. Calley's atrocities, as institutional-functionary Márcio would put it, lacked a standard of proportionality. Yet measured against the CIA Phoenix Program torture centers and its murder quotas, or the scorched-earth policies that leveled whole villages, killed hundreds of inhabitants at a time, destroyed forests with Agent Orange, and left both Vietnamese and Americans exposed to permanent damage, the institutional functionary military operations were not less violent than those of personalistic Lt. Calley—who, it is clear by now, had in fact been ordered to carry out the massacre. However, as long as an image exists that "controlled" violence can be appropriate, even when it generates, secretly encourages, and ordinarily protects other types of violence, the seemingly illegitimate violence workers can be trotted out as atypical violations of the institution's otherwise rational standards.

Relating Theweleit's arguments to our own consideration of masculinity presentations, even though the emotionally frozen and bureaucratically controlled institutional functionary ideal seems to have become the official standard for police behavior during Brazil's military period, the military's internal security system still very much needed (and greatly benefited from) both personalistic and blended masculinity police. Such men guaranteed that a violent task would get done quickly—as when personalistic DOPS official Sérgio invited lower-rank blended masculinity and personalistic police from DOPS to join his newly formed death squad. These policemen would "do the job that other police were reluctant to do," declared Sérgio. Sometimes there were "mistakes" along the way—a torture session might result in an untimely death—but such errors could be hidden and excused as long as the system did not contain too many irrational police who made too many of them.

Having an excess of personalistic or blended masculinity police in a torture complex could result in its operating irrationally, a possibility recognized by several violence workers, as Chapter 10 will illustrate. For example, good torturers had to learn, as institutional functionary Márcio explained, to balance higher degrees of pain against more visible injuries and the amount and value of information gained. Furthermore, if personalistic or blended masculinity police became too predominant within the military's legal-rational social control system, they might, for example, begin to be at odds with the military system itself, as Ignácio did when he tried to form a Civil Police union (illegal by military decree) and as DOPS Detective Fleury did when he refused to turn over his captive to the military's DOI/CODI. Then such police—who could be considered assets in smaller numbers—might become threatening to the system. For example, in Espírito Santo, when the state's initially military-recognized death squad network of blended masculinity and personalistic police—under control of the state governor and his brother, the secretary of public security—began to spin away from even covert military control, the Brazilian military's institutional functionary technocrats opened a statewide investigation (see Guimarães 1978; Huggins 1998).

Varieties of Police Identities

Police culture in general and atrocity systems in particular are not made up of just one kind of perpetrator. Examining varieties of police cultures—and, by extension, police identities—Manning (1978) has discovered two primary police cultural identities among London police: individualist and administrative. The individualists are rank-and-filers who see police work as "entrepreneurial, practical face-to-face activity involving particular people and their problems" (in Crank 1998: 231). Such police, who "develop . . . their own individual priorities and adapt their work to those priorities" (230–231), consider loyalty to partners and responsibility to oneself essential attributes of good police culture—a worldview shared by the Brazilian violence workers whom we have labeled personalistic. In contrast, administrative police culture considers "execution of policy [and] the efficient achievement of organizational goals and the maintenance of hierarchy and [of rank-and-file] discipline" requirements for effective policing. Such an ideal—clearly running counter to individualist expectations—is often met, according to Manning, by efforts to subvert administrative control: independent rank-and-file police form cliques that avoid managerial oversight (232). We would add that the administrative police culture's own creation of elite units, presumably to more effectively combat the dangers thought to lie outside the control of regular police, is in fact a way of officially granting greater autonomy to independent rank-and-filers. This is very likely to subvert the administration's own official ideals and expectations while supporting some of their unofficial ones: personalistic police follow a set of behaviors that violence-facilitating administrators know will get the dirty and dangerous jobs done, albeit through an autonomous culture that formally goes against administrative cultural ideals. Nevertheless, this arrangement allows police administrative culture to blame seemingly atypical rogue cops for any excesses carried out by the specialized units that administrators created and supported in the first place.

Although Manning's findings hint at some of the kinds of cultural and masculine diversity that we have identified in this study of Brazilian violence workers, his insights can be further elaborated. For example, we can differentiate various strains of individualistic police culture just as we have done for violence worker culture. Two of the masculinity presentations we have discussed are close to what Manning describes as making up an individualist rank-and-file police culture. In particular, among the six Brazilian violence workers who manifested personalistic or blended masculinities, four were rank-and-filers. Yet although these men expressed views close to what Manning found characteristic of individualistic police culture, the blended masculinity police also added presentations of themselves that did not neatly fit Manning's formula. For example, they sometimes expressed what Manning would consider administrative cultural discourse. Likewise, the violence workers whose masculinity assertions were closest to that culture—the Brazilian institutional functionary policemen, among whom four of five were police officials—at once resembled and deviated from Manning's categorization. For example, they did not just assert the necessity for administrative control over rank-and-filers but also indicated the importance of administrative hierarchy's regulating their own conduct.

Although it might be expected that those at the top of police bureaucracy—where an official can create and enforce the organization's performance rules while hiding his own transgressions—would be able to express themselves as real people, in fact the institutional functionary policemen (although all but one was a higher officer) were least likely of the three masculinity types to do this. One could argue that these officers had a stake in the bureaucracy that legitimated their status and hence they readily subordinated themselves to it. Moreover, the Brazilian political and higher-ranking military officials needed subordinates to live up to the behavioral ideal that promoted their and the larger organization's goals. In other words, the officers clearly had the most to lose from violating official organizational expectations. As Theweleit (1989) argues for the Freikorps hierarchy, the superior officer functions as a "physical model" for those beneath his status to promote the longevity and legitimacy of the atrocity system.

The real and rhetorical interplay of atrocity role performances that we have been discussing is also suggested in some U.S. literature that sees police violence as rooted in rank-and-file macho culture: the policeman who avoids anything feminine, has a "manly air of toughness," demonstrates unfaltering confidence and self-reliance, and "manifests an aura of aggressiveness [and] daring" (Crank 1998: 181) is the source of much violence. Crank argues that because police have traditionally come from working-class backgrounds, where such masculinity presentations have traditionally received "strong support," the rank-and-file cultural milieu recognizes and highly rewards blue-collar macho masculinity (181). To gain the rewards of his peers, the macho policeman "must be aggressive ... attack first and act with vigor and violence to overwhelm the opposition" (181). Uildriks and van Mastrigt (1991: 160) assert that the toughness associated with such masculinity leads some patrol officers "to feel and act like a 'super-gang,'" providing ample foundation for violence. Acting tough, being a hard man in the right circumstances, increases one's status as a good cop among other rank-and-file police.

But can only one kind of macho rank-and-file police masculinity be the seedbed for police violence? Obviously not, if the masculinity presentations of Brazilian violence workers are any clue to the atrocities that they carried out. Moreover, as we have consistently argued, atrocity systems—whether these are aspects of normal police systems or part of a national security state—cannot be understood apart from the roles of their facilitators. Yet, according to Manning's framework, the facilitator police officials do not ordinarily manifest macho masculinities. Their administrative culture is seen as the opposite of, and counter to, police violence.

Perhaps, rather than pointing to one stereotypic rank-and-file masculinity or to an associated individualist police culture or even to a combination of these as nurturing rank-and-file police violence—and then seeing administrative culture as structured to control or eliminate it—those who study police atrocities (and those of larger security forces as well) might consider how the range of identities among both facilitators and perpetrators can reinforce, assist, and disguise the actions of one another within a violent system.

Indeed, we argue that Brazil's atrocity system (and probably other atrocity systems as well) was made up of a variety of masculinity types that shaped and supported personal, group, and public definitions of one another, of each others' violence, and of the system itself. In the dynamic dramas played out by and within atrocity systems—particularly as these are communicated to outsiders—all actors' performances are needed to set the stage for how different types of insiders will act out their roles and how outsiders will view the play in progress, represent the drama to outsiders, and recollect performances later on. Recognizing the importance of organizational climates to the drama of an atrocity system, including especially the shaping of actors' performances, we turn in chapters 9 and 10 to how Brazilian violence workers were trained and nurtured to carry out their horrific deeds.

CHAPTER 9

Shaping Identities and Obedience

A Murderous Dynamic

The belief in a supernatural source of evil is not necessary; men alone are quite capable of every wickedness.

Joseph Conrad, *Under Western Eyes*

There is horrifying evidence of the violence suffered by victims of security force repression in Brazil. Should we view the police who systematically carried out such atrocities as fundamentally abnormal? Or should we see them as, at least initially, just like anyone else? Perhaps atrocity perpetrators are shaped and molded, particularly as adults, into their violent roles and actions? Is atrocity, therefore, above all a product of certain kinds of ideological messages, organizational structures, and interpersonal interaction systems—all nurtured and legitimized by state action and inaction?

Although it is tempting to see those who tortured and murdered in Brazil as *pathologically* extraordinary personalities, much social-psychological research in other contexts points us away from such a conclusion. A compelling set of recent and older studies that highlight the ordinary nature of those who commit unthinkable acts of evil demonstrates that in many instances such perpetrators are induced or seduced into carrying out atrocities; they have been subjected to powerful situational forces that disengage their usual modes of moral functioning (Bandura 1999). Included in this body of evidence is the research by Browning

(1992) on German reserves who were transformed into mobile killing squads; Chandler (1999), on the bureaucracy of terror in Pol Pot's infamous S-21 Tuol Sleng torture facility; Conroy (2000), on the development of torturers in several different countries; Gold (1996), on testimonies of operatives in the Imperial Japanese Army's infamous Medical Unit 731; Haritos-Fatouros (1998, 2002), on the special training program that created Greek military torturers; Milgram (1974), on the emergence of blind obedience to authority among a broad range of U.S. civilian experimental participants; and Zimbardo (1972), Haney, Banks, and Zimbardo (1973), and Haney and Zimbardo (1977), on the power of a mock prison's institutional structure and norms to turn normal students into neophyte torturers. This rich body of research, which has been further developed in this book's Conclusion, demonstrates that atrocity is more than the act of a few evil perpetrators. Under specifiable conditions, atrocity can be the product of ordinary people who are in certain kinds of work and organizational structures and processes that systematically shape their actions toward violent outcomes.

In the next two chapters we shall examine several versions of this perspective and some alternative explanations in light of our interview data, beginning with this chapter's primary focus on the prior training of those who became executioners. In general, however, we argue here that the social and political contexts in which atrocity work is prepared and carried out are important variables. This perspective directs us to consider not only the direct perpetrators who committed state-sanctioned atrocities but also the facilitators—the political decision makers and social control officials as well as the doctors, notaries, guards, and even some rank-and-file police—who indirectly promoted, nurtured, and protected the perpetrators and kept their evil deeds hidden. This perspective does not shift moral and political responsibility from atrocity's direct perpetrators or decrease their responsibility for such violence. To the contrary, our social-psychological and sociopolitical organizational approach expands responsibility for atrocity by including the auxiliary actors and the organizational entities often omitted from an atrocity equation, a formula that consists of (1) international and (2) national facilitators, (3) bystander communities, and (4) direct perpetrators. By considering systemic atrocity as more than a series of acts by autonomous, essentially evil actors, we will uncover new information about the dynamics of state-sponsored torture and murder in Brazil. We learn from Feitlowitz's analysis (1998) of atrocity facilitators in Argentina how such an understanding directs attention to the wider question of how torture and murder by state agents should be judged and how these atrocities might be prevented in the future.

Conceptualizing Atrocity

This chapter examines the testimonies of the fourteen atrocity perpetrators documented in this study as well as the nine interviewees for whom there is no direct evidence of their having tortured or murdered systematically for the state. While labeling these other nine police as "auxiliary facilitators," we nevertheless recognize that their testimony alone does not guarantee that they never tortured or murdered anyone. At the same time, we know that these facilitator police have maintained that they never directly carried out such violence; we recognize that such denials were initially common from the direct perpetrators as well. However, in the latter case, either the direct perpetrators themselves eventually disclosed that they had indeed committed atrocities, or their documented or lived pasts gave them away. Such information never surfaced in the case of the facilitator interviewees. At the same time, ample evidence exists that the facilitator police were (at least) tacit participants in atrocity—delivering victims to torturers, watching torture or murder, guarding captives, and remaining silent as atrocities were occurring.

In one dramatic example of an atrocity facilitator's role in violence, a militarized policeman explained that in the 1980s, he had worked with a young partner who had a "cruel character." This man would

pick up an individual on the street, take him to the civilian police post where they'd put a black bag over [his] head...and give [the man] a beating. They punched and beat the guy to a pulp. They hurt him so much that he defecated and urinated in his pants.

This interviewee explained that "the [policemen he worked with would] let him watch because [he] was new to the force." Although he thought that his partner who had carried out the beatings was "chicken-hearted" and that "human beings should not be treated that way," the policeman still remained with his violent partner for six months—at the very least, a silent participant in violence. In any case, this militarized policeman's silence was guaranteed by his partner's admonition that if he said anything, he'd die.

Whether, in fact, we can fully believe in each case that an atrocity facilitator did not himself directly commit atrocities, their involvement in such violence never surfaced to the extent that it did for the direct perpetrators. For this reason, we make the analytical research assumption that the facilitator police constitute a viable comparison group for discovering potential differences in life histories, training experiences, and work dynamics between the direct perpetrators and themselves.

Our theoretical perspective for carrying out such an analysis assumes that causal factors develop in orderly sequence over time rather than all coming together at one point to produce a particular result—the latter being a simultaneous model of causality. Social-psychologically, the sequential model postulates that atrocity perpetrators as well as facilitators are shaped within dynamic social interactional and organizational systems. It follows that the identities of people in an atrocity system, whether direct perpetrators or facilitators—as well as the motives encouraging their violence and their self-justifications for it—develop and change over time. In the process, what may have been a cause of violent behavior at one point in this shaping process may not be a cause at another point (see Becker 1967; Toch 1969). This sequential model allows for discovery of the emergent social-psychological and organizational dynamics of atrocity.

For example, we may find the reasons for a policeman's first murder, but these may not explain why he thereafter regularly committed murder as a member of an elite death squad. The policeman may have initially committed murder out of passion, by accident, or because ordered or forced to do so. Yet a policeman's regularly perpetrating murder may respond to a different dynamic. Toch (1996) reports that whether a person is likely to commit an initial act of violence is relatively unpredictable, whereas for the frequent perpetrator of violence the probability of continuing is very high. The serially violent police perpetrator may have been shaped, in the first place, by his merely being part of a murder system—the training or work process has shaped the actor into its loyal servant—and, in the second place, by auxiliary actors who train and protect murderers and punish those unwilling to kill. These atrocity facilitators may promote opportunities to benefit socially, economically, professionally, or politically from murder, for example, through promotions for those who effectively torture or murder wrongdoers. All of these factors will, of course, impact upon different actors in different ways. For example, what causes violence by direct perpetrators may not explain the facilitators' actions. Seeing atrocity as fostered in various ways by people in differentially situated social statuses points to the complexity of atrocity systems and focuses analytical attention on the role of the political climates that legitimize violent social control, its hierarchy, and its specialized units.

Yet there is very little research on atrocity as a *sequentially developing* social-psychological and politico-organizational system made up of facilitators and direct perpetrators. One interesting microstudy that hints at this mix of roles describes attitude and identity changes among prison guards in U.S. death houses. Although most of these men did not choose to work in the death house—having entered prison work to be ordinary guards—Johnson's *Death Work* (1997) demonstrates that once there, they were socialized into an execution culture and an associated vocabulary that shaped the guards into seemingly legal-rational agents of state-mandated murder.

Our organizational approach to atrocity investigates a range of possible relevant causes for systematic state-sponsored and executed violence in Brazil, including whenever possible the reinforcing roles of atrocity facilitators and perpetrators.

Nature versus Nurture:
Being or Becoming an Atrocity Worker?

Having proposed that atrocity may be more than the violence of a few evil direct perpetrators, we must still consider whether they might have been social-psychologically (and abnormally) different from the facilitator interviewees before they began their careers as police. It could be argued that the direct perpetrators entered police work or were recruited into it because, as brutal sadists, they derived pleasure from violence. Starting from such a psychobiological premise, the researcher might compare direct perpetrators' biological and psychological makeup and family backgrounds with those of the less fully involved facilitators. Although our interviews were not designed to address the biological question, nevertheless they do provide some information on whether family background and early life experiences might have contributed to subsequent atrocity.

From interviewees' personal histories, we see that only one man among the fourteen direct perpetrators—Jorge—suffered the kind of consistent and severe childhood trauma and violence that could have led him to enter police service as a way of working through or playing out his own aggressive tendencies. As you recall, he had been separated from his parents during childhood when his father was arrested as a subversive French alien. Jorge and his siblings were subsequently taken from their mother, who suffered a stroke and mental collapse after her own rape by security forces and her husband's imprisonment and deportation. During Jorge's internment in a FEBEM orphanage, he endured years of violence. In his professional police life, Jorge manifested all of the symptoms of a combination of childhood separation trauma and the abuse he suffered in FEBEM. In short, he had learned to live with pain and manifested a desire for revenge. This might have led Jorge to join an organization where he could more easily carry out legitimized violence against others.

However, at the same time, three of the facilitator interviewees who had no apparent direct participation in systematic atrocities also reported moderate-to-severe levels of childhood and adolescent trauma and violence. One of these interviewees remembers his father being very authoritarian, strict, and punitive. Another recalls that his father—a military man and later a "tough" policeman—was violently murdered when the interviewee was in his early teens. This interviewee described his father's murder as a "tremendous shock." The third comparison group policeman recollected that his father, a strict disciplinarian and an alcoholic, regularly beat him and his mother. Although our numbers are small, it still appears that more interviewees among the nonatrocity comparison group category than among the atrocity producers reported the kind of childhood trauma that might have resulted in their becoming police as a way of channeling or dealing with their own aggressive and authoritarian predispositions.

Realizing that both sets of interviewees might have been reluctant to talk about family violence or other traumatic events in their youth, we sought yet another way of determining whether a man might have been initially predisposed toward police work as a way of responding to his anger or other violent predispositions. We reasoned that even if an interviewee did not directly report being drawn to policing because of its association with violence, he might still suggest this motivation in more indirect ways. However, such motives were not communicated by either the facilitator or perpetrator interviewees. As for whether any policeman would ever admit to entering the police because he likes violence and seeks the power associated with that role, Glebbeek (2000) has found that a minority of new recruits to Guatemala's Policia Nacional Civil stated they had joined in order to have the power that being a policeman would give them. In one recruit's words, "I very much like to carry a gun." Another asserted that policing appealed to him because police "have good weapons [and] nice uniforms." A study (Botello and Rivera 2000) of recruits' reasons for entering a Mexico City police force demonstrated their openness to communicate even possibly criminal reasons for joining their force. In Mexico City, police involvement in graft and bribery is common and police salaries low, and a majority of interviewees freely admitted to having joined the force to "make easy money" or to "accumulate capital to start a business." Only a minority of the interviewees manifested an interest in law enforcement, the most common message communicated by our Brazilian interviewees.

Indeed, among the fourteen atrocity perpetrators, the largest single group—six—said that they had entered the police because they liked that kind of work—without citing any particular violence-related reasons for joining: "[It is] a vocation; I joined because I like it"; "I thought that police [work] would fill the blanks in my life"; "I'd seen a movie...*Detective Story,* a film with Kirk Douglas.[1] I was fascinated by the agents, the police station"; "Having just left the army, I was still enthusiastic about military life, so I joined the Goiás State Militarized Police"; "Helping people has always attracted me since I was a child.... so I joined the police." Among the nine auxiliary facilitators, three either remembered becoming policemen because they generally liked police work or gave no specific reason for joining.

Four of the fourteen atrocity perpetrators advanced the next most common reason for joining the police: because they had relatives in the force; two of the nine comparison police also gave this reason. The atrocity perpetrators' third most common reason (two) for becoming policemen was that they were unemployed and needed a job. One comparison group policeman said that he had entered the force to earn a regular paycheck.

The two sets of policemen's testimonies do not suggest that the direct perpetrators were more likely to advance violence as a motive for joining the police. Indeed, both the perpetrator and the facilitator police gave similar reasons for becoming policemen: the appeal of an interesting vocation, because family and friends were police, to get a regular paycheck, and so on. Even Jorge—a documented murderer whose abusive childhood could have predisposed him to become a policeman to play out his anger—apparently did not even himself make the choice to enter the

---

1. This is the only case where we were suspicious that an interviewee was giving some indirect evidence that he might have entered policing for the excitement of violence. In *Detective Story* (1951), Kirk Douglas portrays a police detective who engages in brutality. Interviewee Julius specifically mentioned admiring this film; however, he never directly mentioned the violence and in fact talked more about what he described as the fascinating "puzzles" that Kirk Douglas's character solved.

force. He had been in the army prior to entering the Militarized Police, and he claims that his army superior told him, "Jorge, either we eliminate you because you have become a dangerous person [as the youthful victim of a violent] system [or] you join the police where we can keep an eye on you." Jorge's own career in atrocity hints at how organizational hierarchy can shape an atrocity perpetrator, as this and the following chapter further demonstrate.

Having shown that our twenty-three interviewees entered policing for a range of reasons, not including to play out their existing aggressive tendencies, we continued exploring their life histories. This led us to consider how preservice police training might have shaped relatively ordinary Brazilian police into atrocity perpetrators.

Preservice Socialization

Research on Greek torturers by Haritos-Fatouros (2002) and Gibson and Haritos-Fatouros (1988) has shown that preservice training was used to shape Greek Army Military Police recruits into torturers. This important research offers much to the study of Brazilian atrocity, but it must be acknowledged that the Greek interviews were with men who had become primarily torturers; this study's interviewees were both torturers and executioners. Furthermore, the Greek interviewees were actual soldiers and not civilian police. And although all of Haritos-Fatouros's interviewees had gone through preservice training, only just slightly over half of the twenty-three Brazilian interviewees and, likewise, just over half of the documented Brazilian atrocity perpetrators had either no such training at all or only a very limited amount. However, nineteen of the twenty-three interviewees had gone through army training, which was often very hard.

Yet in spite of these differences between the Greek and Brazilian cases, it is reasonable to explore the possible influence of preservice training in shaping some Brazilian police into certain kinds of atrocity perpetrators. At the very least, preservice training communicates a police organization's mission and expectations and conveys the conduct models required of its members. By shaping new members into the police organization's ethos and communicating its behavioral expectations, training may help prepare the trainee for the violence most commonly perpetrated by his organization.

It can be confidently assumed that different kinds of atrocity require different attitudes, skills, and preparation. For example, the psychological, physical, and emotional techniques required for engaging in long-lasting torture sessions are very likely different from those required for murder. Torturers need to be socialized into small, functionally organized teams that operate indoors in secrecy. Torturers must develop a consciously manipulative emotional relationship with their victims, treating them as individuals without feeling empathy for them. And torturers need to master techniques for securing information quickly and skillfully without killing the victim. They must see each torture subject as part of an incomplete process in which the victim at best provides only some of the information needed to achieve the stated goal.

Within an atrocity dynamic, the torturer's work is relatively slow and methodical, whereas the murderer's is often quick and spontaneous. A torturer's work is never done, but the killer's is provisionally accomplished each time someone is murdered. Killers must learn to see potential victims as aggregated dangerous and faceless 'others' to be eliminated reflexively—nothing personal, just business. Victims are seen as having nothing more to offer the social control system: Killing them is the necessary terminus and appropriate outcome of the murderer's work. Pointing to the partial and always incomplete nature of the torturer's task, one Brazilian torturer—not among our interviewees—asserted that he is "not like the killer who puts a notch on his gun each time he kills someone" (Porão iluminado 1998: 42).

With an eye to the possibility that different kinds of training might be associated with different atrocity outcomes, we began by distinguishing among the interviewees who had been torturers and those who had been murderers. This was not difficult because our subsample of atrocity perpetrators was fairly neatly divided between torturers and murders—with, at most, two police known to have carried out both types of violence. Looking at the organizational affiliations of the two types of atrocity perpetrators, we found that most of the torturers had been civil policemen and most of the murderers had been militarized police. This division of violent labor in fact corresponds to what researchers on Brazilian police have found generally: the Militarized Police—who conduct street policing and arrest suspects—are more likely to commit murder, whereas the Civil Police—who process cases, interrogate, and investigate crimes—are most often associated with physical and psychological torture (see Caldeira 2001; Huggins 1998; Mingardi 1991).

Yet among the nine Civil Police in the twenty-three-interviewee sample—with eight of these being documented atrocity perpetrators—most had no or very little formal preservice training, so their subsequent violence could not be confidently ascribed to it. At the same time, all of the Militarized Police—fourteen in the twenty-three-person sample, six being documented atrocity perpetrators—had gone through four to six months of preservice training, so we examined its possible role in molding them into violence workers; in particular we sought to discover the components of preservice training that might differentiate the eight facilitators from the six direct perpetrators. We examined the role of such training in shaping men to carry out beatings and murder, the atrocities most frequently committed by Militarized Police.

Militarized Police Training: Routinizing Obedience and Aggregating Victims

A primary objective of Brazilian Militarized Police training was to create blind obedience to authority among police who had to use violence automatically against a faceless enemy. However, during the military period such action was legitimated by a culturally pervasive national security ideology that was not necessarily embraced automatically by all trainees. Indeed, even among those who accepted the national security ideology, it is far from certain that this was what caused them to commit atrocities. But to the extent that this ideology helped them to justify their actions, then it contributed to fostering atrocity in the long run. For this reason, this and the following chapter will try to sort out the complicated causal relationship between national security ideology and atrocity.

For example, among our Militarized Police sample, thirteen of the fourteen interviewees had joined the force when the national security ideology was becoming academically entrenched in the Militarized Police training curriculum (see Huggins 1998). At the same time, only five among these thirteen were documented atrocity perpetrators. Furthermore, among such atrocity perpetrators, some remembered accepting and some recalled spurning national security teachings, which suggests that it may have been a necessary but not entirely sufficient factor for turning these trainees into atrocity perpetrators. It very likely had a role in validating and legitimizing the atrocities that the interviewees had been prepared to carry out and were learning to practice.

As for the factors associated with preservice training that may have more directly created a foundation for committing atrocity in general and murder in particular, central among them was the shaping of a trainee's obedience to militarized authority. This seems to have involved a number of deindividuation strategies to degrade and strip away a trainee's previous identity and then reshape it as part of a new Militarized Police–controlled group identity (see Zimbardo 1970). Most important among such factors was hazing, which played a pivotal role in creating obedience, modeling violence as a viable instrument of control, and disengaging violence perpetrators from moral responsibility for their acts.

The process of reshaping the trainee's identity was begun before many of them had even arrived at the Militarized Police Academy. Their degradation of status was very likely first publicly demonstrated when they were unceremoniously transported to the academy on the back of a flatbed truck—like cattle being taken to slaughter. Several Militarized Police interviewees remembered waiting on a corner on the day that they were to be picked up for training: the transport truck pulled up briefly at a street corner, giving them only a few seconds to jump on board. With no railings for hanging on, the fifty to seventy-five strangers on their way to the academy were packed together like livestock. For an hour or more, they bounced along uncomfortably in the back of the overcrowded truck, arriving at the academy dirty, dishevelled, and tired. Their first "greeting" was abusive harangues from a training officer who ordered them to form a line as they piled off the truck, tripping over one another to obey his command.

After the training officer's short welcoming speech, which included a vigorous lambasting of the trainees' disorderly appearance and their lack of military discipline, the trainees marched to a nearby building where they were given a quick shave and military-issue haircut. Next, the drill lines of trainees moved to their assigned barracks, where each man was issued a training uniform and an identification number. One Militarized Police atrocity facilitator remembered that on his first full day at the academy, he got in line and stayed there. He was given a number, as though he were a prisoner of war, and this caused him to comment to the interviewer, "Right off you get a number that's like a kind of a password and you stop existing as a person and become a number." Besides this arbitrary number, which linked the trainee's identity to the homogenized identities of other trainees, the new trainee also got a "war name," which could be a shortened version of the trainee's own name or something completely different. In any case, this new name was chosen by the Militarized Police organization, not by him or his colleagues. Militarized Policeman Roberto, a former death squad leader, remembered that "we all called each other by our military [war] names. It was rare to call somebody by another name." Symbolically, the war name designated the kind of training a man would receive—for war—and the kind of policing that he would carry out—violent generalized repression against an aggregated enemy.

No longer the man that he had been and known only by a war name and a number, the trainee's real identity had been detached from its civil status and was therefore ripe for reshaping into a fully militarized persona.

Military Exercises and Classes

Everything about Militarized Police training smacked of military protocol. The trainees' first full day at the academy began with being rousted out of bed as early as 4:30 A.M. to "screams of 'Hurry, get into shape. Fall in.'" An atrocity facilitator from this group of interviewees recalled that "at sun up, the officers would arrive at the barracks where we were sleeping and start agitating—they'd wake everyone up, throw tear gas, throw water on people, make us line up completely soaked at the crack of dawn." Having only minutes to prepare, trainees had to run half-dressed into the morning dark, putting on their socks and shoes as they fell clumsily into formation. Another policeman from the comparison group recalled that on his first full day at the academy, they "gave us two minutes to get up, get dressed, and get in line. We had not yet had any experience at all in getting totally outfitted, booted up, totally spick-and-span. Two minutes to get all this information and be in line for training!" Militarized Police trainees were embarking on an experience much more like boot camp than preparation for peacetime civil policing. But then, Brazil's military government was at war with subversion.

Once in line, the trainees were expected to respond professionally to marching orders, but as one atrocity perpetrator remembered, "I was a civilian; I didn't know how to march. We couldn't stay in step. Our group was sort of awkward." A policeman from the comparison group recollects that the superior officer's "provocations" began right away:

He...[had] a mean, scowling face—very macho, very much the man. He starts out by saying that he is better than everyone else, demonstrating that he has authority, showing that he has the power and that we must submit to it...to do whatever he wants to us within legal limits. After that, everyone's ego is hurt; everyone feels belittled.

After being assigned to a platoon, the trainees began rigorous physical drills and exercises—before or after a thirty-minute breakfast. The trainee's normal physical exercise routine involved a mix of close-order drills, calisthenics, countless sprints and chin-ups, carrying others piggyback, and charging a barbed-wire fence. The training cycle was broken at midday by a thirty- to ninety-minute lunch. The workday usually ended at five or six, followed by dinner at seven—fourteen or more hours after the trainee's day had begun.

As for the academic side of their training, classes were cycled throughout the day in between physical and operational training. The rank-and-file trainees studied Portuguese, criminal sciences, the Brazilian penal code, personal defense, hygiene, public relations, and theories of crowd control and population management. Those training to be officers took courses in criminal legal procedure, criminal law, and "sociology, public human relations, [other] subjects in the social area." They had tactical training as well. Recalling his academy training, a Militarized Police officer who later committed atrocities observed that his program had been primarily "oriented toward [a combination of] training, discipline, and hierarchy." Another Militarized Police atrocity perpetrator recalls that his training involved the normal "close-order drills [and] field maneuvers [and also] training for confrontations in war [and] guerrilla and counterguerrilla warfare." This interviewee maintains that Militarized Police training became "very militarized" after the coup, reaching a peak in 1967—the year that he entered the force. An atrocity facilitator from the comparison group agrees that Militarized Police Academy preservice training had been "much more military than real professional police training." Recalling a training experience of his own that was similar to a police operation against subversives, another comparison group policeman disclosed that a trainee was "made to roll in the weeds on top of thorns, wood, rocks, like he was a pig.... [If he] hurt himself.... the instructor thought it was funny. He was training the policeman to go to war, not to protect the public.... [Tear] gas bombs were thrown in the classroom for people to get used to the gas."

Hazing and Obedience

Although the overt operational objective of academy training was to teach prospective Militarized Police how to operate in warlike combat conditions, what gave this training its distinctly military quality was its underlying operational objective—to shape obedience. This was carried out through physical and psychological hazing, a process that announced and reinforced the trainee's position as a subordinate within the Militarized Police organization. Hazing most generally involves the members of an organization employing physical or psychological pain to initiate prospective members into the group's consciousness and operating culture. Its most specific objective is to create obedience to and unthinking support for organizational authority, which, in the case of Militarized Police training, meant obeying an authority promoting and legitimizing violence. The hazing was aimed at deindividuating the trainee—an outcome that separates the person from him- or herself by punishing any behavior that is not derived from or related to an organizationally controlled group identity.

Most hazing in Brazilian Militarized Police training took the form of "status degradation" (Becker 1967), rituals that announced a trainee's transition from normal and unsoiled to debased and dirty. In addition to replacing a trainee's given name with a number and war name, other mechanisms for accomplishing this included the use of abusive name-calling, physically exhausting drills and punishments, inconsistent commands, and divide-and-rule orders. Through this psychologically or physically violent hazing, Militarized Police trainers extinguished a trainee's individuality and subordinated him to a hierarchy that arbitrarily promoted and legitimized violence. In the process, the training in general and hazing in particular provided lessons in the acceptability of violence for achieving desired ends and disengaged violence from negative legal, social, or moral appraisals. It is interesting to note that such degradation rituals are commonly practiced against prisoners in the United States when they first enter a correctional facility.

Abusive name-calling, a common hazing strategy in Brazilian Militarized Police training, frequently involved the technique of designating a new trainee as the "beast" of an older militarized policeman. Fernando, an atrocity perpetrator who looked favorably on this practice, remembers "beast" being the "name they use[d] for the person who is beginning [his training]—You're my 'beast'.... Each veteran chooses his beast to help and to harass." Fernando recalled a training incident where "we were in the mess hall and there were two veterans and two beast [trainees] sitting there.... When it was time to serve the meat, the trainees' meat was taken by the veterans. The trainee's dessert was theirs as well. So we had to eat what was left over.... The first two months [of training] were a massacre." Another atrocity perpetrator remembered a time when his platoon had to "crawl on the ground like snakes; they step on you, call you names like 'animal' and a lot of things that do not have anything to do with human beings. They teach you how to be mean."

Pointing to the social control function of such derogatory labeling, another former atrocity perpetrator explained that the "older students were hierarchically superior to the newer students, and all of us were hierarchically inferior to the school's officers." The label "beast" left no confusion about the new recruit's lowly position within Militarized Police organizational hierarchy. Resurrecting his painful memories of pre-service name-calling, one policeman from the comparison group described his academy training as totally degrading: officers would yell, "Hey, you're a faggot"; "You're a monster"; "You're an idiot." When the trainee answered the officer—and he had to answer him—he had to repeat that he is a monster."

Physically punishing drills and exercises were also used to degrade trainees. The standard exercises were tough, but trainees who were unable to live up to the demands of a hazer would be ordered to perform even more—and more demanding—exercises. A militarized policeman from the comparison group remembered "being punished by [having to] do exercises. Everything [was] based on exercises or, sometimes, giving you night duty, detaining you overnight. Sometimes we were even detained for not running well in the streets." Another policeman from that group recalled that "sometimes an individual would fall down exhausted during maneuvers because he couldn't run that much.... [This man and] those who [came in] last [on exercises] already knew that they'd be staying on the base over the weekend. This happened constantly." Another militarized policeman from the comparison group asserted positively that "exercises prepare[d] us physically. [They were] a form of discipline, never a form of punishment."

Nevertheless, one militarized policeman from a death squad, critically recalling the antithetical nature of his training, explained that officers would "tell you to sit down, then almost immediately they have you stand up; you're standing up and they order you to sit down again. This sit-down/stand-up session, which is a form of torture, physically exhausts a person." It is also a means to create adjustment to a totally arbitrary universe, an Orwellian environment where authority's irrational actions define rationality and where only mindless discipline makes sense. Furthermore, as one documented murderer explained, "Generally, [if we failed to adhere to a command or rule, we were given] fifty push-ups. If you repeated the offence, you'd be restricted to base during the weekend." The only way that a trainee could get a weekend pass was to consistently demonstrate obedience to the Militarized Police organization. As a result, the organization and its officers used withdrawal of the weekend pass to control a trainee's conduct. Bernardo remembers that "everyone tried to maintain very proper conduct so they could see their girlfriend, visit their parents, on the weekend." The ultimate punishment for failing to live up to academy expectations was being sent to the academy's lockup or dismissed from the program, a threat that loomed strong for those who could not be shaped into the Militarized Police organization's culture.

A trainee's life at the academy might not have been so difficult if he had only to adhere to an *attainable* and *consistent* set of organizational demands and rules. He would have been able to figure out what to do and not do to stay out of trouble. However, one of the biggest hurdles for trainees was apparently the contradictory nature of most academy hazing. In fact, the very essence of hazing was its inconsistency: a trainee could not succeed at one command or expectation without breaking others. Therefore, no matter what a trainee did, he would deviate from some rule. One result was that trainees constantly faced punishment. Because officers' expectations were usually far higher than what a new recruit could successfully or realistically achieve, it was not even necessary for a trainee to actually break a rule to be punished; he had only to fail to measure up to impossible standards.

By establishing problems that trainees could not possibly surmount or by giving an order that required breaking another one to carry it out, Militarized Police trainers were creating "learned helplessness" (Seligman 1974). This promoted a trainee's obedience to authority by making him totally dependent on those who judged his performance and rewarded him for being a "good little boy." In the process, learned helplessness engendered trainees' dependence on the organization whose agents were doing the hazing. The trainee who failed to become sufficiently helpless by resisting being stripped of his individualism was a threat to organizational integrity. One militarized policeman from the comparison group remembered a trainee who had been ordered to do difficult physical exercises:

[He got] totally outraged [at the difficulty of the tasks and] told the sergeant that he wouldn't do any more because he was totally dead from training.... [The sergeant] pulled him off the line and took him to the lockup and decided to throw him out [of the training program]. They decided he wasn't a good policeman—that he didn't obey orders—because a good policeman has to obey orders, has to do whatever he is told to do unhesitatingly.

A trainee who was unable to perform a particular hazing task had to be left alone to wallow in his failure.

Most important among the hazing mechanisms for accomplishing deindividuation were divide-and-rule strategies that punished trainees for helping one another. Several interviewees remembered not being allowed to assist another trainee who had fallen down during a group exercise—under penalty of their being punished for doing so—a tactic that pitted trainees against each another. Roberto, a militarized policeman who spent years in a Rio death squad, acknowledged that in his training program "they pitted one friend against another." He maintains that training officers "punish everybody if [you] make a mistake, so that everyone will be against [you]." A militarized policeman from the comparison group observed that "we were encouraged, through the system of hierarchy, to be divided." He now believes that "whoever invented this form of exploitation knew what he was doing." He seems to recognize that discouraging trainees from helping one another and therefore from bonding against the organization itself reinforced hierarchical authority and decreased the development of extraorganizational solidarity among trainees—that is, from developing what Manning (in Crank 1998) might label an "individualist" police culture.

Running the Gauntlet

Perhaps the most important lesson that hazing imparted in Militarized Police preservice training was its modeling the acceptability of violence. One atrocity perpetrator dismissed as "unimportant" the violence that he had seen in hazing: "Some people yanked on the freshman [trainees'] ears, slapped them on the head, but nothing very traumatic [happened] beyond the limits of a rude joke." This police official maintained uncritically that there was "nothing exaggerated" about hazing trainees by beating them "without leaving marks" as they ran through a gauntlet of other police trainees.

Painfully recalling his own preservice experience with the gauntlet, one militarized policeman from the comparison group described this hazing:

[There are] two lines of policemen, one on one side and one on the other side, and the policeman [trainee] has to run down [the corridor between them]. If he...doesn't [get hit], he's saved. But rarely does the guy run down the middle without being hit. I recall getting punched in the stomach—don't know if I was punched or kicked. I just fainted on the floor.

In contrast, a Militarized Policeman from a death squad justified this and other such training violence:

[It makes you] lose your fear because you become accustomed to just about any-thing...I saw what happens—the humiliation, the head clubbing, the pushing, the face slapping...to create that...inner hate, the anger so that [the police-man] will be ready for everything.

In fact, the gauntlet was also regularly employed by Brazilian police and military during the military period against captured political subversives themselves.

By using violent hazing against and between trainees, ostensibly for preparing militarized police to fight a just war, the academy curriculum "morally disengaged" (Bandura 1999) police violence from its negative political and moral implications and consequences. It was common—par-ticularly for murderers—to claim that because they had carried out their violence in a group, no single group member needed to feel any direct re-sponsibility for the outcome. With every policeman in the group shoot-ing, no one person had direct responsibility for the killing. In fact, under such circumstances of complete diffusion of responsibility, no one even knew who had shot the bullet that killed a suspect. Most firing squads use a similar diffusion strategy by having many blanks and a few live bullets.

Effects of Atrocity Training

Having identified the components of Militarized Police preservice train-ing that could have engendered atrocity, the question still remains as to whether it actually did. One step toward answering this question is to examine whether atrocity perpetrators and facilitators accepted hazing any differently. Although our interviewees had all made it through pre-service training without being dismissed for trainee insubordination or weakness—one sign that the hazing was working on them—we still need to explore both sets of trainees' attitudes about preservice training, including hazing. If approval of hazing is better preparation for atrocity work than nonapproval, then we should find that those militarized po-lice who did not commit atrocities should be less accepting of preservice training over all.

Indeed, we found that among our Militarized Police interviewees, the atrocity-facilitating comparison group was less likely to be openly supportive and most likely to be explicitly critical of the deindividualizing and dehumanizing aspects of preservice training. For example, one policeman from this group observed that his training had been "for the exclusive and sole purpose of torturing, degrading people. There was no teaching going on.... [The trainees] had no guns, no helmets, no equipment at all." Another Militarized Police atrocity facilitator explained critically that his academy training had focused on teaching men how to "fight the people" and not criminals. In his words, the objective of Militarized Police preservice training was not "to make strong men [but] to have men go out into the streets and do the [government's] bidding. They raise irate policemen . . . [who] leave the base feeling bitter."

In contrast, the six documented Militarized Police atrocity perpetrators had very few explicit criticisms of their preservice training and much praise for it. Bernardo, a Militarized Police murderer who as a Civil Police official later oversaw torture, describes quite favorably the use of physical exercises for implanting authority: It created "discipline . . . [and the] military abilities [that] were highly demanded [by the Militarized Police]." Through punishing exercises "we [would] really acquire that professional disciplinary awareness." Another atrocity perpetrator, Roberto—a former death squad leader and a murderer himself—believes that "discipline has to be rigorously enforced" in Militarized Police training because it builds a disciplined policeman. Militarized Police officer Fernando, another murderer, attributes his men's strength under fire to their tough training at the Militarized Police Academy: They learned "humility, and you must be humble." Fernando remembers humility as being inculcated primarily through hazing: "You're going to polish my boots, do what we order. You have to know how to obey." Fernando sees hazing as "a type of value-building [activity]. It creates respect."

A good deal of research supports Fernando and the other atrocity perpetrators who championed hazing for its role in reshaping trainees' identities and engendering their obedience to Militarized Police authority. Van Gennep (1960) illustrates how preindustrial societies' hazing-like rites of passage serve much the same purpose. Haritos-Fatouros (forthcoming) has shown how preservice training transformed Greek Military Police recruits into torturers and how similar training shapes U.S. Marines into elite fighting units. Yet what precisely is the role of hazing in reshaping identities? It is well known that U.S. college fraternities have long used "hell week" and a final "hell night" as an integral part of their admission screening and for creating a sense of uniqueness among those fraternity initiates who succeed in surmounting the organization's degrading rituals. As research on cognitive dissonance shows, people like best those things and those groups that they have to suffer most to join (Aronson and Mills 1959).

Moving into Society

As Militarized Police trainees neared the end of their preparation period, they faced the most intense and gruelling hazing of all: Hell Week, a violent climax to training that made no pretense at being a skill-imparting phase of police preparation. It was quite simply a final test of a man's courage and will to fight. The trainees were cursed, humiliated, and hit; their faces were pushed into dirt as they did endless push-ups; and they were subjected to anything else that the officers could think of as an appropriate test of their resolve. As one policeman from the comparison group remembered Hell Week, "Everyone went through a 'washing'":

I wouldn't say it was brainwashing, but it was a physical washing.... The whole troop rolls around in the grass and then goes through that oil trench. All that suffering so that on the day of the [graduation] ceremony they can put on their uniforms—washed, starched and ironed—as if nothing had happened.

Hell Week often culminated with a baptism-like ritual performed by a training officer at a makeshift altar. During one part of this ceremony, trainees were required to "receive the Eucharist," which involved drinking blood, urine, or some other equally dangerous and noxious liquid from the trainer's ceremonial cup. ("Receiving the Eucharist" was also the euphemism for a notoriously violent form of military and police torture, involving a strong electric shock being administered to a victim's mouth or genitals by a live wire.) Trainees were dressed in a manner and given hazing tasks that further punctuated their degradation and powerlessness: with their nude bodies wrapped by a shroud and unprotected from the elements, they were ordered to fall to the ground and roll in a trench:

There's this trench where cars get oil changes. It's completely full of oil...that dirty car oil. In training we had to crawl through it on our bellies in order to get to the other side. You were a piece of sludge by the time [you finished].

After this, trainees were ordered to crawl through a sewage ditch and next through a dark, almost airless tunnel; as filth swaddled their bodies, a tear gas grenade was tossed in. This quintessential test of suitability for Militarized Police service measured their determination and courage under fire: The man who fled the trench gagging from gas and desperate for air would then get double or triple the number of hazing challenges. Those who could not withstand this final test were deemed unsuitable for Militarized Police service. Many injuries and sometimes deaths were, and still are, the outcome of Hell Week hazing.

The trainees who survived these final rituals were eligible to become full-fledged militarized police. The Militarized Police Academy's formal graduation ceremony usually lasted almost an entire day and included colorful, patriotic marches; religious and national songs; and speeches from prestigious public and military officials. At a sumptuous luncheon, there was another round of speeches and a series of toasts for distinguished guests—to honor the officers and their families as well as the trainees and their immediate kin. The new militarized policemen, dressed in their formal police uniforms, fortified by the strength of their organization, and emboldened by the harshness of their training, by all accounts left the graduation ceremony proud, energized, and ready to confront anything. Having come through training that demonstrated their courage, the new policemen could take their place among other brave Militarized Police professionals.

Reflecting this stout-hearted attitude, an atrocity perpetrator argued that preservice training had made him "lose [his] fear because you become accustomed to just about anything.... You have the feeling that you can confront anything and anybody of any proportion—even [prize fighter] Mike Tyson." A policeman from the comparison group recalled having such omnipotent feelings on graduation day that he "wanted to intervene in all kinds of problems. I felt like a superhero... powerful and unbeatable. I believed that... authority is not... to be questioned. That's what I'd learned."

The Secret World of Hazing and Violence

Hazing clearly played a crucial role in creating a complex set of feelings and attitudes among trainees that may have predisposed some of them toward violence against enemies of their state. By shaping Militarized Police trainees into an army at war against subversion, hazing in particular and other preservice training in general—especially that which promoted unthinking obedience to commands—could have laid a seedbed especially for aggressive beatings and quick-fire shootings. At the very least, by hazing's sending a message that violence is normal, instrumentally effective, and organizationally acceptable, the Militarized Police gave trainees a violent formula they could take into the field; among the eight militarized police who openly admitted to having been hazed during academy preservice training, five were among the six documented atrocity perpetrators. Even the one atrocity perpetrator who did not claim to have gone through hazing during preservice training—Jorge— had been subjected to a great deal of brutal hazing during his many years in a state-run orphanage. In contrast, among the facilitator militarized police, only three of eight admitted to having been hazed in their preservice training. This would seem to suggest that the hazing experience might have contributed, at the very least, to creating a potential for perpetrating atrocity.

However, the relationship of hazing to atrocity is not as clear as it might seem. First, among the militarized police who did not mention being hazed either prior to (Jorge) or during preservice training—or who flatly denied having gone through it—there is good reason to suspect that most of them had in fact been hazed. But what is the evidence that the comparison group police had in fact been hazed? Everything that we have derived from the militarized police interviewees about preservice training, whether these interviewees were officers or rank-and-filers, or from journalist exposes of this training, suggests that during both Brazil's military and redemocratization periods, hazing was an integral part of Militarized Police training. Therefore, we propose that some interviewees' silence on this matter indicates that they were very likely withholding this information. The reasons for their secrecy lie in expected punishment for discussing hazing, the threats to group solidarity from disclosing it, and our own linguistic difficulties in soliciting information about it.

Indeed, perhaps the most compelling reason for interviewees keeping their academy hazing a secret is that during our interview period there was a great deal of negative publicity in Brazil about the Militarized Police organization's brutal, dangerous, and racist hazing. The organization responded across Brazil by prohibiting its members from talking about any aspect of preservice training, including in particular Militarized Police hazing. Officials warned that such disclosures would result in fines at the very least and imprisonment or dismissal from the force at worst. Yet Militarized Police protest groups across Brazil still leaked information about past and current hazing practices to the Brazilian press, including releasing clandestinely videotaped documentaries of violent and racist Militarized Police Hell Week activities in Brasilia and Minas Gerais. These exposés left little doubt that hazing has been and remains a central component of Militarized Police preservice training.

However, the threat of violence was not the only thing keeping some interviewees from talking about hazing. An even more compelling motive for remaining silent about hazing may be that secrecy about hazing bonds victims to one another and to the larger organization and protects an organization's inner core from critical outsiders. As Simmel (1950) has pointed out, once a group's secret is disclosed, the group loses some of its identity. In the case of Militarized Police Academy hazing, this practice attaches trainees to an organizational entity whose very existence is defined and reinforced by secrecy about violence.

Finally, given the formally and informally enforced secrecy about hazing, it was naturally difficult to frame interview questions that would secure information about it. For example, we learned very quickly that the Portuguese word for hazing, *trote,* provoked either silence or an argumentative polemic. For example, a former Militarized Police atrocity perpetrator responded angrily that his preservice training "wasn't hazing [*trote*] at all." Sure, his officers' training group had to "shine thirty-two pairs of muddy combat boots," but this was different from "hazing, [which would be] doing push-ups...running around the barracks for ten minutes." For this interviewee, boot polishing was not hazing because it gave future officers "a kind of lesson in humility.... Before giving orders, you have to be able to obey them." Nevertheless, he was counted as one of those admitting to hazing's occurrence.

From this reaction and those of other interviewees to our questions about hazing, we learned on the one hand that we could not assume that we and an interviewee had the same definition of *hazing* and on the other that if we limited instances of hazing to what interviewees gave as the definition most politically acceptable to them—and used these responses as a description of hazing—we would fail to capture most of the hazing that had gone on. Because we could not find any single Portuguese word for hazing that got at all of its various manifestations, we used a variety of words to probe its existence in Militarized Police training. For example, we asked about the kinds of "physical training" a trainee had experienced? Had "physical exercises" been used as a punishment? What kinds of physical or psychological "discipline-building activities" had a trainee gone through? This line of questioning helped uncover information about activities that would normally be labeled "hazing." Yet, even with this more indirect approach, some militarized police who were very likely to have been hazed still did not disclose information about it in their preservice training experience.

However, if we assume from this theoretical and empirical argument that hazing was and is ubiquitous in the Militarized Police training curriculum, this complicates the presumption of a relationship between hazing and atrocity: The facilitators were also hazed but apparently did not carry out systematic atrocities. We therefore face a thorny theoretical problem: if the comparison group police were hazed yet did not commit systematic atrocities, then what is the relationship of Militarized Police preservice hazing to atrocity? Because we cannot assert that hazing actively creates atrocity perpetrators, we propose that by fostering unthinking, group-minded obedience to authority, it established one important institutional girder for *certain kinds* of atrocity. Hazing shapes Militarized Police trainees into atrocity *teams* by modeling violence, creating blind obedience to authority, bringing about group bonding for reflexively meting out violence, and nurturing the moral disengagement that disguises and justifies such violence. The uniformed militarized police, many of whom carried out beatings and murders collectively in public view, had to present themselves and be seen by outsiders as acting legitimately *in concert* against a social and political enemy. Hazing is one mechanism for institutionalizing the team solidarity, group action, and hierarchical control for convincingly demonstrating such operational legitimacy. As one militarized policeman from the comparison group explains,

We had to be physically strong. We had to prove ourselves as men through physical strength.... We had to stand, put up with all types of exercises and an absurd number of repetitions, like 100 push-ups.... Then after a lot of exercise, you run outside. We're going to show the people out there that we are united, happy.... We demonstrate [through exercise] that we are a group of...strong valiant men.... It's part of the brainwashing that you get.

If Militarized Police are to carry out "politically legitimate" street beatings and shoot into crowds and murder faceless suspected (not legally adjudged) wrongdoers, then their violence must appear as disciplined, professional teamwork. The *quality* of group action itself (e.g., organization, preparedness, uniformity) in part confers legitimacy on the group's violence. Under such conditions, no single member of a team can deviate from the group's militarized script; its violence must appear an unvarying group product. By inculcating obedience to Militarized Police authority and to its social control and political goals, preservice training in general and hazing in particular help mold trainees into more predictable and controllable agents of the state. The former trainees may not have all been made into institutional functionaries, but in their public performances they had to at least appear like them.

Summing up the obedience-shaping process, Roberto—the man who claimed to have "lost his control" when he stepped outside group discipline and gunned down four people as a militarized policeman in a death squad—explained that Militarized Police officials "consider[ed] discipline essential: The policeman at school is trained to stand everything; he's humiliated and suffers psychological pressure that... tests his level of police training." Of course, as Roberto's case suggests, the outcome of such violent discipline may be summary executions, on or off duty, contributing in his case to his status as a blended masculinity policeman.

However, because preservice training was carried out at the beginning of a militarized policeman's career, which may have been several years and a few promotions before he began *systematically* committing *serial* beatings and executions, we must examine other possible subsequent factors that led some militarized police to perpetrate these atrocities. Moreover, because most Civil Police atrocity perpetrators did not receive preservice training and because they tended most often to engage in torture, not murder, we need to look into the factors that may have shaped their later careers. Finally, we need to seek commonalities in the careers of the Militarized and Civil Police atrocity perpetrators that bridge these organizations and explain serial atrocity more generally.

In the next chapter, we extend our analyses of how violence workers are shaped by demonstrating that Brazilian police atrocities were commonly the outcome of certain kinds of organizational affiliations that defined atrocity perpetrators' careers—whether in the Civil or Militarized Police. Within this finding we uncovered new layers of information about how work structures and processes shaped the organizational and interpersonal dynamics of the policemen who became serial atrocity perpetrators. Thus, although this chapter has focused on what could be labeled the explicitly abnormal and "evil" experiences that influenced some Brazilian police, the next chapter looks at the banal structures and activities that more informally fostered and reinforced serial atrocities, whether torture or murder.

CHAPTER 10

Secret and Insular Worlds of Serial Torturers and Executioners

Cruelty has a human heart,
And jealousy a human face;
Terror the human form divine,
And secrecy the human dress.

William Blake, "The Divine Image," *Songs of Experience*

Whoever chases monsters should see to it that in the process he does
not become a monster himself.

Rafael Perez, convicted CRASH Unit policeman,
Los Angeles Police Department Rampart Division

This chapter looks at the structural and interactional factors that shaped relatively ordinary Brazilian police into serial atrocity perpetrators. We begin this exploration with a description of several Brazilian policemen's entry into specialized police organizations, social control units, or informal death squads. Clearly, such career moves—which locked their members into an isolated, all-embracing, and operationally violent culture— began their transformation from ordinary working cops into repeat killers. Seeking the actual processes that explain the connection between membership in one of these agencies and the perpetration of regular and systematic atrocity, we examine violence work organization as well as the associated informal social-psychological processes.

We discovered that *serial* atrocity was nurtured out of an interrelated dynamic that included three spheres: the politics of an internal security

ideology; the specialized hierarchy and competitive organization of social control units; and the associated social psychology of deindividuation, obedience, dehumanization, modeling violence's acceptability, and
moral disengagement. These processes, which in the last chapter were
identified as official aspects of formal Militarized Police training, are examined in this chapter as indirect aspects of political and organizational
structures and processes and of informal work socialization. When
speaking of the banality of evil, scholars of atrocity are pointing to how
seemingly normal and pervasive systems of social organization and social psychology can foster, hide, and excuse abnormal outcomes.

Violent Turning Points:
Atrocity Unit Recruitment and Promotion

In addressing how specialized violence organizations might shape human
conduct, Robert J. Lifton (1986: 425) argues that these are "so structured...institutionally that the average person entering...will commit or
become associated with atrocities." Our interview data lend compelling
support to Lifton's proposition: among the twenty-three interviewees, we
found that the careers of the Militarized and Civil Police atrocity perpetrators were marked by similar identity- and behavior-transforming initial
and continuing assignments that differed from those of the facilitators of
atrocity. In particular, the most clear-cut introduction to systematic torture and murder turned out to be joining an elite operations or interrogation organization, team, or squad. All six of the documented Militarized
Police atrocity perpetrators had been in at least one specialized social control team or squad, compared with only one of the eight facilitators. In
fact, almost all of the atrocity facilitators, whether militarized or civil police, were rank-and-file beat cops throughout their careers. The pattern of
direct perpetrators' holding elite-service membership was true for the civil
policemen as well: Six of the eight documented Civil Police atrocity perpetrators had been in special units or teams. However, one Civil Police
atrocity facilitator had also been in such a special organization. In any
case, within the sample of twenty-three police, twelve of the fourteen direct perpetrators had been in special police organizations or squads, compared with only two of the nine auxiliary facilitators.[1]

1. Although our initial sampling strategy was to seek interviewees from elite squads (see
Chapter 3) with the assumption that these might be likely to contain atrocity perpetrators,

But knowing that atrocity perpetrators were more likely to have been in elite units does not explain how such organizations actually fostered violence. Let us examine how they did in Brazil, beginning with a hypothesis based on psychological predisposition: torture and murder organizations attract already sadistic individuals who volunteer for them and then use their positions in these units to play out their violent propensities. However, as we shall see, most of the routes into atrocity organizations do not easily lend themselves to this argument.

The policemen who served in specialized social control teams entered their assignments through a variety of routes, none of which was related directly to any predisposition to cruelty. Those in such organizations or units were selected or promoted by others (especially if considered trustworthy) or fortuitously chosen, that is, by chance, or through just following orders to carry out violence. In fact, a policeman's movement into a special team or unit usually resulted from several of these factors coming together.

Some policemen were assigned to a special atrocity unit or team immediately after academy training—a career move not of a trainee's own choosing or even preference but resulting from a superior's decision. Militarized Police official Fernando believes that he was selected during preservice training for his first special unit—a SWAT team—only because of the tactical skills that he had demonstrated. Armando, too, was placed in a Militarized Police SWAT team as his first postacademy assignment without his indicating such a preference. He remained there for four years, with two promotions for his excellent operational performance.

Other atrocity-committing interviewees neither asked for nor desired their first assignment to one of the specialized, violent organizations. For example, without explicitly seeking such an appointment, Civil Police official Márcio was told by São Paulo political officials that he was being assigned to an elite RONE motorized squad because, as a former newspaper reporter, he would be able to deal with press attacks on RONE. Thus, although Márcio presents his own career progression as based solely on meritorious rewards for professionally rational police work, the evidence points to Márcio's movement into elite policing as a result of higher-level police and political officials perceiving him as able to effectively promote their agenda.

---

we did not know that this hypothesis was correct. However, because we also obtained a number of interviewees who had not been in elite squads, we were able to use these police as a comparison group for examining our original hypothesis.

In some cases, movement into a special operations team was quite by chance. For example, early in Eduardo's career, he remembers that Civil Police officials "just threw me [into the DOPS political police]... without asking if [I] wanted [it]": in fact, DOPS officials believed that Eduardo's "baby face" would enable him to infiltrate student organizations without getting burned. Eduardo's career in violence thereafter took many twists and turns; his progression was neither direct nor linear. After many successful DOPS infiltrations and agitprop smear operations and with a new law degree in hand, Eduardo applied and took examinations to transfer to either one of two prestigious internal security organizations—the National Intelligence Service (SNI) or the Federal Police. But Eduardo's bid to enter the Federal Police was turned down for physical reasons, and his application for the SNI thrown out for failure to meet residence requirements. With his career in intelligence stalled—and physically and emotionally exhausted by DOPS intelligence and operations—Eduardo moved first to prison work and then to the Civil Police stolen cars division, both of which were notorious for utilizing extreme violence, including murder and torture, in their operations.

In the end, Eduardo's committing certain kinds of violence, such as beatings and torture, rather than more indirect violence, such as primarily overseeing and ordering torture, was in fact a product of his not getting into elite social control organizations where, as a high-level official, he would have become primarily an atrocity facilitator. Being rejected for elite intelligence service and feeling unable to keep up the pace of DOPS operations, Eduardo got himself transferred to social control settings where he would continue directly perpetrating the murders and physical and psychological coercion that he had already carried out as a political police operative.

Jorge was moved out of the military and into the police in the first place because military and police officials suspected his psychological instability and felt he needed to be kept more closely under their direct control. Apparently given an ultimatum, Jorge could either join the Militarized Police, where he would be regulated by a police hierarchy and then subordinated to the armed services, or be assassinated. However, Jorge apparently backed into his first Militarized Police murder assignment, which then led to his assignment first to an elite murder squad and then to his trial performance in a torture squad and then to his being detailed to an elite execution team. Illustrating that careers into atrocity are not always direct and not invariably by choice alone, once

Jorge had killed the members of a religious group (described in Chapter 7) as a rank-and-file militarized policeman under orders from his senior officer, he had no recourse but to accept his superior officer's next assignment: not only had Jorge committed six murders, but he knew that his officers were covering them up for him as well as themselves. Assigned after the murders to the Militarized Police Reserved Service, where officers could continue keeping tabs on him, Jorge was just one advancement away from his final career placement as a DOI/CODI murder operative.

Eduardo's and Jorge's careers also suggest that experience in units that specialize in one kind of violence—for example, murder, rather than torture or vice versa—usually resulted in promotion to specialized units engaging in similar types of violence. Militarized Police atrocity perpetrator Bernardo, for example, recalls police being "chosen [for special units] according to...experience": Some police are better at "overt operations [beatings and murder]. These were the more courageous policemen who also knew how to use the equipment and weapons better." Even though such police were sometimes already "very cold...[and] aggressive," in fact, according to Bernardo, this alone had not made them atrocity perpetrators.

DOPS official Sérgio argues that he sought "hard-nosed," aggressively violent police for his informal death squad by selecting them from among the men who "liked staying up all night, doing all those things you see in the movies." Sérgio maintains that as regular civil policemen, such men were not inherently aggressive; he merely took advantage of the fact that they they had gotten brutal after years of carrying out direct physical violence, often at his direction. Fully knowing what to expect from these men's nurtured propensities, Sérgio—in his role as atrocity facilitator—dispatched his death squad into the night knowing that he could count on this team's following orders. As Sérgio explained, the "policeman who is outraged [that is, bestialized by carrying out years of atrocity]...will commit murder if he has the opportunity." But note that Sérgio chose only men with years of such experience, not neophyte psychopaths.

As for torture squads, indeed, being too cold, too ruthless, or even too sympathetic might contribute to a man's disqualification from such service. Jorge, for example, was initially groomed to enter a torture unit after he had executed the religious devotees. However, during his brief preparation for this transfer, in which Jorge was assigned to observe torture sessions, officials apparently decided that he was unsuitable for that kind of work. Arguing that Jorge's background made him a better murderer than torturer—a role that he had already successfully demonstrated—officials assigned him to an elite DOI/CODI execution team. Once in the DOI murder squad, Jorge expressed great relief that "[now] at last [he] can quit seeing stupid things" like torture. This violence worker preferred to put the hood over the head of his victim and shoot—a process that was clean, easy, and direct, involving no positive or negative psychological relationship with the victim.

Those adjudged sadists or brutes were seen among several of the interviewees as bad torturers. As one admitted torturer interviewed by Brazil's national news weekly *Veja* (Porão iluminado 1998: 48) explained, he had personally fired two sergeants whom he "did not want working with [him]" because they were sadistic. Likewise, Civil Police official Márcio believes that the most rational torturers were those without "character disorders"; they could become predictable torture functionaries only if their violence could be regularized and guided by professional administrators. Such operatives, however, needed to learn how to personally handle the sometimes negative consequences of their violence, a process that was integral to the violence worker's daily police duties, as this chapter illustrates shortly.

Remaining in a Special Unit

After their initial placement in a specialized unit, some interviewees actually requested transfer to another even more specialized one or were willingly promoted into one. For example, Armando, after four years in the Militarized Police SWAT team—which he asserts "psychologically prepared [him to] contain [street] disorders created by large numbers of people"—volunteered for Rio de Janeiro's GOE. This elite special operations team, organized by a state public security official infamous for brutality, Army General Luis de França Oliveira, was made up of men selected from the army, police, and fire departments. Fernando, another friend of Oliveira, could also parlay his two years in the elite Rio SWAT team into a promotion to the GOE special operations unit. Fernando believes that public security officials chose men for GOE operations who had "already demonstrated [courage] during their professional life"—they wanted men who had "some experience in...combat." However, in fact, rather than Fernando's skills alone qualifying him for GOE service, this policeman was picked for his bureaucratic trustworthiness: Fernando could be counted on to do whatever political officials wanted.

But operatives in specialized atrocity work who wanted to transfer out often found that it was very difficult to do so—their desires were rarely taken into account by officials. Sérgio, as a civil policeman, was selected by his state's governor (who "absolutely trusted" him) very early in his career to head the São Paulo DOPS, which at the very least made him a torture and murder facilitator. Initially very enthusiastic about this prestigious appointment, he ended up being emotionally and physically exhausted by the many demands it imposed on him, and he desperately wanted to resign. Yet each time Sérgio requested release from his DOPS post, the governor countered by expanding Sérgio's scope of operation and even promoted him to a higher police position.

Roberto, who initially joined an informal Militarized Police death squad to avenge himself on the men who had violated his family's honor, maintains that he wanted to quit after several years as the squad's driver. But, like Jorge, he alleges that he could not leave the death squad without becoming a murder victim himself. Warned that because he had availed himself of the death squad's services, he "was part of the group," Roberto had to accompany the death squad on murder rounds "whenever [the death squad] needed [him], ... or [he and his] family would be killed." Ernesto, a Civil Police atrocity perpetrator with death squad connections, believes that it was even dangerous to leave the police system: "As an expoliceman you are at the mercy of those you arrested, those you did not arrest, ... and even other policemen who could be [your] enemies." Ernesto, who entered the Civil Police with distinction and left it a convicted murderer, maintains that he was framed for murder by disreputable police officials who were protecting their drug connections. These examples illustrate that just as entry into a violent social control organization or squad was not always a policeman's direct choice, so leaving one was sometimes also outside his control.

Atrocities against others cannot be excused just because these men entered specialized social control units not necessarily by choice or because of others' nurturing their careers or because extracting themselves was difficult or impossible. Our findings instead suggest that Brazilian state-sponsored atrocities were apparently not the result of individual actors' sadistic predispositions. This opens the door to examining the role of organized states' ideological campaigns, their social control organizations, and the social-psychological dynamics that are produced by and shape serial atrocities.

Internal Security Politics

Most of the police atrocities that are the focus of this book occurred in an authoritarian, military-controlled state. Its national security ideology supported, promoted, enforced, and justified police and military repression against those deemed its enemies. This ideology, which "manufactured contempt for the perpetrator" (Morales 1999: 5), encouraged bystander communities to accept or at least to fail to act against state repression, and it reinforced inaction through implicit and explicit messages that those who challenged national security would suffer violence against themselves and their families. Notwithstanding the culture of fear that was created by real and threatened state repression, the national security "emergency" still demanded new and improved social control organizations to enforce its mandates. These incorporated serial atrocity into a highly routinized and segmented (i.e., "Taylorized") division of violent labor that misrecognized atrocities as something other than what they were. The organized system of violence was supported by "respectable" and powerful facilitators who legitimized atrocity through their support for or membership in the system itself.[2] The usually less powerful and generally less respectable direct perpetrators who carried out the system's violent directives were encapsulated within the internal security system's organizational cocoon. Social-psychologically, violence came to define these men's self-perceptions and those of their colleagues, especially as these operatives were transformed by membership in violent specialized police organizations.

Training for Atrocity

A fundamental premise of organizational sociology, that the work process shapes the worker, is as valid for unconventional and antinormative occupations as for mainstream ones. Having already found that Brazilian atrocity perpetrators did not start out in the police with abnormal predispositions toward violence and that Militarized Police atrocities could be

2. "Taylorization" suggests Frederick W. Taylor's "time-study" theory of scientific management. It proposes a strategy for work organization that features a strict division of labor between workers and management within a ranked hierarchy of task specialization that includes clear delineation of authority, separation of planning from operations, and the breakdown of production tasks into their constituent parts—the latter a piecework approach to worker output that became a foundation of the assembly line.

only partly explained by these operatives' preservice training—with most Civil Police atrocity perpetrators not even going through such training—it made sense to explore both Militarized and Civil Police atrocity perpetrators' in-service training. Assuming that formal ongoing training was given to all specialized police, we were surprised to discover that, in fact, such training was received only by a portion of the interviewees and by only a segment of the atrocity perpetrators among them.

For example, seven of the fourteen atrocity perpetrators and five of the nine facilitators did not receive any structured in-service training—almost the same proportion for both groups. At the same time, however, those atrocity perpetrators who had been in specialized organizations were much more likely to have gone through formal in-service training. For example, almost twice as many (seven) of the eleven perpetrators who had been in special units had also been through in-service training, compared with only four perpetrators in special units who had not received any. In contrast, the two atrocity facilitators who had been in special units had both received in-service training, whereas among the seven other facilitators who had not been in special units, only two had gotten formal in-service training. These comparative data suggest that although in-service training could not have been the single determining factor in shaping serial atrocity perpetrators, it may have played a role in their socialization—especially in conjunction with membership in a specialized police organization or squad.

But the in-service training of police interviewees was relatively narrow in scope—focusing primarily on technical skills—and very restricted in duration, lasting only about two weeks. Just the same, it is useful to examine its content. Fernando's specialized training for the GOE operations unit, which imparted both techniques and attitudes, featured technical courses on "chemical warfare... [and] bomb and antibomb explosives." In a sophisticated commando course, physical punishment was used on the trainees to "summon a man's will to fight": they were sent "into the woods where they would get beaten on the knees and...back." Fernando believes that this kind of training taught men "to look for [their] limits." In the process, such aggressively violent preparation eliminated the men with "fragile spirits—the men who shouldn't be there," men unable to endure the demanding physical and psychological abuses that would toughen them up to carry out physical beatings and murder.

Later in his career, as a Militarized Police training official preparing others for the specialized operational units in which beatings and murders were common, Fernando taught a guerrilla warfare course. Challenging his own students to expand their physical and psychological limits in this advanced "operations course," he maintains that his students began to fully benefit from the training only after they had gotten seriously hungry and exhausted. Fernando stretched his men's endurance by having them carry "rifles on their back[s], cross...obstacles, and swim," continuing to push their limits until men pleaded, "I cannot take any more." Only when his men had "reached the point of exploding" would Fernando let up. According to Fernando, this taught trainees "what a difficult situation is and that [they] can endure it," presumably excellent preparation for a Militarized Police battalion that spends long periods in the streets or countryside battling subversives.

Sérgio, a Civil Police DOPS atrocity perpetrator who spent most of his career in intelligence work, received some in-service training from the CIA in the United States. His instruction included, besides such academic subjects as how the Soviet KGB, French Sureté, and CIA operate, demonstrations in "how [political police] should work." Sérgio also took a range of technical classes, including learning how to "bug... phones, install...microphones [and other] listening devices, and infiltrate." But for Sérgio the most important element of this coursework was "swapping ideas" with the CIA personnel about tracking subversives across national boundaries—as Brazil's security forces would do in Operation Condor, a violent international security initiative that linked the CIA with the security forces of Latin America's Southern Cone military-run countries in a war against subversion. After Sérgio's stay in Washington, D.C., he remembers feeling more enthusiastic about tracking Brazilian "students who would go to Paris [or]...Russia."

A Militarized Police atrocity facilitator remembers his in-service training as primarily imparting a particular set of operational social control techniques. He was able to "learn how to make handcuffs...out of a [policeman's] club" and a piece of leather or twine: turning the club puts more and more pressure on the person's pulse and causes sufficient pain to restrain the suspect. This policeman also learned to use his club to "hit specific parts of the [suspect's] body where black-and-blue marks don't appear." This leaves "no proof of an aggressive act [or of] abuse of [police] power."

A Civil Police atrocity facilitator who may have actually tortured as well got in-service training in such subjects as how to apply "self-administered pain- and panic-blocking techniques."[3] This policeman

3. As we explained in an earlier chapter, the distinction between perpetrators and facilitators in this study leaves some room for error. Although in most cases we feel confident

also observed his trainer grab a hot charcoal and say, "Look, it doesn't hurt. I'm not feeling any pain." The atrocity facilitator says that he was taught how to control his mind so that he would not feel pain if tortured—a process that undoubtedly also hardened him against others' pain. The combination of developing high pain thresholds and experiencing various kinds of abuse very likely contributed to a loss of empathy for torture victims.

These interviewees' testimonies about the content of their in-service training suggest that it could play a role in shaping some police into certain kinds of atrocity perpetrators, but perhaps not consistently and in all cases. Such training imparted the skills for making atrocity more refined and systematized and helped to shape the attitudes that numbed a policemen to his and others' violence. In-service training very likely also strengthened a trainee's commitment to his specialized social control organization and its violent mission. That such training was often given as a reward after good service, usually in association with promotion to a more prestigious position, not only lent institutional respectability to the content and outcomes of the training but also recognized an atrocity worker's commitment to violence. In any case, the training group reinforced its members' pride in being part of a unique cadre of men with a mission; they shared experiences that no one in ordinary society could ever know or appreciate.

However, although formal in-service training had a potentially important role in generally shaping atrocity perpetrators and in nurturing certain kinds of violence, we cannot assume that it produced serial atrocity in and of itself: only little more than half of the atrocity perpetrators and just under half of the facilitators received it. Instead, what continues to most distinctly mark the careers of serial atrocity perpetrators—whether in the Civil or Militarized Police—is ongoing membership in a specialized social control organization or squad, whether or not this was also associated with in-service training. With an interest in how such specialized squads may have nurtured atrocities, we examined informal daily socialization in elite police organizations.

---

that the atrocity facilitators were just that, and clearly not *serial* atrocity perpetrators in any case, we feel least confident in this assumption about L. O. In his role as a civil policeman and as an operative for the federal-level SNI, L. O. may very well have tortured. However, because nothing in his testimony directly connects him to such activities and those who knew and worked with him did not indicate this involvement, we have included L.O. in the atrocity facilitator group.

Work Socialization for Atrocity

A potentially very important component of atrocity work organization is the informal socialization that prepared police technically and developed the attitudes and behaviors that explained the reasons for their violence for themselves and associated others. The socialization that has most consistently shaped violent modes and outcomes has taken place for Brazilian police while engaging in the daily work of social control. In fact, research on policing in the United States (Bayley and Bittner 1984; Bittner 1993; Prenzler 1997; Rubenstein 1973; Skolnick 1966) confirms that police generally learn much of what they know about social control techniques, criminal detection, and self-protection, as well as the situationally appropriate responses to danger, from those with whom they work most closely. What police actually learn in their work settings, of course, derives from the kinds of social control they carry out. If police are in operations work, then learning to accept and to appropriately carry out beatings and murder may be the grist of their learning curriculum. If police are in intelligence or interrogation, then psychological and physical coercion for information may be the raw material of their learning environment. Where policing is well integrated into a network of corruption and graft, as in Mexico City, informal socialization focuses on implanting the correct attitudes about protection rackets and bribes and teaching police how to work safely and effectively within such a system (see Botello and Rivera 2000).

Taking these insights as our starting point, we present what Brazilian interviewees disclosed about informal socialization's role in shaping their attitudes about and learning the appropriate uses of violence. We recognize that such socialization will vary according to a social control organization's dominant ideology—in this case, an internal war against subversion—and according to a police organization's formal jurisdictional mission—whether predominantly investigative (where torture occurs) or search-and-arrest (where beatings and shootings are most common).

We quickly discovered, however, that the information most difficult to obtain from interviewees was precisely what they did each day in police work. Either they could not remember or they held back to protect their pasts. Nevertheless, we still acquired a number of valuable insights into when, how, and which policing techniques and attitudes had been informally communicated to atrocity perpetrators. Suggesting the normality of this process, police specialists will quickly recognize that the process and much of the content of this learning does not differ radically from what is taught within regular police organizational climates. Indeed, looking over the interview narratives, we saw that the situations and venues in which the Brazilian interviewees had learned relevant police techniques and attitudes could be grouped into four sometimes-overlapping categories that can be seen in normal police socialization as well. In one situation, interviewees explained that they had learned day-to-day policing from a teacher—usually an older policeman in a routine, nonemergency setting. In another, they had learned from an oral tradition. A third learning situation was generalized long-term, nonemergency, on-the-job experience. The fourth teaching venue was emergency environments where speed or danger were perceived or emphasized as making learning immediately necessary.

THE POLICEMAN AS TEACHER

Many interviewees indicated that the most consistent and useful information they gained about policing had been from other police in routine settings—the station house, on patrol, or in a police car or van. There, a younger or newer policeman—the interviewee—was usually schooled by an older partner or colleague. Civil Policeman Ignácio believes that "your real [police] education...is always through someone with more experience, the older one." Márcio, too, as a new Civil Police station chief in a rural area, relied on support and information from other, usually older, police: this statewide network of police chiefs shared "information as a duty, a moral obligation."

Civil Police atrocity perpetrator Bruno, even before his induction into the police, was introduced to the police division where he would begin his career by his older cousin, a tough operational cop who worked in arrests. So Bruno "began to hang out" with his cousin and very quickly discovered that this was where he wanted his career: it was action-charged and exciting. Once in this specialized arrest division, where he would in fact become a detective, Bruno was informally schooled in "persistence" by another, older civil policeman. Bruno learned that "the policeman must persevere: If he has a lead on an address, something must be there, so you have to go to the bar on the corner, to the neighbors; you have to sometimes spend two or three days on the street." Bruno recalls the older policeman as an excellent "on-the-job teacher."

Civil Policeman Ernesto's partner would "wait for situations to arise" and then teach Ernesto how to use "care when approaching a criminal."

Jacob learned from his partners during interrogation sessions that "you can't trust anybody's tears." Ignácio found out how to profile criminals by walking a beat with his partner, who would point to someone passing by and say, "Look at the way that guy is...he looks like a mugger, an embezzler, a gambler." Márcio and his Civil Police partner would walk down the street and play a guessing game: "'I think he's Portuguese and a doorman.' 'No, I think he's Portuguese and a banker.'" The two policemen would then stop the person, ask for identification, and begin an on-the-spot interrogation—"as if we were doing police supervision." From then on, whenever Márcio saw "someone [not] justified at being [there] at the time, that person [became] a suspect."

Interviewees also were taught by partners how to identify and protect themselves against a corrupt or dangerous partner. Ignácio learned who would make an "ideal partner" by working with a range of different policemen until he found the right one—a man who, like Ignácio, did not "work by the clock." Jacob learned to differentiate trustworthy from dishonest fellow police, a skill that he had been taught by his older cousin—the aggressive civil policeman who had recruited Jacob into policing. Ernesto found out that if the "policeman who works with you...is involved in crooked things, [he] is dangerous. [He] can shoot you, ambush you."

ORAL TRADITION

Márcio explains how his civil police learned to torture, asserting that nothing is written about how to use the shock box: "It comes from an oral tradition. Someone tells someone else [and] that [policeman] passes it on to another." Ignácio indicated that he had learned how to predict his partner's reliability in an emergency in similar fashion:

In arrest vehicles, patrol cars, [the policemen] would begin telling stories. Someone would say, "Do you remember what happened yesterday?" [Or we'd talk] about what to do when we get [to an arrest location]. Alternatives start coming out: "If this happens, do this, that, the other." Those discussions provide security because you find out your colleague's reactions, for example, if he is likely to defend you.

ON-THE-JOB EXPERIENCE

When Civil Policeman Ignácio, an operations man who sometimes tortured as well, was thrown totally unprepared into his first surveillance-and-arrest operation, he had to figure out what to do as the dangerous work progressed. Civil Policeman Eduardo and his partners learned through trial and error how to conduct political investigations: officers would give them a mission, and they would have to do it any way they could.

Ernesto, a civil policeman, maintains that "if you're...a student of human behavior, you begin to develop a perception [of guilt or innocence] just talking to somebody. It seems like there's a sign written on the person's forehead." Civil Police DOPS official Sérgio explained that "political reasoning, everything that you learn,...you only learn from on-the-job experience. You have to work a long time to acquire that quickness of thought,...that mistrust" of others. Bruno, in a Militarized Police operations team at the beginning of his career, claims to have been initially "extremely nervous" when he went out on violent arrest operations, but by "doing [these operations], we lose our fear." He maintains that experience taught him how to "disconnect" and do the job of violence, an apparently necessary step for him and other atrocity perpetrators as we shall see shortly.

EMERGENCY ENVIRONMENTS

Situations rife with potential for fostering a violence worker's being able to carry out serial atrocities were usually relatively short lived and almost always fraught with danger and tension. Violence and force were the means and the message of this setting's informal social control curriculum. For our violence workers, these emergency-charged environments included their secret interrogation or torture sessions, where speed in securing information was the norm, as well as the security force operations that were carried out in a climate of presumed or real danger. In both of these contexts, the social control attitudes nurtured and the techniques imparted and refined were grounded in the notion that Brazil was in the middle of a national security emergency.

Within these circumstances, the violence worker discovered and worked out his relationship to a police unit and the wider environment. Explaining how he felt when his DOI execution team was on an elimination mission, Jorge discloses that

it was as if everyone was carrying a liter of nitroglycerine and there was no way to get rid of it. It was total tension...no one could speak, nobody joked around, there was no relaxation. [We avoided] anything that could represent a risk.

Within such a setting, murder operatives not only had to uncover and eliminate threats from outside the atrocity team but also to recognize and neutralize those from within the group itself. As Jorge explains, "During every operation you really risked your life. Whenever anyone was careless, he...died." He also recalls that "the deaths of members of [his execution team] resulted [mostly] from violating the norms" against being an individual.

Pointing to a form of individualism that could undermine the unit, one atrocity facilitator explained that he learned from emergency situations that even asking too many questions could pose a threat to the group. This interviewee, attached to the SNI though apparently not a torturer himself, remembers having been cautioned that he should "never try to know too much, because if you do, your life...and your country can be at risk." The interviewee now realizes that he "should have [asked] 'why'" more often, but he "just kept quiet" for the sake of the group's, the country's, and his own safety. Asking too many questions could, at the very least, call into question the taken-for-granted premises about group solidarity and, at worst, get you killed.

Civil Policeman Márcio, who had carried out torture and overseen torturers, explained the importance of torturers' maintaining personal and emotional control. Police who demonstrated this had discovered what Márcio labels "the limits to effective torture." He believes that a policeman must be "completely aware of what he is doing" and be guided by a recognized formula: "[Torture] must cause suffering, but it must not cause injuries."

The technique is to make the suffering compatible with the lack of injuries. Injuries can cause the policeman to be held responsible.

In other words, the out-of-control atrocity perpetrator who lets his emotions get in the way of rationally torturing is not an effective worker. As a French interrogator explained about his nation's torturers during the 1954–1962 Algerian War, "Those who got the best results were those who neither got angry nor had pity on their victims." (Book of French torture resurfaces 2000: 6).

We can recall that Jorge's superior decided that he would make an unfit torturer because the superior assumed that Jorge would not be able to forget his own history and would thus end up "helping" his victims by killing them outright just to put them out of their misery. Likewise, when Civil Policeman Ignácio began crying with a criminal he was interrogating, his partner laughed and warned Ignácio that he "ought to be arrested along with the crook for being so soft." Ignácio explained—

without convincing his partner—that his own background in poverty always made him pity those who committed petty thefts out of need. If true, this emotionality may have kept Ignácio out of torture work and in police street operations: He did not have the emotional control to torture, but he had the hair-trigger responses to beat and shoot the alleged criminals who violated his sense of right and wrong.

Settling into a Proper Role

One important step in becoming a serial atrocity perpetrator, rather than a policeman who commits "just" one or two acts of violence, seems to have been the individual's discovering and working out his proper emotional and operational role within a team or organization. Another essential step seems to have been discovering how to cope with the immediate negative emotional by-products of committing or watching atrocity. Jacob recalls that after some of his first shoot-outs, he returned home and had to leave "everything outside the bathroom [before taking] a shower." This helped Jacob separate himself from his morally polluted clothes. Yet after a shooting, as Jacob was sleeping in the middle of the night, his legs would start shaking, and he would awake extremely upset. It was Jacob's cousin who taught him to cope with these inconvenient negative effects. Jacob would talk over each shooting with his cousin in the police car: "He used to drive me home and we'd talk for, let's say, half an hour. It helped very much." Thereafter, Jacob apparently no longer needed to go through such extensive moral cleansing at home to avoid his viscerally traumatic reactions to violence. Jacob could just shower and go to bed after a murder; a good night's sleep and he was ready to return to murder again the next day.

Eduardo also remembers having to learn to handle the emotional repercussions of his shootings. Recalling a joint mission early in his career that involved his own DOPS team, a squad of militarized police, and some federal police, Eduardo says that he shot four times at a fleeing seventeen-year-old suspect, leaving him "shaking [and] nervous: [It] shook me up, really shook me up." Eduardo did not rejoin the operations team until a Militarized Police captain who had noticed him off by himself remarked, "Hell, you are nervous." The captain was able to reduce Eduardo's anxiety by saying, "You are shaking: calm down, be calm." Eduardo was then able to again take his place in the team's ongoing search-and-capture operation.

Perhaps such forms of interpersonal socialization explain why some research on violence has demonstrated that if a person has never committed a violent act, it is difficult to predict whether she or he ever will. However, after the fourth or fifth violent act, the probability of recidivism is very high (see Toch 1996: 108).

The rewards for learning how to continue engaging in violence were certainly there for the police in our sample. Bernardo remembers that as a young rank-and-file operations policeman, he knew when he had done a good job because a police official would send him "on another mission that had a certain importance." Indeed, Bernardo's sense of personal and professional accomplishment was greatest when each mission was more dangerous and important than the previous one, an expectation that must have encouraged him to learn how to make each new one live up to his superiors' expectations. Within such an other-directed framework, elevated danger and effective violence became guideposts for Bernardo's measuring his work's success. Likewise, Roberto gauged his own and his death squad's accomplishments by death ratios: "Our group was successful [if there were] no casualties on our side, [when] people on their side died but not on ours."

Assembly-Line Violence

Like any other bureaucracy, Brazil's authoritarian social control system had an elaborate division of labor: external and internal control were allocated, respectively, to Brazil's military and police. There was also a division of violent labor between and within the two main police organizations themselves and among these and the new elite internal security organizations. Just the same and in spite of each social control organization's formal jurisdictional mandates and boundaries, there was still a good deal of operational overlap.

Considering first the division of labor between Brazil's two main types of police organizations, the uniformed militarized police were supposed to primarily conduct operational street policing, not to investigate crimes or interrogate suspects, which was the job of the nonuniformed civil police. Contrariwise, the civil police were not to be involved in arrest operations, only in the investigation of crimes. Of course, both police organizations routinely violated their jurisdictional mandates—for example, the civil police in São Paulo State had the murderous RONE, and the militarized police conducted interrogations after arrests either on the spot or through the Reserved Service.

Each police organization also had specialized social control units and teams with their own internal division of labor. For example, the DOPS had special units for investigation and surveillance, capturing suspects, and interrogation. Moreover, within the DOPS interrogation section itself there was a division of labor: some operatives delivered victims to interrogators, others strapped down and guarded these suspects, and others interrogated them. And as an interrogation proceeded, some operatives tortured while others facilitated by advising on the physical limits of pain.

One particularly revealing locale for operationalizing the national security ideology was in the division of labor between specialized atrocity groups. Some such units were to evaluate information derived from other specialized units' surveillance, interrogation, and torture. Such data were then to be passed to field operations arrest teams—either those of the regular police organizations or to one of the new state and federal internal security organizations (e.g., Operação Bandeirantes or DOI). These teams were then to capture more prisoners for interrogation or kill the suspects no longer of use or dangerous to the system. The squads that specialized in execution were very often further subdivided into the drivers who brought killers to their victims, lookouts who watched for intruders, assault units for killing the suspects, and backup teams for protecting the killers. Of course, the informal death squads that operated alongside of and within the formal social control system also had an internal division of labor, and they also formally (even though not always in fact) respected the one between themselves and the official police system.

This elaborate division of labor can especially be seen in DOI/CODI, the top-ranking federal internal security organization. Because the DOI/CODI division of labor formally mirrored the internal security system's more general one, closer examination is useful. Although DOI/CODI did not always operate according to its formal jurisdictional mandates, the specialized social control units in its segmented assembly line were each formally dedicated to a different set of violent tasks. For example, DOI had different units for capturing suspects, interrogation, and "neutralizing"—that is, killing—subversives. CODI had entities for analyzing information from infiltration and interrogation and for planning new operations (Dossiê de repressão 1978: 32). Jorge, the former Rio de Janeiro policeman in a DOI murder team (*grupo de quebra*), explained his squad's particular division of labor: The assault team "goes up front. It has the people who are going to enter the house...check out things, search...and bring out [the captives]." The support team "isn't seen; it is there to protect" the assault team. The murder squad itself waits for captives to be delivered up—presumably some were withheld for questioning under torture by a DOI unit. Once its information has been passed on to CODI, the DOI murder squad then eliminates them all.

Such a Taylorized social control situation—where there is not only routinization of procedures but also an elaborate and jurisdictional subdivision of tasks—carries several consequences, including competition, police operational illegalities, and dramatic violence. Although bureaucracies in general, and Brazil's violent social control bureaucracy in particular, inherently pit one functional entity against another, the ramifications of this were especially lethal where the Brazilian military was engaging in an internal war against subversion. In Brazil's assembly line of repression, where each separate social control organization, team, or squad was competing for the rewards of capturing the greatest number of or the most high-profile subversives, competition frequently spilled over into violence among the various groups as well as against the captives being brought in.

For example, although theoretically DOI/CODI was bureaucratically subdivided to eliminate jurisdictional overlap, confusion, and conflict, in fact its division of labor often fostered inter-security-force violence. DOI interrogators were supposed to secure confessions and then turn their information over to CODI's intelligence and planning analysts, who in turn were to pass on their information to the relevant DOI capture teams, but it was apparently common for CODI intelligence agents to be on hand during the preceding DOI team's interrogations—just to make sure that all relevant information was turned over to CODI (Ustra 1987). In fact, DOI interrogation units often failed to pass on information to CODI in order to use it to carry out another capture themselves. With valuable information from an interrogation in hand, the DOI interrogation unit could make a name for itself by becoming an ad hoc capture team. In the social control numbers game, what furthered an operative's or his unit's career was a greater number of suspects arrested, the relatively high importance of a captured subversive, the quality of information obtained through interrogations, and the speed with which all this was accomplished. Each social control entity gained most from competing successfully with the others.

A particularly dramatic example of how such competition nurtured security force violence occurred in São Paulo on March 1, 1970. A DOI/CODI team raided infamous *delegado* Sérgio Paranhos Fleury's São Paulo DOPS facility to "rescue" and interrogate its prisoner Shizuo

Ozawa ("Mario Japa"), a Japanese-Brazilian militant of the Vanguarda Popular Revolucionária guerrilla group, in one of DOI's own torture facilities. But DOPS Detective Fleury had no intention of letting this happen. As the DOI/CODI team stormed Fleury's DOPS facility, Fleury—knowing that Ozawa might supply DOI/CODI with information that Fleury wanted to keep for his own purposes—rushed with his guards into the jailhouse cell and ordered Ozawa on the floor: Fleury jumped on Ozawa's chest, breaking several of his ribs, with the intention that Ozawa would thus be too injured for DOI/CODI to torture information out of him (Fon 1986).

Notorious for creative brutality in extracting information from suspects, Fleury's atrocity calculus turned on getting quick results at any cost. Indeed, success within Brazil's war against subversion and crime was contingent upon security forces' getting captives to confess as quickly as possible (Wright 1987). In the words of a former São Paulo regional DOI/CODI commander, General Ustra, "We all lived in a race against time and against the unknown. Speed was vital...to discover and neutralize [terrorist] actions that could cause deaths and great material damage" (1987: 71). Several interviewees asserted their belief that torture was the fastest way of getting information from captives.

Ramirez (1999) maintains that where danger and competition are rife, aggression and violence are likely means for promoting one man's masculinity over another's. As we argued in Chapter 6, patriarchal Western masculinity expectations contain implicit pressures toward violence, beginning with the perception that there are zero-sum masculinity resources. That is, rather than a fixed gender characteristic, patriarchal masculinity is in degrees: displaying less masculine traits calls into question a man's overall masculinity. In a successful masculinity performance, a man consciously or unconsciously demonstrates his masculinity attributes by consistently displaying the requisite amount and degree of them. Competitive interactions—especially those involving danger—are an important locus for masculinity to be tested and validated and for new masculinity presentations to emerge. With respect to the latter, for the personalistic and blended masculinity police, the ultimately successful masculinity handles and conquers danger through physical toughness. The institutional functionary police demonstrate their successful masculinity by not manifesting its traditional patriarchal elements: they subordinate emotions and brute force to bureaucratic rationality. As we argued in Chapter 8, within an interaction climate fraught with danger—whether real or perceived—the small, elite police unit wages its war by means of a range of masculinities that, although formally seemingly contradictory, are, in fact, complementary.

In contests where one person's respect is derived from another's degradation, the thin line between some manifestations of normal masculine aggression and physical violence is very easily transgressed; this is especially true where compounded by pervasive competition over scarce and elusive masculinity resources. And where competitive masculinity is swaddled within an elite police unit's social cocoon—creating a secret, clublike atmosphere in which each man is constantly having to prove his courage and toughness to others in the unit, physical violence may be the only way of successfully demonstrating manhood (see Uildriks and Mastrigt 1991; Skolnick and Fyfe 1993). This is very likely to have been part of the dynamic behind the Los Angeles Rampart Division CRASH Unit's illegalities, as we shall see shortly. In any case, when masculine competition is heightened and legitimized by a climate of politically validated internal war, atrocities are extraordinarily likely.

As we have argued previously, although Brazil's national security state needed loyal and predictable "organization men"—the institutional functionary police—the repressive system's own violent dynamic—a toxic mix of pressure for speed and competitive bureaucracy—constantly created pressures toward and informally validated some go-it-alone personalistic or blended masculinity policing styles. Such police sometimes operated outside of and parallel to the official national security system, while at other times—often under pressure from their work team to stay within the group's usually unstated interactional guidelines—they operated according to their elite group's own violent imperatives. Thus, even though, as argued in this and in previous chapters, Brazil's social control system formally encouraged police to subordinate their personalism—including the traditional physical masculinities associated with it—to the system, it was in fact inherently structured to promote the personalistic and blended masculinity aggression against which it was formally and informally socializing. In the end, we shall propose that the volatile chemistry of national security, bureaucratic competition, and functionally supportive masculinity performances together promoted high levels of aggression and violence.

Social-Psychological Dynamics of Atrocity

Having explained how internal security politics and the social control bureaucracy's division of labor helped to generate and support atrocities in Brazil, we now examine the social-psychological factors that were nurtured by, and supportive of, regular atrocity work. We propose that the secrecy and insularity of atrocity work organizations shielded operatives from potentially dangerous outsiders, guaranteed operatives' anonymity, disguised victims' humanity, and morally disengaged an operative's sense of responsibility for his violence. Particularly, in their totality, such processes contributed to moral disengagement.

MORAL DISENGAGEMENT

In part, moral disengagement resulted from the segmented jurisdictional nature of the atrocity system itself (see Bandura 1999: 203–204). Illustrating how institutional segmentation and the organizational division of labor fostered moral disengagement, Roberto, the Rio militarized policeman who was also in an informal death squad, maintains that even though he had witnessed forty-five killings, he himself never killed anyone. Using his murder squad's division of labor to disguise his own role in violence, Roberto maintains that he only drove the death squad's car and was its lookout as the murders occurred. Yes, Roberto kept the car's headlights trained on the murder scene so that his colleagues could see to make the kill, but because Roberto was just the death squad's driver, he was not a "real" murderer. In fact, Roberto was both a perpetrator and a facilitator, sliding easily between one status and the other in any given night's operation.

When Fernando was asked if he had ever interrogated his squad's captives, he could assert legalistically that "the person who is operational is operational, and the person who works in information, works in information." According to Fernando, who saw his work as operational, anyone who captured and then interrogated suspects would be "completely violating professional principles." Consequently, Fernando maintains that he could not have tortured anyone—even though he very likely did—because he was not in a unit that did that sort of thing. Whether or not Fernando is telling the truth, the system's tightly woven division of labor—as understood and elaborated by Fernando himself, the consummate bureaucratic functionary—allowed him to argue, and even to convince himself, that he could not have been a torturer. Indeed, Fernando admits only to having had "a conversation with [a] prisoner" that he had arrested.

Likewise, Jacob was able to disconnect his arrest operations from their violent consequences by describing himself as a professionally neutral social control filter: his team would simply arrest suspects "and leave them to be 'officialized' in the police stations." Jacob's team just "gave [interrogators] the 'material' to work on." Then interrogators (i.e., torturers) could further their careers by getting the necessary information out of suspected subversives. Jacob—by presenting himself as a mere operative in a system that transformed humans into cases to be investigated and interrogated—relegates his captives to the status of nonhuman material to be bureaucratically processed. By deindividuating and dehumanizing his victims, Jacob did not have to concern himself with nagging questions about the legality or morality of his violence. As a legitimate social control operative, Jacob was merely passing on "favors" (i.e., potential torture or murder victims) to other operatives, much as a medical doctor refers patients to a colleague as a professional courtesy. However, doctors' reciprocities are supposed to focus on preserving and treating human health, whereas atrocity's competitive system was powered by reciprocities that maximized the destruction of human flesh and will. This system, of course, includes some medical doctors in its evil dynamic.

SOCIAL-PSYCHOLOGICAL DISGUISE

Within Brazil's atrocity system, violence workers' moral disengagement from victims was also created, sometimes literally, by concrete disguises themselves. Whether in DOI/CODI or some other intelligence or operations unit, police frequently conducted their work undercover—taking a code name, wearing hair pieces, putting on fake or real beards, or using a hood to cover their face. For example, Bernardo, the Militarized Police operative–turned Civil Police intelligence official, reported that when he began working in intelligence, he let his beard and hair grow to ensure that he "was seldom identified or perceived as being a policeman." Jorge remembers arriving at work for his first day of DOI duty in his Militarized Police uniform. As he stood proudly in the inspection room, his superiors "looked [him] over from top to bottom and said, 'Look, you don't need that here. Leave, spend three days at home, and come back without having shaved; don't get any more haircuts and forget that you've ever put a uniform on. From now on, no uniform...just civilian clothes.'" On the other hand, other DOI/CODI violence workers reported wearing an Army or a Militarized Police uniform during a mission to avert public suspicion that DOI/CODI had captured someone: onlookers would think that the agents were from the armed services or the regular police.

Hooding captives was common. Jorge remembers that his team's DOI operations "lasted [only] a minute. [We] invaded the house with lightning speed and came out with the people already wearing hoods [and] handcuff[s]." For high-profile daytime arrests—where a hood might have called undue attention to a police operation—an arrest team might place what appeared to be regular wraparound sunglasses on captives, except that they would in fact fully block the captives' vision. Anyone seeing the captive being driven away in an unmarked car by men in civilian clothes would not necessarily suspect that the victim was in police custody. This victim could not identify his captors, and the captors did not have to be concerned with the victim's humanity. Disguised, the victim was disembodied—something less than a full person—enhancing the perpetrators' moral disengagement.

Bernardo remembers many a "mission where we couldn't even identify ourselves to the [local] authorities." Only the immediate head of the sector knew who they were; "you didn't even really know the [other] agent who [carried out] a mission" with you. All this secrecy made Bernardo feel "safer to act. I felt more secure, because the moment that I showed myself openly,...I would run the risk of being discovered." Jorge also felt more safe because his murder operations were anonymous. Indeed, his team went to great lengths to ensure their members' anonymity: "On a raid, we're [all] just 'Pompeu'" (a fairly common surname in Brazil). "No one [else] could identify us," he said with obvious operational delight.

ANONYMITY AND INSULARITY

Group anonymity encouraged the elite squad's insularity and supported violence workers' bonding, dependence on one another, and separation from outsiders—including other police, nonpolice friends, or even family. Jorge recognized that by all members of his murder team taking the same name, there was assurance that "everybody's life—each one's personality—[was tightly] identified [with the group]." Jorge contrasted such anonymity favorably over against autonomous individuality, which could "represent a risk to your life: if I'm not comfortable around you, you're not comfortable around me, and we become targets"—for dissension, for getting shot by suspects, even for leftist thinking.

It strengthened the atrocity group's control over its members that they had very little time to be alone or to spend with nonunit friends or even their families. Elite unit police spent almost all of their time with each other. For example, although police were to have forty-eight hours

off for every twenty-four hours that they worked, many atrocity perpetrators in specialized units reported working around the clock and for
weeks at a time. The former head of São Paulo DOI/CODI reports
that his men "sometimes spent night and day in the stake-out van." (Ustra 1987: 131). Bernardo, the former intelligence operative, remembers
working nonstop:

I would spend ten days on duty—twenty-four hours a day, for ten days. We'd
sleep in the police station itself. We were called any time during the night. I
would work the whole day; at night we'd take turns sleeping. [Sometimes] we'd
stay...on duty for thirty days [at a stretch].

Julius, who maintains that he "lived in the police for thirty years," described his work as "a passion that demands a lot of time: It's an un-
grateful lover."

Former São Paulo DOPS official Sérgio remembers having "no real
life apart from...work. Even on those rare days off, I still lived,
breathed, ate, and slept (when I could sleep) information collection."
Before long, he was taking drugs to keep from falling asleep on the job:
"When something extremely serious was eminent, how could I sleep?"
The pressure on Sérgio reached a point where he felt completely lost. A
DOI operative not in the interviewee sample remembers that he spent
"many nights [on the job] without sleep," completely controlled by his
nonstop life in intelligence. (A lei de bárbarie 1992: 30). Jorge, the murder operative, reported that "we would frequently go on a mission that
would take...weeks or months. We were literally...away from contact
with people."

It also helped to ensure a violence worker's loyalty to, and control by,
the specialized unit that many of them kept their work entirely secret
from family and nonpolice friends. Jorge remembers not having "any
friends back then. Nobody [in the group] could say they had friends—
no one. Anybody who said that was soft." Reflecting on the impact of
such isolation, a DOI operative not in our interviewee sample recalls
that his group's secretiveness made him feel "trapped,...without
friends, [unable] to even unburden myself to my wife" (30). Jorge remembers being called in to work late at night. "Going...away for days;
even up to a week," Jorge would tell his wife, "I'm going out to buy
some medicine"; she knew that he meant: "I'm going to work" because
Jorge would take his weapons and drive away in his car.

A startling parallel situation showing the effects of high levels of security force isolation and insularity recently emerged in the United

States. The Community Resources against Street Hoodlums (CRASH) Unit, established in the 1980s in the Rampart district west of downtown Los Angeles, focused exclusively on ridding the area of gangs. The police in this elite unit were given a free hand to fight fire with fire. The unit itself, which over time had from twelve to twenty officers, identified itself by the logo of "a skull with a cowboy hat and a poker hand of a pair of aces and a pair of eights—the dead man's hand." Its mission was unquestionably violent, and its violence was rewarded: CRASH Unit police gave plaques to their colleagues who shot gang members. Its operatives could wage their war against gangs as they saw fit, given an attitude higher up that nurtured their operational independence and organizational insularity.

When overcrowding at the main Rampart police station house resulted in the CRASH Unit's being moved to a substation nearby, it became even more independent—ignoring the requirement that its operatives work in uniform and disregarding some officials' warnings to go easier on the district's residents. CRASH even changed the lock on its new station house door so that other police could not enter: it had become "its own police department with its own rules" (Cannon 2000: 34). CRASH carried out false arrests; shot at unarmed people and constructed stories to justify these shootings; extorted suspects' drugs and weapons and kept them for themselves; framed alleged perpetrators; and beat, tortured, and murdered gang members. The CRASH Unit's illegalities were supported by a host of auxiliary facilitators, including a bystander community in the form of local residents tired and afraid of neighborhood gangs who condoned the unit's harsh practices. High-level facilitators such as the city's mayor and executive-level police officials, including the chief of police, left CRASH alone or quietly encouraged and rewarded its excesses. Los Angeles District Attorney Gilbert Garcetti, who saw ridding the city of gangs as a reelection boost, facilitated CRASH atrocities by closing his eyes to its illegalities and then using these to secure convictions.

CRASH Unit policeman Rafael Perez, one direct perpetrator who has been convicted for extortion, false imprisonment, maiming, and murder, explained that in his antigang work he had been consumed by an "us-against-them ethos.... My job became an intoxicant that I lusted after. In the end, I cheated on my wife,...on my employers,...and on the people of Los Angeles." Pointing to the institutional structure that had created and embraced his police persona, Perez maintains that he had been seduced by the "pressure of status, numbers, and impressing supervisors." Considering how this competitive dynamic shaped him into a violence perpetrator, Perez warns of the long-term consequences of violence work.

Personal Transformation

The insular and secret world of the specialized atrocity organization or squad clearly facilitated the violence worker's becoming morally separated from the consequences of his behavior. A dramatic example for Brazil of the consequences of nonstop atrocity work comes from the testimony of the adult daughter of a former Militarized Police sergeant. Although her father was not one of the police in our own sample, we still learned from her how drastically he metamorphosed after joining DOI/CODI (Sargento do DOI matou colega antes de desaparecer 1985). She explained that as a regular policeman he had returned home enthusiastic about his work—the police rounds and patrols, his own "heroic deeds." But her once easygoing father changed after getting into DOI. In a life dominated by secrecy and disguises, he assumed a false name and identity and switched cars almost daily. Working day and night and seldom with his family, he went on frequent trips out of Brazil—particularly to Paraguay, Argentina, and Chile, three of Brazil's politically repressive Southern Cone allies. Very likely this DOI operative was involved in Operation Condor.

Separated from any relationships outside the violence juggernaut and completely encapsulated by it, this DOI operative, according to his daughter, experienced a "profound personal change." Her father became obsessed with capturing left-wingers, warning his family "not to speak against the [Brazilian] Government [for fear of] becoming a Communist." (Sargento do DOI matou colega antes de desaparecer 1985). The man had become a true believer who feared not just that his family might be denounced as communist for speaking against the government but that it might in fact *become communist* by doing so. This DOI operative's obscured identity had come to eclipse and erase all other former and parallel identities—a reality undoubtedly facilitated by a repressive system protected by anonymity and granted impunity at every turn.

"Normal" Violence

Examining more generally the roots of police lawlessness, Skolnick's research (1966: 42) on policing in the United States and Europe reveals what he calls a policeman's "working personality." A set of "cognitive tendencies unique to the policeman," this way of looking at the world is shaped by three elements of the police working environment—danger, authority, and efficiency. Recognizing that a police working personality lays the seedbed for deception and violence, Skolnick points out that danger makes police attentive to "signs indicating a potential for violence and lawbreaking." Suspicion—whether the result of training or nurtured by the work environment itself—encourages police to distrust civilians, a quality that can isolate them from family and nonpolice friends. Police may be reluctant to develop friendships if anyone could be a lawbreaker.

Police autonomy grows out of enforcing laws against a community that regularly engages in a range of behaviors labeled illegal. Under such circumstances, the community can come to see police as a potential enemy, a double-sided process that helps turn police organizations into defensive bureaucracies as the isolation resulting from police–community conflict encourages police to limit their friendships to others in the profession. Their own working norms come to determine appropriate police conduct, constrained only by their own superiors, who may be secretly encouraging their violence.

According to Skolnick, when authority and suspicion are then combined with administrative and public pressure for police "efficiency"—defined as quickly catching criminals, clearing crimes, and making streets safe—police lawlessness is a likely result. In Skolnick's words, "the demand for police 'efficiency' creates a type of 'professional' police practice in which the concern for legality is minimal" (1966: 110). It could be argued that where police are isolated from nonpolice communities and organized into insular, specialized units whose raison d'etre is efficiently eliminating a community threat—whether such units operate in a dictatorship or a democracy—the potential for police lawlessness, including torture and murder, increases.

Continuum of Police Inviolability

It can be confidently added that as Skolnick and Fyfe have pointed out, the more a police department is divided into small units, with each under pressure to produce and excel, the greater the likelihood that competition will produce abuse (1993). A former Special Forces combatant in the Dominican Republic and Vietnam, Jenkins (2000) would agree:

[Special units] are assigned missions considered difficult and dangerous and requiring extraordinary measures. This fosters 'creativity'; it can also breed contempt for the 'desks.' [Elite unit police] tend to view the world in terms of combat.... They cultivate an image of toughness. The profound sense of mission, the action,...can become intoxicating. Members of elite units...often operate outside normal organizational Controls. Pleased with the results, the top brass may choose not to inquire too closely just how [their success] is being accomplished. The members stick together; their behavior can sometimes border on defiance.

This dynamic has been dramatically illustrated in the Los Angeles Rampart Division CRASH Unit and by the New York City night-operating street team that executed Amadou Diallo. For Brazil, the lawlessness bred by specialized, autonomous squads has been vividly illustrated throughout this chapter.

That policing contains inherent pressures toward lawlessness even in democracies suggests that the Brazilian atrocities may be part of an organizational continuum of police violence. It could be argued that in democracies under standard policing situations, rather than in specialized emergencies, police violence grows out of the pressures associated with a normal police working personality. This police outlook nurtures the suspiciousness that can promote violence and isolates police activities from some of the outside social controls that might regulate behavior.

But as Skolnick (1966) and Skolnick and Fyfe (1993) have argued, such a working personality is even more likely to generate violence when encapsulated within an elite, insular police unit or team. That police violence in modern Western democracies has not reached the level of either military or postmilitary Brazil under routine circumstances may be the result of constitutional checks on the police. However, these checks can be reduced or eroded where specialized squads are given unsupervised (or covertly promoted to carry out) crime control mandates to efficiently regulate dangerous others. Their expanded (if not legal) right to accomplish this for the protection of society can even produce a margin for legal police violence that is expanded by policy, administration, law, or by judicial decisions (see Gordon 1990).

In Brazil, where, during the military period, police violence was legalized through national security laws, the war against subversion had no effective limits. With danger seen as ubiquitous, there was an emphasis on teaching Brazilian police simply to recognize and demolish it. Operatives had to learn how to predict danger and mistrust others, including sometimes those in their own work teams: The enemy could be anyone.

This in turn helped to confirm for police that Brazil was in the midst of a national security emergency, which granted almost total impunity to the police (and military) who waged the military government's war.

In an authoritarian work climate requiring violent action without reflection—where potential victims were dehumanized as subversives and terrorists and instrumental operational results were rewarded over concern for human consequences—torture and murder came to be defined as something other than what they were. Indeed, as our interviews have demonstrated, the Brazilian atrocity perpetrator's own absolution from responsibility for violence was almost total: only one of the fourteen direct perpetrators of atrocity assumed full personal responsibility for his past violence by confessing to it. The other thirteen deflected personal responsibility for their violence onto "bad" police or victims or into vague cultural and social circumstances, or they saw it as deriving from a just cause or as either resulting legitimately from professionalism or illegitimately from professionalism gone wrong. Pointing to the latter, Justin A. Volpe (Excerpts from sentencing hearing in the Louima torture case 1999: B-5), the former police officer convicted in 1999 of torturing Haitian immigrant Abner Louima in a Brooklyn, New York, station house, explained his violence as resulting from horrors he had seen as a policeman:

I witnessed misery on a nightly basis...so many dead bodies in all forms of decay and mutilation. I have seen innocent babies dead, lying in trash next to incinerators. I have seen assaults with guns.... I have been charged at by men wielding butcher knives...[and] guns. I've even had a newborn baby thrown at me by its parents.

Although horrific, such accounts do not justify Volpe's atrocities against Louima. Nevertheless, as Chapter 11 illustrates, this kind of discourse reduced the violence worker's own sense of moral responsibility for past atrocities.

CHAPTER II

Moral Universes of Torturers and Murderers

Those who would treat politics and morality apart will never understand the one or the other.

Henry David Thoreau

We have great freedom to carve up the external world into named categories, and then analyze the categories to suit our social convenience.

Edmund Leach, *Culture and Communication*

Having examined the political, organizational, and social-psychological factors that nurtured atrocities in Brazil, this chapter investigates how violence workers explained, justified, and excused their own and others' violence. Among our interviewees, we discovered four strategies for explaining and excusing atrocity: diffusing responsibility, blaming individuals—whether victims or perpetrators—citing a just cause, and asserting that professionalism had correctly guided their and other's violence. From these static categories we could make out a more dynamic system of moral reckoning that defined some atrocity as acceptable, some as unacceptable but understandable, and some as totally unacceptable. Leaving behind their former status and values as agents of an authoritarian military government, most violence workers couched their recent statements about atrocity in a rhetoric compatible with the expectations of modern police in a democratizing state.

Sérgio's Police Life

The richest of the violence workers' justifications for torture and murder were those of Civil Police DOPS official Sérgio. His moralities about this violence were like the overlapping circles created by stones skipping briskly across a still lake. Sérgio, who entered the São Paulo Civil Police in 1957, quickly became an important intelligence operative for the governor. Without any particular initial training, Sérgio began his intense, all-consuming life in intelligence, spending days and nights tapping phones, installing surveillance microphones, and infiltrating unions and political parties.

On the eve of Brazil's 1964 military coup, Sérgio says that he was already "worn out" from seven years of intelligence and operations. Fed up, he delivered his resignation to the governor, who not only rejected Sérgio's proposal but also promoted him to the interstate police intelligence section of Serviço de Polícia Interestadual (POLINTER). The governor claimed that he needed Sérgio too much to let him resign. In POLINTER, Sérgio helped the governor and military coup conspirators engineer their national takeover from São Paulo State.

In the late 1960s, again finding himself isolated and exhausted, Sérgio tried a second time to resign. Rejecting Sérgio's resignation once again, the governor appointed his close confidant as director of São Paulo State DOPS, a position that placed Sérgio in charge of all countersubversive intelligence in Brazil's most populous and politically important state. During a period of mounting internal turmoil and repression, Sérgio worked twenty-four hours a day—directing and carrying out intelligence and in operations himself. Sérgio found this work "intense and permanent"; remembering the "strike[s] every two, three days, [with] vandalism," he was held responsible for predicting and quashing them. Feeling unable to delegate much of this work, Sérgio ended up taking part in all of the important operations, "infiltrating literally everywhere, every movement, the [Communist] Party" and other progressive political groups. According to Sérgio, he "had to pick up on everything" and couldn't even assign much of the work to trusted subordinates.

Feeling "lost in the midst of [that] shit, [knowing that] tomorrow anything could happen" and considering himself impotent to effectively control the future—sometimes even finding himself under death threat from officials the governor had sent him to investigate—Sérgio pleaded with the governor to let him resign. This time, the state's highest official transferred Sérgio to the DEIC, the Civil Police robberies and thefts division. Known for its liberal use of torture in interrogation, the DEIC got its job done quickly and efficiently. Apparently finding the DEIC's normal strategies falling short of their goal, Sérgio set up his own death squad to accomplish what on-duty police were "reluctant" to do.

Totally drained from his many years in intelligence and operations, constantly under the pressures of the DEIC robbery division and his own death squad, and "unable to think, sleep [and feeling] totally absorbed by [work-associated] problems," Sérgio finally retired from the Civil Police in 1971. Interviewed in 1993 in his expensive and lavishly decorated apartment in São Paulo's exclusive Jardims district, Sérgio was by then severely debilitated from two heart attacks and a mild stroke. Yet even two decades after his period of political police service, Sérgio still presented us with a clearer and more complex system of justifications for torture and murder than any other interviewed violence worker. His tightly woven labyrinth of explanations for violence— sometimes congruent and sometimes contradictory—covers the entire range of moralities in the accumulated discourse of the other thirteen direct perpetrators of violence.

Sérgio's Moral Universe

Sérgio emphatically denies having personally carried out torture, citing his opposition to such violence as was routinely "used by [by other agencies like] OBAN and DOI/CODI." By diffusing responsibility for torture into other organizational entities, Sérgio draws attention from his own culpability. He maintains that he "didn't work the way" OBAN and DOI/CODI agents did, adding that if he had, he "would have been revolted" by their practices. Yet Sérgio—offering a justification for atrocities that places the onus on perpetrators as individuals—apparently sees no contradiction in calling many of the men transferred from his command into OBAN and then DOI/CODI "close friends." He argues that men invited into these violent internal security organizations were "all very hard-nosed" (physically and emotionally tough) to begin with. But he adds that the extreme violence they meted out in DOI/CODI further "bestialized" them. Sérgio excuses their violence as simultaneously part of their nature and as shaped by structural forces, including his own, beyond their control.

In another account about violence, Sérgio recalls regulating his subordinates' violence by saying, "Okay, slow down," implying that if bad behavior can be controlled by good and rational police officials, then it is not really so bad after all—a professionalism justification that makes some violence acceptable. Indeed, he believes that much excess police violence could have been avoided if there had been more police training, overlooking the fact that Sérgio, who considers himself a professional and who had been extensively trained, had knowingly allowed torture under his command. Presumably, the justification lies in its having been skillfully regulated—controlled by a plan, rules, and procedures and overseen by a rational (and trained) police official.

Concerning his own torturing, Sérgio grants limited acceptance for it if there is a just cause, arguing hypothetically that "if a little girl's life were at stake and if by torturing someone [he] could save her life," he would "torture—or order his men to do so." Such noble ends justify ignoble means. At the same time, Sérgio considers it wrong to use violence against a person who has "a political ideal: I never used violence against anyone in the Communist Party.... I always respected their ideals." Yet at the same time, he "almost beat [a student] to death" for denying that he was in the Communist Party. According to Sérgio, the student was "so cynical. If he had [just] said, I took the [guerrilla] course...but he was uppity," so Sérgio lost his head.

In Sérgio's moral universe, torture, generalized violence, and beatings are each permissible under different problematic situations. Although it is clear that Sérgio would (and did) torture, he seldom used the "T word," usually waltzing around or mislabeling it. Indeed, Sérgio's explanations for torture point to irreconcilable contradictions in his moral universe: he would not torture, yet he does, albeit under a different label. This policeman's narrative about violence implies the complicated richness of violence workers' moralizing about violence, as this chapter further illustrates.

Discourse of the Violent

We discovered that it was difficult to ascertain and then even harder to systematize how involvement in torture and murder was reflected in perpetrators' discourse. As Chapter 4 illustrated, the violence workers skillfully manipulated language to cover up, prevaricate, deny, and lie to themselves and others. Out of their socially constructed maze of secrecy, we not only had to discover violence workers' secrets but also to seek out and generate meaningful patterns in their painful revelations about

TABLE 11.1. Accounting for Atrocities
(Harm or Death to Others)
(n = Total Cases)

Admitting Act Is Wrong	Accepting Responsibility for Act	
	Yes	*No*
Yes	*Confession* (Admitting personal guilt) $n = 1$	*Excuse* (Blaming others— perpetrators' or victims' individual characteristics) $n = 13$
No	*Justification* (Professionalism) $n = 14$ (Just cause) $n = 7$	*Denial* (Diffusion of responsibility) $n = 12$

SOURCE: Adapted from Scott and Lyman (1968).

NOTE: Table totals exceed total number of cases because some cases fall in multiple categories.

atrocity. This process began with an analysis of the fourteen violence perpetrators' narratives.

Initially, ten explanations were uncovered for a person's having committed torture or murder. Finding this list too long and unsystematic to clearly communicate its patterns, we sought underlying similarities among the explanations. Four inclusive accounts emerged for a violence worker's having engaged in violence. The least commonly asserted explanation identified just causes for torture and murder. Another less common justification diffused responsibility for violence into sociocultural or organizational contexts. Somewhat more common was an explanation that blamed individuals—whether victims or perpetrators—for torture or murder. The most frequent justification for violence identified professional imperatives and pressures behind its acceptable use and "unrealistic" pressures behind its unprofessional use.[1]

1. Haritos-Fatouros, Huggins, and Bozatzis (2000) discuss similar categories as identity constructions—"the bad professional," "the good professional," and "the policeman as victim."

TABLE 11.2. Moral Reckoning about Torture

Casual Evaluations	Morality about Torture		
	Acceptable	Not Wholly Acceptable but Understandable	Unacceptable
Perpetrators' Described Characteristics	Professionally trained and controlled	Youthful, aggressive, stupid, ignorant; lacks training; temporarily out of control	Sadistic, irrational, cruel, cold bloodedly vicious
Assumed Proximate Causal Influence	Psychological cunning and intelligence	Exploited by superiors; acted under "bad" orders	Out-of-control character disorder; judgment impaired by drugs or alcohol
Assumed Larger Motivating Conditions	Just cause to get information; belief that only violence will succeed; uncooperative victim	Under brutalizing social conditions; having to be actively present (but not actively participating)	Hedonistic satisfaction or economic greed

These four post facto explanations for violence were further summarized as denials, justifications, excuses, and confessions (Table 11.1) and reveal a hierarchy of moral reckoning that labeled some torture acceptable, some not wholly acceptable but understandable, and some unacceptable (Table 11.2).

Explaining Violence

The least commonly offered explanations for torture or murder assert that the police who committed such violence were either responding to a generalized declared war, state of siege, internal war, or war on crime or were acting in a situation where a specific good citizen's life was in peril. Only seven of the interviewed violence workers advanced a just cause argument, with the majority of these interviewees giving only one or two such justifications during their three-hour interview. The just cause accounts either legitimized violence to save a life or to save Brazil from an internal enemy, with the latter less commonly advanced than the former.

Two violence workers who perceived themselves as fighting for an ideology labeled their deeds as "good" and themselves as "heroic."

We worked as if at war. We were patriots, we were defending our country, we were proud of that, so they were adversaries, the enemy. We were proud of what we did...working in DOPS...[and] ridding the country of a threat, of a Communist regime.... [We were] people doing a patriotic job, a big job, an important job.... We were a religious people, a Christian people.

If I arrest someone who has kidnapped a little girl who might be killed in four hours, I'm not going to waste time by questioning him for two or three days just to wear him down. So...I'll hang that guy up [on the parrot's perch], work him over, and he'll tell me in five minutes.

Another set of explanations assign blame for atrocities to other people or factors. These violence workers cited no clear source of personal responsibility for torture or murder. Eleven of fourteen interviewees presented these diffusion-of-responsibility arguments, with most advancing between five and seven such explanations during their interview. No violence worker ever actually denied categorically that violence had never occurred, at least in their presence while in the police. Some placed the roots of torture or murder in other colleagues' behavior or within a police unit other than the interviewee's, even though in most cases the interviewee had been present when violence was taking place. For example, one violence worker asserted that

it was shocking...the first time to see someone hanging on the parrot's perch with a water hose in his mouth. I didn't agree with that, but I was inside the room and the [other] guys were [torturing him].

In a more classic diffusion of responsibility argument, another violence worker stated that

some guys died, but I don't know who killed them. There were many guys shooting...I don't know who hit the guy and who [didn't]. You just know that people died. Fortunately it was the other side.

Another version of the diffusionist argument, offered by two atrocity perpetrators, placed responsibility for violence on sociocultural conditions:

Living in an aggressive environment affects you, contaminates you little by little, without you feeling it.

Brazil is a Catholic country. In Brazil they are used to this kind of behavior—like torture, for example, because Catholic churches tortured people for years and years, centuries and centuries.

Yet another diffusionist strategy was to cite a suddenly altered state of consciousness as accounting for the violence. As two violence workers stated:

The first time I traded shots with someone...was like when you fall asleep at the wheel of the car. You're there and it frightens you so much that it scares the sleep away for minutes.

[When I killed those five people], I went totally blank. I didn't see anything clearly. I only saw a reflection...I didn't know who had shot me with the gun. So I took my gun and shot one, then the other, then the other, then the other.

Blaming individuals, whether victims or perpetrators, frequently surfaced as an explanation for torture or murder. Among the thirteen violence workers who advanced this argument, the majority gave between three and four individual responsibility accounts in the three-hour interview. Locating the roots of torture and murder in "bad" victims, some interviewees asserted that violence occurs when victims fail to cooperate with police or through their "stupidity" or because of their antisocial behavior. For example, Sérgio reported that he "almost beat [a left-wing student] to death because he was uppity." It was in the victim's hands to avoid torture: if he had just admitted his "guilt," he would not have been beaten. In two other versions of this bad victim argument, two police argued that victims were

tortured because they were stupid.... [We said] you had the opportunity to talk without being tortured, but you preferred not to talk. If she had confessed, she would have remained a prisoner but without any torture.

[Torture] is used on thieves and assailants because... sometimes the evidence is so obvious and they deny things so cynically that if a policeman working with him doesn't have a certain balance, he'll slap him around a little [on the parrot's perch].

A parallel but contrasting explanation saw such violence as carried out by policemen who were either permanently bad (almost always someone other than the respondent) or only temporarily out of control (sometimes implicitly including the interviewee), driven by strong situational emotions and bad judgment, in which case they were partially exonerated. These police had tortured or murdered out of stupidity or because of their youth:

[The torturers] were a bunch of guys doing stupid things,... young guys who didn't know what they were doing.... Most of these guys were not well prepared; they [just] wanted to show off.

On the other hand, the permanently bad police either derived illicit pleasure from violence, were given to excess drinking or drug use, or were overly aggressive and dangerous. Their violence was due to a character disorder, or they were just inherently dishonest. In most cases, these violence workers—who, for example, murdered "for the simple joy of killing" or who tortured because they were "very cruel"—were portrayed as exceptions rather than the rule. As two atrocity workers explained:

There [were] certain men in the police, on my team—I knew one—who got pleasure out of killing [a crook]. It wasn't in self-defense, and we couldn't even say, 'Let's get rid of this guy [the captive], he's bad.' No, he really wanted to kill—when one or two bullets was enough to kill someone, he'd wind up taking five rounds—pow, pow, pow.... [He'd] kill people as coldly as you'd kill a chicken.

There's the torturer [who] wants to torture to find out about evidence and extort... other people. He catches a thief and beats... him so the thief will tell him who he sold his things to. He'll... go to those people... and take money from [them to keep quiet].

A more subtle argument in this category was that although police who became torturers and murderers were indeed initially more aggressive and cold, it was the higher police officials who had recognized these characteristics and selected and trained these police to do the institution's dirtiest work.

People who are more identified with... [torture and murder are] very cold by nature,... very aggressive... [These qualities are] noticed... [by superiors].... Certain people who have that quality for working in a certain [violent] fashion really are exploited by their bosses, by those who want to get the job over with quickly.

Paradoxically, these arguments shade into justifications that place responsibility for violence on the system itself and its goals.

The most common explanation for torture and murder cited occupational mandates and pressures as the causes of atrocities. This account was given by all interviewees, with the majority advancing between five and seven such explanations during their interview. A fundamental assumption of professionalism accounts was that torture or murder were sometimes necessary and acceptable, with those carrying out such violence neither good nor bad but just professionally attuned to their organization's policies and practices to a greater or lesser extent.

[Such police] aren't unbalanced;... they show good conduct in the police, they reach retirement and don't have disciplinary problems. [That they torture] doesn't mean that they're monsters.

According to this argument, violence is "normal" (i.e., natural and acceptable) if carried out in the "proper" circumstances by police professionals who know when and how to use it. Whether or not their violence is acceptable can be assessed by a rational calculus:

You can't [just] react [emotionally] to kill [properly]; you have to act with reason. Police work [requires] being intelligent, it's [about] reasoning, technique, information.... You only kill when... either you [do so] or someone else dies. Beyond that, you don't kill, in my opinion.

This discourse presents acceptable police violence as a difficult balance between the policeman's rational calculation as a professional and the possibly disruptive organizational pressures and imperatives that he faces on the job. As one Civil Police official explained:

Torture is zealousness in trying to discover, unravel a crime. [The police] handle a lot of work. [But] we don't have the resources to work on an investigation... [so] the shortest route is by torturing.

Embodying and Disembodying Violence

The four rationalizations for torture or murder implicitly represent different ways of incorporating body and mind into explanations for violence. The first three—just cause, diffusion of responsibility, and individualism—embody violence by including references to a victim's body or to someone or something that explicitly acts on a victim's body. This was more common among the personalistic and blended masculinity violence workers than among the institutional functionaries. Specifically linking violence to human physicality, the personalistic and blended masculinity police rendered it more visible to outsiders. In contrast, the professionalism accounts disembodied violence by substituting non-human organizational actors (either perpetrators or victims) for human agency and by justifying violence through a dispassionate calculus. In the process, the agent of violence and its human impact are rendered considerably less visible, a way of talking about violence most common among the institutional functionary violence workers.

The most dramatic example of the disembodying nature of professionalism discourse can be seen in Gold's research (1996) on Japan's notorious Unit 731, a medical experimentation team that used the term *maruta* (wooden log) to refer to prisoners designated for vivisection and murder. By stripping victims of all humanity and turning them into scientific material, the experimenter was absolved of responsibility for human destruction. As one Japanese experimenter explained dispassionately, "The *maruta* I was working on was on the verge of death. It would be disastrous if he died. Then I would not be able to get a blood sample, and we would not obtain the important results of the tests we had been working on."

Besides the presence or absence of physicality in Brazilian violence workers' discourse about torture and murder, another pattern was these interviewees' framing their statements in a manner that made past violence compatible with Brazil's postdictatorship human rights climate. As we shall propose in this chapter's conclusion, this discursive process draws on a culturally available "vocabulary of motives" (Mills 1940) to make past deviance more compatible with current normative expectations, a process fostered by what sociologists call "aligning actions."

Aligning Actions

In a study of convicted rapists, Scully and Marolla (1984: 274–275) found that interviewees reconstructed their deviance so as to neutralize another person's expected negative evaluations of their violence. Rather than such accounts being random, they are "standardized within cultures..., [and] routinely expected." The accounts are then drawn upon in problematic situations. Some of their incarcerated interviewees negotiated "a moral identity for themselves by presenting [their] rape as [having been] idiosyncratic rather than typical"—it had been beyond their control. Other rapists brought past deviance in line with assumed cultural expectations by describing their violence as "controversial"—the rape, although not quite morally correct, was appropriate for the situation: a bad woman had gotten what she deserved. In both cases, the convicted rapists' aligning accounts used culturally available stereotyped patriarchal scripts about women to construct justifying discourse about violence. Through these scripts, the interviewees situated their past behavior within the current moral climate.

Scott and Lyman (1968: 61) have found that most aligning accounts are of two types: excuses and justifications. Excuses assume that "an act...[is] bad, wrong, or inappropriate [and there is a denial of] full responsibility" for it. "Idiosyncratic" and controversial rape discourse, for example, excuses this criminality as having been an accident or as having resulted from a "special state of mind," from uncontrollable biological drives, or from the victim's "badness." Such accounts were also part of our violence workers' individualism discourse.

Accounts that take the rhetorical form of justifications recognize the unacceptability of a deviant act "but claim...[that a] particular occasion permit[ted] or require[d it]" (Scott and Lyman 1968: 51). Justifications most commonly neutralize deviance (Sykes and Matza 1957) by denying any injury and violence to the victim, by condemning the condemners, or by appealing to a higher loyalty. Cohen (1993: 107) argues that such neutralizations come "into play when you acknowledge (admit) that something happened but either refuse to accept the category of acts to which it is assigned (e.g., 'crime' or 'massacre') or present it as morally justified." Among our violence workers, those who appealed to professionalism and to a 'just cause' included the kinds of accounts sociologists label justifications.

Accounting for Violence

Yet neither Scott and Lyman's nor Scully and Marolla's typologies by themselves explained the range of discursive patterns among Brazilian violence workers. Besides justifying or excusing their violence, the fourteen perpetrators of violence also either denied or confessed to it. Taking these two additional categories into account, we created a four-celled taxonomy (Table 11.1) to capture interviewees' vocabularies of motive. These confirmed that violence workers clearly utilized some normative accounts more than others.

For example, all fourteen violence workers gave one or another account that justified police atrocities. These explanations most commonly advanced professional mandates to account for police atrocities. Next most frequently, interviewees excused torture and murder, recognizing that such violence had been wrong while refusing personal responsibility for it. Their strategy in this case was to blame victims, perpetrators, or perpetrators' superiors. Almost equally as commonly, the interviewed violence workers denied violence, a category that our interviewee testimony suggests but that the other cited researchers did not indicate. In denial discourse, a violence worker rejected both the deviant nature of torture or murder and disclaimed any personal responsibility for this violence. The most common form that a denial took was to diffuse responsibility into professional organizational structures or vague sociocultural contexts.

Least common among violence workers' accounts was to openly and unequivocally confess to violence. Yet even Jorge, the only violence worker who fully admitted to having murdered for the state, qualified his confession with the caveat that his violence, carried out as a DOI murder team operative, had been preferable to colleagues'. Jorge had "only" murdered his victims; he had not tortured then first.

Acceptable and Unacceptable Violence

The morality scale implicit in Jorge's confession points to evaluative distinctions made by all fourteen violence workers. Pointing to the relative permissibility of torture and murder, interviewees assigned their violence to one or another of three moral categories: acceptable, excusable but not wholly acceptable, or unacceptable, depending on its situational context (Table 11.2). By placing their past violence in a reconstructed social context that took current moral expectations into account, the violence worker could align his past actions in a way that negotiated for himself a seemingly more normatively acceptable moral identity.

Although not all interviewees included all three categories of moral judgment in their aligning discourse about violence, all such discourse shared several features in common. Interviewees had a clear notion of when violence was acceptable and when it was not. All had remarkably similar criteria for assigning past violence to one or another moral category. Each interviewee's moral calculus was sufficiently flexible to make violence acceptable in one situation, excusable in another, and totally unacceptable in a third. Finally, the status of perpetrator, victim, or hero shifted according to the sociopolitical context so constructed. Only subtle nuances in Portuguese separated one moral classification from another.

An interesting foundation for most interviewees' moral calculus was that torture had to be kept operationally distinct from murder: torturers who did their jobs properly should not kill, and killers should not dirty themselves with torture, as Jorge so clearly elaborated. The tendency for violence workers to operationally separate torture from murder led us to focus our next analysis exclusively on assertions about torture.

Moral Reckoning by Torturers

"Good" police torturers were described by accounts that justified their violence: trained and "rational" police who had tortured acceptably had a clear knowledge of their limits or were being directed by a "rational" superior. Under such circumstances, torture was legitimate for fighting a just cause and for professionally interrogating bad suspects (Table 11.2). Within such a framework, the good torturer's violence was justified by organizational or ideological necessities or as guided by a rational mind.

"Bad" police torturers had illegitimately used violence for pleasure—they were deliberately sadistic, permanently lacked self-control, or had tortured under the temporary influence of drugs or alcohol or for dishonest economic ends. Such unacceptable torture was seen as a biologically driven result of "irrational" human physicality.

Torturers in the moral middle ground—where torture was not wholly acceptable but understandable—were described by a mixed discourse. Torture could excusably result from a temporary loss of emotional control, where the system had selected an overly aggressive policeman to carry out its violence. In the moral middle ground, where torturers were frequently seen as victimized, physically driven perpetrators, their unacceptable torture was excused as biological or social in origin.

Changing Accounts: Explaining Past as Present

Because Brazil's official democracy now formally condemns torture—even though it is still regularly practiced against the poor (see United Nations Commission on Civil Rights 2000; Jovem photografado em "pau-de-arara" confirma tortura 1985; O poder de pauleira e do chocque 1995)—current accounts about past violence could be expected to explain it through a vocabulary that neutralizes a policeman's presently unacceptable conduct. Furthermore, if as Cohen (1993: 107) argues, motivational accounts are "drawn upon in advance from the cultural pool of... vocabularies [currently] available to actors and observers," then the same accounts that legitimately motivated, justified, and excused torture or murder during Brazil's military period should not be as socially and politically acceptable today. In this case, motivational accounts will change to embrace the shifting cultural, social, and political realities of the era in which judgments are being conjured up and presented.

Discussing the relationship of discursive content to societal conditions and change, Foucault (1979; see also Sheridan 1980) suggests that to be taken seriously, motivational accounts must today be grounded in a scientifically grounded writing of rules, techniques, and the instruments for establishing "truth." Throughout much of the industrialized world, believable accounts are now couched in scientific, rational, pragmatic, and organizationally instrumentalist terms. Putting this another way, C. Wright Mills (1940: 910) wrote that "in a society in which religious motives have been debunked on a rather wide scale, certain thinkers are skeptical of those who ubiquitously proclaim them." In other words, with a shift from the ideological hegemony of religion and the sacred to that of science and secularism, explanations that rely on the former will not have the credibility of those based on the latter. Recognizing that the users of language incorporate such cultural expectations into their discourse, Cohen (1993: 108) points out that built into an individual's accounts "is the knowledge that certain ones will be [more readily] accepted [and] will be honored by the legal system and the wider public." Let us apply this argument to violence workers' varying discursive patterns.

From National Security to Professionalism

Much research on Brazil's military period (Black 1977; Huggins 1998; Langguth 1978; Lernoux 1982; Pinheiro 1991) demonstrates that at that time cold war notions of national security were commonly invoked as justifications for state repression. Security forces divided Brazil's population into subversives and good citizens, with police and military and their elite secret squads in an all-out just war against subversion (Alves 1985; Black 1977; Huggins 1998; Lernoux 1982; Skidmore 1988; Weschler 1987). Relying on a just war argument, President General Ernesto Geisel (1974–1979) explained in the early 1990s that "there are circumstances in which a person is forced to engage in [torture] for obtaining confessions and, thus, to avoid a greater harm [to society]" (Fundação Getulio Vargas 1997). The retired general's postdictatorship argument for torture is, in fact, perfectly congruent with what was an acceptable justification for atrocity during Brazil's military period.

Having expected our interviewees to predominately advance such an account, we were surprised when only seven of the fourteen actually did. In fact, among those who offered a just cause account for torture or murder, only four specifically advanced a national security justification for such violence. In contrast, as we have shown, all fourteen interviewees offered one or more professionalism accounts for torture or murder. It could be argued that the dominance of such discourse reflects a reduction in the cultural and political legitimacy of just war accounts for violence and an increase in the cultural resonance of professionalism for justifying police abuses of power. As we have argued, this shift may point to a deeper cultural change in the industrializing world toward an appeal to ideologies that are rooted in rationality, instrumentalism, and science (e.g., professionalism) over those appealing to passion and emotion (e.g., just war). But what are the consequences of such a reliance on disembodied professionalism for police training, police conduct, and for evaluating and legitimizing police violence?

Professionalizing Police Violence

Equated with scientifically guided action, professionalism is understood to include specialized training in a particular body of knowledge, a rigid division of labor, hierarchy of decision making, self-imposed occupational standards, and impersonal and universalistic rules for appointment, promotion, demotion, and remuneration. For policing in Brazil, professionalism has been operationalized through crime-control ideologies and technical militarization (see Chevigny 1995; Huggins 1998, 2000a; for the United States, see Skolnick and Fyfe 1993). Militarized professionalism, in turn, justifies creating an ever more hierarchical police, fortified by technical crime-fighting squads and the militarized materiel to combat a generalized enemy. By dividing a population into good citizens and criminals, the militarized crime-control orientation retains the Brazilian military's older Manichaean division of the population—with "criminals" transformed into rule-violating outsiders to be managed through heavy and generalized police repression.

Seen as the opposite of unreason and unpredictability, professionalism is thought to reduce police violence by increasing rational action. In fact, however, militarized professionalism can both increase (see Chevigny 1995; Skolnick and Fyfe 1993) and disguise police violence (see Huggins 1992, 1998). In any case, the assumption that legal-rational methods guide police behavior ipso facto rules out the possibility that true professionals could act with inappropriate violence. This relegates the police who violate professional standards to the status of exceptional: they are bad apples in an otherwise conforming, right-thinking institution.

As for how militarized professionalization fosters police violence, professional domains grant wide autonomy to occupational insiders, in this case allowing the police to define and evaluate for themselves what is and is not excessive. Because a secular ideology of professionalism, which defines professionals as most qualified to help clients eliminate, stabilize, or improve a problem or situation, places professional decisions outside alternative viewpoints, dependent clients—whether the larger society or alleged law violators—must respect the moral authority of those in a professional position (see Bledstein 1976: 87). The autonomy of professionals in general and the relative isolation granted professional police in particular establishes a climate for abuse of power. As death squad leader Vinnie explains, he "never killed anyone off duty."

Legacies of Military Rule: Authoritarianism in Democratic Transitions

Writing about the causes of torture, Crelinsten (1993: 5) argues that its systematic routine use "is only possible within a closed world imbued with an alternate reality separated from that of conventional morality." Although Crelinsten is correct that torture occurs within and is fostered by isolation, it would be misleading to view torture as outside conventional morality. One such conventional morality—professionalism—is a modern, secular moral ethos that includes a set of principles about right and wrong in which science and reason supposedly guide attitudes and conduct. The professionalism ethos allows relatively autonomous police professionals to decide the acceptability, accessibility, or unacceptability of gross human rights violations. Seen as a scientifically based standard for assessing the appropriateness of torture and murder, the secularized, tautological morality of professionalism provides a legitimate justification for police violence. If carried out by professional police acting professionally, violence is acceptable. Or as Armando, the chief of Rio's Municipal Police, explained, "I don't use...violence outside the standard of my conscience as a human being. I'm a conscientious professional. I know what to do and when to do it."

Atrocity Burnout: Doing Violence and Living Lies

Can the fragile cocoon that psychologically disguises and protects the atrocity worker from the realities of his past remain intact indefinitely? Even though atrocity perpetrators may be able to explain away their violence to themselves and outsiders and even escape prosecution for their violence, how do such perpetrators live with the consequences of what they have done? What happens physically and psychologically over the long run to those who carry out state atrocities? What happens when the work of repression becomes too stressful for the policeman and his family? Chapter 12 examines these questions within the framework of an analysis of job burnout, where carrying out repression results in the psychological tail wagging the physical dog—where perpetrators become the prey of their own violent careers.

CHAPTER 12

Hung Out to Dry

Nothing begins and nothing ends,
That is not paid with moan;
For we are born in other's pain,
And perish in our own.

Francis Thompson, "Daisy"

Whatsoever a man soweth, that shall he also reap.

Galatians 6:7

Policemen all over the world are trained and employed to protect citizens, enforce laws, and serve decision makers. Particularly in authoritarian regimes they are primarily expected to protect and serve the powerful—that is, to do their dirty work, usually acts of violence in the name of an ideology that is supposed to better the nation. But what happens when this work of repression becomes too stressful for the policeman and his family? What consequences arise when occupational accomplishments and the positive self-definitions attached to them are challenged by changes in social and political conditions? How do police react when old assumptions and accomplishments are called into question and earlier social support from occupationally significant others is neutralized or reversed? We explore some possible answers to these questions in this chapter.

Job Burnout

Job burnout is a prolonged response to chronic interpersonal stress at work (see Maslach 1981, 1982, 1998). The three defining dimensions of

210

this psychological response are feelings of being overextended and depleted of emotional resources (emotional exhaustion); a negative, cynical, or excessively detached response to other people and the job (depersonalization); and a decline in feelings of competence and productivity at work (a sense of ineffectiveness and failure). The experience of burnout has been linked to several negative outcomes, including problems at work (e.g., employee turnover, absenteeism, interpersonal conflict); troubles with family life (e.g., emotional distancing, interpersonal conflict, violence, divorce); and reduced physical and mental well-being (e.g., insomnia, alcohol and drug abuse, depression).

Researchers usually assess people's level of burnout through the Maslach Burnout Inventory (MBI) (Maslach and Jackson 1986). On this self-report measure, high burnout is reflected in reports of emotional exhaustion and depersonalization and feelings of low personal accomplishment. An average burnout response is reflected in middle-range scores on all three factors. Low or absent burnout is indicated by low emotional exhaustion and depersonalization and high feelings of personal accomplishment.

The burnout syndrome has been studied mainly among people working in health care, teaching, psychotherapy, and social work (see Maslach 1982), where depersonalization in particular would seem to run counter to the very nature of their positions. However, professionalization (and the threat of burnout) calls for some emotional distancing from clients. In policing, where depersonalization is often demanded by training and within the working environment, we might expect it to be a normal component of a police personality. However, more pronounced degrees of depersonalization may be evident among the more burned-out police.

Indeed, in a study of a normal sample of U.S. policemen and their families, Maslach and Jackson (1979) have found that police with higher rates of emotional exhaustion reported more anger and other symptoms of affective strain. They were emotionally distant from their families and had other emotional problems. Depersonalization, exhibited in police tendencies to dramatize citizens' complaints as of their own making, was associated with policemen having fewer nonpolice friends, seeing their children as emotionally distant, and in being absent from family celebrations. Their lowered sense of personal accomplishment was indicated by a tendency to rate their job performance a failure. Greater use of alcohol and medications as well as insomnia were also correlated with higher scores on burnout. Other research has shown that police in general are more at risk for psychological, circulatory, and digestive disorders as well as divorce and suicide (see Guralnick 1963; Friedman 1967; Kelling and Pate 1975; Kroes 1976; Paton and Violanti 1996; Stevens 1999).

But who is the most burned out among U.S. police? To the extent that burnout derives from identified forms of work stress, some academic evidence (Stevens, 1999) suggests that the most stressed-out U.S. police are primarily those involved in investigations of violence—such as homicide detectives—or in the special units at war against crime or drugs. At the same time, some research (Machell 1993) also demonstrates that general police work, rather than violent and dangerous "critical incident" (e.g., high-risk) policing, creates the greatest stress. However, most past studies of police stress and burnout have failed to systematically explore whether these outcomes are more likely for police in elite violent units than for rank-and-filers. Although it is outside the scope of this chapter to compare these two U.S. police groups, we can compare burnout among the Brazilian sample's direct perpetrators of atrocity—who, for the most part, were in special units that engaged consistently in critical incident policing—and among the atrocity facilitators—who were largely rank-and-file beat cops. Certainly, all of the conditions usually associated with job stress and burnout were present for the Brazilian police perpetrators from specialized squads: official pressure for results, a pervasive image of danger and action to combat it, physical absence for extended periods from family and nonpolice friends, depersonalizing of citizens, short-run elusive rewards for their operational successes, and sometimes long-run condemnation and punishment. Indeed, in the long run, these violence workers faced possible betrayal by the very system that had mandated and supported their violence in the first place.

Yet if it is difficult to locate studies on the impact of systematic violence on those in elite units who carry it out, it is even more difficult to uncover studies on the impact of committing extraordinary, systematic state-sponsored atrocities on the operatives attached to an authoritarian state. Only psychiatrist Frantz Fanon (1963), in *The Wretched of the Earth,* which focuses on the French war against Algerian independence, and physician Aldo Martin (1995), in his study of torturers among his Uruguayan patients, describe instances of what could be seen as occupational burnout among active or former torturers. Both of these therapists reported their patients' having had violent episodes with their families while actively torturing. As one torturer informed Martin (1995: 13), "When I find opposition, even outside my work, I feel like I want to harm those who stand in my way." Martin also found many depressed from guilt and through having left the occupational networks that had supported their atrocities.

Although these clinical observations offer us a beginning, we must recognize that no sample of police who have routinely tortured or murdered has been studied systematically. One reason may be that these ordinary atrocity perpetrators are difficult to locate and then even more difficult to interview, as we pointed out in chapters 3 and 4. Moreover, as Chapter 2 argues, philosophical and theoretical assumptions about the legitimacy and morality of studying and taking seriously the storytelling accounts of atrocity perpetrators militate against even examining the negative impact on the perpetrators themselves. Avoiding doing research on violence perpetrators for reasons of moral sensitivity is associated with the assumption that the disreputable cannot be expected to tell the truth—because such people are too low on a hierarchy of credibility to be believed. Thus, there are solid arguments against considering the possible impact of atrocity on perpetrators themselves. Ultimately, the researcher who examines the possibility that perpetrators of atrocity are themselves victims may be inviting charges of bias. It may appear that atrocity perpetrators are being excused for their violence when, in fact, research on burnout serves as a warning to those who would follow in their footsteps: you may do it only at physical and psychological risk to yourself, with no guarantee that those you serve will support you in the end. Indeed, some of them may even facilitate your prosecution—if only to save themselves from it. In the end—with your identity soiled and your familial and friendship networks destroyed by your atrocity work—there may be nowhere to turn for support.

Some human rights interpretations of atrocity perpetrators' violence blame it on their being born sadists, which implies that they would not be negatively impacted emotionally or physically by their violence. Because they are biologically scripted to carry out atrocity, they must therefore enjoy it. This leads to the conclusion that they need not be studied for any negative feedback effects of their violence. However, as we have demonstrated throughout this book and as research in contexts outside Brazil has shown as well (Browning 1992; Conroy 2000; Haritos-Fatouros 2002), official torturers and killers are made, not born—they are typically ordinary human beings who perform violent and abhorrent acts under particular sociopolitical situations and work circumstances.

If one is prepared to accept that under the right conditions anyone can become a torturer or murderer, then it is possible to assume

that committing this violence regularly could have negative consequences for the perpetrator. Particularly in light of our findings that
police from Brazil's special squads were more likely than the rank-
and-file atrocity facilitators to be physically and socially distant from
family and nonpolice friends and that the atrocity perpetrators
spontaneously reported outcomes that are associated with burnout,
we resolved to examine this syndrome systematically among our interviewees.

In this chapter, therefore, we attempt to answer questions about the
degree, sources, and consequences of burnout among interviewees.
But due to the special conditions surrounding our interviews, the particular characteristics of the interviewees, and the limited number of
subjects, we did not administer the MBI to our interviewees. Instead,
we relied on a more direct assessment of burnout by measuring the
number of times an interviewee mentioned the following in his interview narrative: difficult job conditions, emotional problems, health
problems, quitting a job, and the impact of job on family. In addition
to these five outcomes, we added a sixth—feelings of betrayal (see
Table 12.1). On the one hand, betrayal is a factor that could affect feelings of personal accomplishment and job satisfaction—two components of the standard burnout inventory; on the other hand, with formal restoration of democracy in Brazil, many of our interviewees'
"accomplishments" for the military government were now being condemned.

Interviewees who presented five or all six of the negative outcomes
were rated as having high burnout. Those who had between two and
four were rated as having moderate burnout. Those with up to two outcomes were rated as having no burnout. According to this index, two-
thirds of our twenty-three interviewees ($n = 15$) showed moderate-to-
high burnout. Among the interviewees with no-to-low burnout—eight
interviewees—two reported only one burnout outcome, and six gave
evidence of no such outcomes at all.

Most of the interviewees who demonstrated moderate-to-high
burnout were direct perpetrators of violence. Eight of them manifested
moderate burnout, and four demonstrated high burnout.

Looking at the burnout figures another way, only two of the fourteen
atrocity perpetrators demonstrated no burnout at all; these two policemen had begun their careers in the Militarized Police and were still in
official police positions, having transferred to the Civil Police. As for the
interviewees who facilitated atrocity, just one manifested high burnout

(a militarized policeman), whereas two others (both militarized police) demonstrated moderate burnout. Thus, in contrast to the high burnout of the specialized atrocity perpetrators, the majority (six of the eight) of those who presented very low burnout were rank-and-file atrocity facilitator police. Very few of the facilitators, therefore, manifested any significant burnout outcomes.

To understand the conditions associated with this syndrome, we will focus especially on the interviewees who demonstrated moderate-to-high burnout. Noting that within this category, different levels of burnout were associated with carrying out different kinds of violence, we divided the perpetrators into torturers and murderers. We hypothesize that the torturers would have paid the highest price in burnout because, as Jorge pointed out, the torturer must develop a personal, dyadic psychological relationship with the victim. In contrast, because the killer eliminates his victim before any such relationship can develop and usually works in murder teams or squads, the killers should have been burned out less severely. The murderers were usually in less direct personal contact with their victims, so it was easier to dehumanize victims (although not without such depersonalization contaminating the perpetrator's own emotional life). Furthermore, murderous teamwork may have provided the collegial support to mitigate some of the negative personal impacts of sustained violence work. Because killing was most often done collectively, the effects of potential burnout from guilt could be transferred onto the murder group itself, lowering personal, individual guilt.

With these possibilities in mind, we turn now to our analysis of the burned-out atrocity perpetrators, beginning with three emblematic high-burnout torturers.

Torture Burnout

Sérgio, whom we met in Chapter 11, was seventy-three at the time of his 1993 interview. A successfully retired Civil Police official with a university degree, Sérgio has divorced and is now remarried. He served two decades in the DOPS. Proud that he supervised "efficient" and "successful" policemen, Sérgio believes that he guided them in administering measured and appropriate violence. He admitted having used excessive violence "once," specifically torture, while denying that he used such violence unnecessarily or regularly.

TABLE 12.1. Burnout Reactions

Interviewee's Name or Initials	Burnout Indicators						Total Number of Indicators	Burnout Level
	Difficult Job Conditions	Emotional Problems	Job Affects Family	Health Problems	Quits Job or Leaves Post	Betrayal		
Jorge	+	+				+	3	*
Armando							0	
Bruno	+	+	+	+		+	5	**
Sérgio	+	+	+		+	+	5	**
Fernando	+	+	+				3	*
Jacob	+				+		2	*
P.	+						1	
Eduardo	+	+	+	+		+	5	**
L.O.	+		+			+	3	*
Ignácio	+					+	2	*
L.U.							0	
Vinnie			+			+	2	*
O.							0	
Ernesto	+	+				+	3	*
Bernardo							0	
M.							0	
A.		+		+	+	+	4	**
I.	+	+				+	3	*

M.E.	+					1	
Roberto	+	+	+	+	+	5	**
Julius	+					2	*
Marcio	+	+		+		3	*
L.U.C.						0	

** = High burnout.

* = Moderate burnout.

No star = No-to-low burnout.

NOTE: Atrocity facilitators are indicated by initials; direct perpetrators, by names.

Sérgio began to manifest several signs of job burnout relatively early in his career. Exhausted by the tension to which he was constantly exposed, Sérgio asked the governor several times to allow him to resign:

"Fed up" is what it's called. I couldn't take any more. I didn't want anything to do with it any longer. I wanted out.... The work is intense...and permanent. You sleep, wake up, dream; everything [is work-related].... There was a [labor] strike every two, three days. It was crazy. I'd say that I'd infiltrated literally everywhere.

Sérgio remembers often not being able to think straight on the job because of his many responsibilities:

Sometimes I wouldn't sleep for three nights [in a row]. I took Perbidim to keep from falling asleep. When something extremely serious was imminent, how could I sleep? You can't afford to. It reached a point where I wasn't.... Everything was piling up.

Like the other highly burned-out violence workers, Sérgio indicated that such difficult work conditions created problems for his first wife and family. At one point in his career, Sérgio even refused promotion in order to stay near his family, especially his children. In his words,

I never spent time with my daughters. They went on trips, went out, and me, never. I didn't have any vacations. There were none, so it was a draining, exhausting, absorbing job.

Sérgio began fearing for his children's lives when his investigations into official corruption made him a target of military "justice." With threats against his family and the constant demands of his work, Sérgio was by necessity socially isolated: "You begin not trusting your friends." He learned that the governor's private secretary was working to do him in: this man told "lies" about Sérgio and tried to get him "to rebel and quit." By the time Sérgio resigned as DOPS director, he felt totally betrayed by the system.

Sérgio's work clearly affected his health: He felt constant anxiety, suffered from sleep deprivation, got hooked on amphetamines to stay awake, and became increasingly paranoid as well. Despite retiring, Sérgio suffered a heart attack and a stroke. He clearly shows all the symptoms of job burnout even a decade or more after his retirement: he could still remember how stressful and difficult his job had been, and he made many references to feelings of social isolation, to emotional and health problems, to the devastating and lasting effects of his job on family life, and to his betrayal by some superiors and colleagues. Although he never used these symptoms and complaints to justify his atrocities—relying primarily on "bad" victim and "bad apple" perpetrator arguments—Sérgio believes that he sacrificed his youth for his job. Therefore, instead of taking pride in his accomplishments, Sérgio looks back at his career with a low sense of professional achievement.

Eduardo, introduced in Chapter 1, was in his mid-forties at the time of his 1993 interview in his administrative office. A Civil Police official, he had very slowly worked up through the ranks of his police organization, beginning at nineteen as a DOPS field operative. A university graduate with a law degree, he completed his university education during many years in DOPS police service.

Along the way, Eduardo suffered two major career disappointments: his transfers to the elite SNI and to the federal police were blocked—transfers that Eduardo claims to have sought because his DOPS service was making him physically ill. Although over the years Eduardo has had marital problems, a fact that he attributes to having been away from home for long periods, he is still married.

Eduardo describes his emotional life in the police as a roller coaster, with ups and downs and distressing twists and turns that seem to have caused him much turmoil. He describes his work as having been very difficult, mainly because he had to improvise how to carry out his potentially life-threatening police operations as he went along—without any backup from higher officials. He reported feeling fear and terror each of the many times an operation placed his own life in danger. He described as painful a "serious incident" when he nearly killed someone; he recalls reacting by trembling all over.

In his interview, Eduardo reported a number of health problems, attributing these in part to the pressure of his work: "Stress...had an influence.... I had emotional problems, hypertension,...insomnia..., nervousness." He was already suffering from hypertension by his early twenties, only a few years after starting work in DOPS. He also became an alcoholic, which led to gastrointestinal problems. Eduardo believes that his alcoholism resulted from a volatile mix of police culture and work pressures:

I started drinking because everyone in the police drinks: we'd get off work and everybody'd drink but me. I began to get isolated. [So] I drank for fifteen years, until I had to quit drinking because I'd reached my limit. It was one of the things I learned in the police, to drink.

Yet although Eduardo admits that his DOPS work was stressful, fear provoking, and generally difficult he still argues that he liked his work. Eduardo sees himself as a good policeman, dedicated to his job. Eduardo copes with the fact that policemen commit atrocities by blaming out-of-control individuals who are pressured for results.

Although Eduardo reports having many friends, even outside the service, he thinks that people no longer respect or appreciate police work. Like Sérgio, Eduardo now feels somewhat betrayed by the police system and by society at large. He sees Brazilian society in general as not merely unappreciative of but hostile toward the police.

Eduardo, who has been rewarded by the police system itself with the directorship of Civil Police for an important Brazilian city, seems to have a high sense of personal accomplishment. Thus, although aware of how his work contributed to his unpleasant physical and psychological symptoms, Eduardo still reports pride in his job—while admitting to the "mistakes" he made, a vague reference to his torturing and killing. He declares that he would never think of resigning from his job—a political appointment that would in any case end as soon as Eduardo's superior, the state's governor, lost an election.

We know that Bruno, described briefly in Chapter 4, is burned out, not so much because of what he said in the interview but by how he acted and spoke outside of it. Bruno was the civil policeman and former prison warden who at the time of his interview was a police official in an important southern Brazilian state. Now nearing the end of his police career, Bruno, in his mid-fifties, had been an operative during the early part of his career—when he was primarily a killer—and then a prison warden during the latter part of Brazil's military period—when he mostly oversaw torture or directly took part in it himself.

Bruno was careful and emotionally guarded during his interview in his large office at his state's police administrative headquarters. He claimed that he could not have been part of "political repression" because, on the one hand, he did not believe in operating "that way"—"beating someone *for nothing* is sadism," he asserts, with the implication that beating for "rational" ends is appropriate—and, on the other, because later in his career he was a prison warden and such violence does not occur there. In fact, of course, much torture has occurred and does occur in Brazilian prisons (see United Nations Commission on Human Rights 2000). In any case, not only does Bruno's name appear on lists of denounced torturers, but a former police colleague (who suggested that Bruno be interviewed) also indicated Bruno's past history in violent po-

litical repression. However, the closest that Bruno himself came to talking about his own role in atrocity was to explain generally that in operations "sometimes we'd get intoxicated from our work" and do things
that should not be done. Bruno says that he "felt like a demigod," a kind
of high that came from "dictat[ing] the rules." Bruno says that he now
realizes that "all [such] intoxication is negative" because it causes the policeman to be "irritable, aggressive, [prone to] having problems at home
[and] drinking."

On the day after Bruno's interview, he fell apart and manifested a
range of symptoms that he had identified the previous day as associated
with psychological "intoxication"; we recognize these as burnout outcomes. Bruno arrived at midmorning, smelling heavily of alcohol, to
pick up the interviewer, and spoke in disjointed sentences—less from
the alcohol and more from anxiety and emotional confusion. On the
verge of tears, he recounted the failures of his personal and professional
life after explaining that the previous day's interview had made him look
at his life through a new moral lens.

After discussing Bruno with one of his police colleagues, the interviewer learned that this atrocity perpetrator—who is widely known to
have serious alcohol and emotional problems—was undergoing therapy.
His colleagues feared that Bruno might attempt suicide because of his
ongoing anxiety and depression. Apparently, Bruno had for some time
been dogged by his earlier career in atrocity; he was not living well with
what he had done.

Reflecting such feelings of betrayal by the system, Bernardo explained that many police he knew "feel frustrated because they believed
at the time...they were doing a relevant job [that those in the government wanted done] and benefited from. And now they are thrown into
the background. They then feel highly frustrated." This attitude clearly
signals feelings of low personal accomplishment—that life has been
wasted—an attitude common among the most burned-out perpetrators.
As one betrayed interviewee put it, "We are society's toilet paper."

Burned-Out Killers

On the other hand, most of the killers, in contrast to the torturers, manifested only moderate burnout. Indeed, of all the killers, only Roberto,
the militarized policeman in a death squad who was described in Chapter 8, exhibited high levels of burnout. But because his profile diverges

from that of the other interviewed killers and mirrors much more closely that of the torturers, it is useful to examine his narrative as an exception that seems to prove the rule. It can provide clues into those factors in atrocity work—whether carried out by torturers or murderers—that tend to create burnout.

Roberto—now in prison—is the only Militarized Police murderer who joined the force after the end of Brazil's military dictatorship. He actively criticizes the postmilitary police system, which in terms of violence does not seem to operate very differently than during the military period. Roberto was interviewed in prison, where he was serving a seventy-two-year sentence for killing five people while on duty.

Roberto, in his thirties at the time of his interview, has a secondary school education. He has been married, divorced, and remarried, with a daughter by his first marriage. After a short stint as a rank-and-file militarized policeman, Roberto was promoted to a Militarized Police Special Operations Battalion (Batalhão de Operações Especiais, or BOPE) in south-central Brazil, where he was trained in crowd control, including the use of deadly force. Roberto also joined an informal death squad to avenge his family's honor by capturing those who had robbed his brother's house and raped his sister-in-law. The roots of this death squad lay in his own BOPE battalion.

Roberto spoke repeatedly of the stress associated with his work. Because of his formal role in the Militarized Police and his informal one in the death squad, Roberto explains that he "was a policeman every day, even when I was off duty." Pointing to the pervasive influence of the death squad on his life, Roberto explained that the it seemed to get "bigger and bigger and bigger and before you [knew] it, [all] the police [were] inside the death squad. Just about the entire police force [was] involved."

Roberto felt trapped: if he denounced the death squads, he would come up against not only these killers but the police system itself. This could result in his or his family's murder, which surely left Roberto feeling vulnerable and impotent—conditions that very likely contributed to his very high level of burnout. But the stress he felt about having one foot in a police organization and another in an associated death squad was exacerbated by the normal stress associated with Militarized Police operations.

Roberto admitted that killing itself was highly stressful and that he saw the death squad kill a lot of people. For Roberto, the sheer number of murders that he participated in contributed to his physical and psychological problems:

I saw a lot of dead people at the scene of the crime; I'd go there to pick up dead bodies and guard dead bodies until the investigators arrived to do their job. You could see killing while you were on the job and killing while you were off duty. I think that during that period something started happening to my head...[a] kind of [psychological] disturbance.

Roberto fearfully recognized the distinct possibility of getting shot himself. Indeed, during a murder operation Roberto frequently asked himself, "Is it going to be my turn [to die] this time? I would tremble a little [and] feel nervous, but...had to...get used to it. I escaped from death...about five times with bullets flying inches over my head."

Roberto's nervousness about killings was heightened by also being vividly aware that he could be deliberately shot by the squad: "There were a number of attempts on my life; a lot of things were going on." Roberto increasingly found himself "getting sick" of going out with the death squad, and he learned to cope with such feelings by developing strategies for handling them, recalling, in particular, the value of silence during a murder operation: "I didn't need to talk to anyone. [The squad would] remain in a way silent—quiet—after committing [murders]." Of course, Roberto's coping strategy was also part of his group's process of keeping it secret by isolating its members from one another and from outsiders—so Roberto was cut off from any social support or alternatives, which undoubtedly contributed to his high level of burnout.

Roberto's social relations gradually deteriorated during this period. But ironically, the murders themselves led Roberto to maintain some contact with his family: after a murder, he often suggested to his second wife, "Let's go to my ex-mother-in-law's and pick up my daughter and go out." This distraction strategy of visiting his daughter helped Roberto "forget what we'd just done."

It must have heightened Roberto's burnout that the family member who could best provide him support—albeit for torture and murder—his brother, a Militarized Policeman as well, in the end betrayed him. After Roberto had shot five suspected criminals, his brother refused to vouch for him. Roberto was charged with the murders and ended up in prison.

By this time, Roberto clearly was already well on his way to becoming a fully burnt-out case. Explaining the five killings, Roberto recalled that when he shot at the suspects, "Something happened to my head, I don't know what it was. I'd really like to take a psychological examination, to really study and see what happened to my mind, because I got so nervous." Roberto's violent reaction—in a man who had carried out and seen scores of murders during his relatively short career—might be attributed today to posttraumatic stress disorder—the delayed stress syndrome associated with Vietnam War veterans' immersion in unremitting violence.

In his narrative, Roberto presented various symptoms of emotional exhaustion and communicated his feelings of low personal accomplishment. His many hours in the death squad and the atrocities that he observed or directly perpetrated have been powerful influences on his life. Roberto's nonstop work seems to have affected his health and to have created family problems: his second wife left him (he is still remorseful about that), and he has an ulcer. Roberto was distrustful of fellow policemen because he feared they would kill him. He still feels betrayed by his brother, who abandoned him just when Roberto needed him most. Sitting in prison with no parole in sight, Roberto is worried about his future, although he still holds out some hope of being released from his seventy-two year sentence.

Ignácio, a sixty-year-old rank-and-file civil policeman from a working-class family, was first introduced in Chapter 6. A secondary school graduate, he has been married to the same woman for his entire police career. Joining the police during the military period because he "knew that he would like the work," Ignácio was trained for operational activities: his Civil Police career in the south-central part of the country was in crime investigation. Ignácio admits that some of his interrogations involved violence, including torture and killing, and he recognizes that he frequently used it to get results, with beatings and killing more his modus operandi than systematic torture.

After Ignácio's first decade of police service, he lost his political rights and his job for ten years, in part because—as an active member of the General Association of Civil Police, basically a police trade union—he fought for higher police salaries and better working conditions. As he puts it,

[In the] association ... we had the support to struggle for salaries, working conditions, all of those things. During the military government, labor questions were considered illegal. Anybody struggling for better salaries, working conditions was considered illegal. And I was prosecuted under the work antistrike law, because I was creating many movements, ... work stoppages, in the Civil Police. I'd say that the Civil Police was going to stop, and they'd really stop [on strike]. ... And [the military] didn't like it.

Ignácio's unionizing activities fostered his pariah status with the military, so much so that he left the Civil Police for a position in the private sector. It was during this period, as assistant to the director of security for one of Brazil's largest banks, that Ignácio suffered threats on his life: "They [the military] kept me under surveillance at night." Ignácio remembers living in terror as the system of repression turned its violence against him and his family: "They invaded my home, beat my wife and children, broke up everything in my house." He maintains that "the military government tried to kill me [by] staging an accident." According to Ignácio, the military's pattern in such cases was to

pick someone up, break him on the parrot's perch...and the guy...[would] die. [Then] they'd take the guy and stage an [automobile] accident right in the street. They'd isolate the area to do a technical investigation. Since...the coroners belonged to [the military], they testified the way [it] wanted.

Ignácio is still angry about the military's repressive national security atmosphere. He believes that this undermined the police system and unnecessarily politicized it. He decries the military's use of operatives to infiltrate police academies and precincts. Such "police pretenders" were not professional police, he says; they were just spies.

Ignácio spoke freely and frequently during his interview about his difficulties being a committed policeman. The policeman, he says, is usually away from home; his work causes stress that can be mitigated only by a close working relationship with the "right kind of partner." Because Ignácio had great difficulty finding such a person, he was a loner carrying out difficult and dangerous work. Ignácio compensated for his occupational isolation by developing social support networks inside the communities he policed—poor people who "work hard," are "honest," and are "exploited by the system" became Ignácio's weekend drinking buddies and informants. Ignácio was increasingly frustrated by his superiors' judging his hanging out in slums as unprofessional.

Despite everything that he has been through, Ignácio shows only a moderate level of burnout. He does not mention any health problems that he believes were specifically caused by his job. He probably owes his relatively lower levels of burnout to several factors that linked him to people and communities, including the collegiality associated with union organizing, the time he spent during the military period away from policing, and his continuing weekend trips to visit the network of poor people who served as his support group, all of which provided him appreciation and social-psychological maintenance.

Jorge, introduced in Chapter 7, was a man in his late thirties at the time of his interview. Born into a working-class family, Jorge is a secondary school graduate. Unmarried, he was living with the mother of his two daughters before his imprisonment for murder. Jorge maintains that his life as a policeman in south-central Brazil did not allow him the time or the personal security to have a "real" family life. In prison for a murder that Jorge was supposed to have committed while on duty after Brazil's military dictatorship had ended—and after he had already carried out countless murders for that previous military government—Jorge alleges that he was framed.

Jorge's interview provided a window on the impact that the emotional turmoil of his past has had on his present condition: Separated at a very early age from his parents, Jorge had tears in his eyes and almost started to cry audibly when he talked about his mother's sexual assault by the soldiers who were arresting his father. Jorge also vividly described the abuse that he suffered as a young child in the FEBEM orphanage after his mother's breakdown. Jorge manifested less emotion but expressed a great sense of disappointment and betrayal about his violent life in the Militarized Police: "They taught me how to kill; [they] used me. I gave them almost my entire life, and I've never had anything. I don't have a house and I've got two daughters."

Jorge is afraid that the government, even though no longer a military one, will eliminate him: "When I get out of here, they'll try again [to kill me] because I'm an archive of everything, all of those excesses they committed in that period. I know a lot.... I know that I'm going to be murdered." Jorge talks a lot about these threats against his own life and his family's.

Yet Jorge is an interesting case because he displays only moderate burnout, even though his potential for it should certainly be high. He expresses emotional exhaustion and strong and persistent feelings of betrayal, but he does not refer specifically to any health problems. He condemns the military for eliminating his chance for a family or social life and now feels that his entire life in the police was a waste. This means that he has a very low sense of personal accomplishment for what took place during that important phase of his life.

There are probably three reasons why Jorge manifests only moderate rather than high burnout. First, the FEBEM orphanage, whether consciously or not, probably socialized its children into becoming a Praetorian Guard for the military state: they were brought up under abusive military discipline, trained to obey authority and to withstand the violence committed against them and therefore to cope better with the atrocities that some of them would later mete out. In addition, by claiming that he was just following orders when he murdered, Jorge reduced his sense of personal guilt and promoted the idea that he was merely a victim of the system: Others were to blame for what Jorge did because they had "used" him. Finally, Jorge has taken on a new identity in prison. As a born-again Christian, he sees himself as a different man from the one who committed murder for the military state. The life that Jorge had before "coming to Christ," the life that ought to have led to very high burnout, has been eclipsed by a new identity that no longer allows most of his earlier anxieties, frustrations, and betrayals to shape his discourse and definition of self. Joining a community of Christian believers, Jorge now has the support that makes his "evil" past discontinuous with his new-found salvation in the present.

Who Did Not Burn Out?

The violence workers who showed little or no burnout present a number of common characteristics. First, they were very cautious as interviewees, offering little information about their lives in general and policing in particular. What this signals is unclear; it could even mean that rather than having been relatively unaffected by their past careers, they were so burned out that they feared disclosing anything about themselves. However, most of these police were atrocity facilitators, rank-and-file cops on the beat, and thus generally had little direct responsibility for and experience with the kinds of sustained violence and the associated work and lifestyle climates that could have nurtured high levels of burnout.

Second, the interviewees with the lowest levels of burnout tended not to mention difficult job conditions, talking instead with enthusiasm and pride about their work. They generally failed to mention the job factors frequently identified by the most burned-out interviewees. They were also very unlikely to manifest a sense of betrayal about their police past; indeed, they saw police work as having improved rather than hindered their happiness.

Furthermore, among these low-burnout police, there was relatively little depersonalization of victims, that is, less of a tendency to blame others for their own problems, commonly expressed by those exhibiting the most burnout. Clearly, depersonalization in burnout means social and psychological distance from others. In the case of such police, depersonalization can even mitigate their stress through labeling victims "criminals" or "deviants," with the people who fall into such dangerous categories deserving less consideration than good citizens. Haritos-Fatouros (2002) has identified this coping mechanism among Greek torturers as well. She has discovered that these atrocity perpetrators "situationally compartmentalized" their violence work to reduce the negative effects of their violence: "I work for the state"; "I am a civil servant"; "I protect my country and society"; "I was only a bureaucrat." Such rhetorical psychological withdrawal allows violence perpetrators to hide behind a social or work status regulated by others' rules or orders. The police with high burnout can therefore use depersonalization of victims as a psychological defense against the danger to their integrity from admitting the violence that they have perpetrated; it serves to morally disengage highly stressed perpetrators from the possible consequences of their self-abhorrent behavior. Yet at the same time, it tends to isolate them from their colleagues and their family and friends, which is part of burnout.

We cannot claim that all of the low-burnout police had viable connections to family and friendship communities. Nevertheless, the contrasting evidence among the moderate- and high-burnout interviewees reveals that the more personally and professionally isolated they were, the more they also tended to display burnout outcomes. Overall, supportive family, especially a supportive wife, could and did play a role in mitigating the outcomes of burnout. However, because our high-burnout interviewees commonly kept their violent work secret from wives and other family members, these potentially positive roles were significantly reduced. Ironically, the way a wife could best support her perpetrator husband psychologically was to become an active facilitator for his atrocities, a role that Julius's wife very clearly assumed (see Chapter 4) although without sufficiently mitigating Julius's moderate burnout.

Social and professional isolation, combined with emotional or physical health problems, therefore, tended to characterize the most burned-out police, who complained of feeling as if they were losing their mind as well as of excessive drinking, insomnia, physical pains, marital breakups, and feelings of professional and social rejection and isolation.

Violence Turned Back upon Itself

Those atrocity perpetrators who retained connections with one another, their families, and nonpolice friends were better able to commit atrocities without burning out so completely in the process. They either paced their work in order to have time for nonatrocity networks, or they developed tight networks with other atrocity perpetrators and supporters. Although these contacts with other outsiders might under some circumstances call their atrocities into question and thus possibly lead perpetrators to question their careers, the ties with others involved in atrocity definitely fostered their continuing involvement by providing support for violence and by softening its social and personal consequences.

Yet everything that we have learned from this Brazilian study about atrocity systems suggests that their training programs, social and work organization, and social-psychological dynamics are so organized as to discourage and punish any collegiality that could create the moral introspection that not only might call atrocity into question but might also mitigate the effects of burnout. Atrocity systems operate by nurturing operatives' unthinking reactions, thriving on secrecy and political and juridical impunity and gaining sustenance from fraud and disguise. These factors, in turn, hide the identities of perpetrators, facilitators, and their victims—with horrible consequences for the victims, their families, and for a political system attempting to punish those responsible for atrocities.

Obviously, the highest price for state-sponsored and -sanctioned atrocity is paid, first and foremost, by its direct victims and only secondarily by the political system and its members who sustain terror. Yet as this chapter has demonstrated, even atrocity perpetrators themselves are not exempt from the moral, psychological, social and, one hopes, political consequences of their violence. Those who would carry out state-sponsored or -condoned atrocities should eventually be able to recognize that their superiors—the officials who order this violence—will inevitably change themselves to suit the shifts in the dominant political ideology. In this process, the past loyalty of atrocity perpetrators to a system that encourages such actions will be forgotten and even punished. Either way, as Jorge and Sérgio have pointed out, atrocity perpetrators will have wasted their youth for a system that in the end protects and rewards only select elite perpetrators and most of the higher-level atrocity facilitators, who despite political changes may well maintain their professional status and sense of personal integrity. Even Chile's Pinochet, still free from official punishment, has not been fully and conclusively condemned for the massive violence he ordered and directly facilitated.

Only in some cases are the very powerful crushed under the weight of the violent system that supported their power—and even then, in most cases, their fall from grace has primarily only personal consequences. Consider the story of Erich Mielke, former head of the German Democratic Republic's feared secret police, the Stasi. A man by all accounts feared by his nearly 100,000 subordinates and loved by no one, he believed that he "needed to keep watch around the clock on everyone. [Mielke] managed to poison an entire society, making husband spy on wife, brother on brother, child on parents" (Schneider 2001: 32). Just days before Mielke's death in his apartment in reunified Germany on May 22, 2000, visitors found him alone, shouting orders to invisible agents on an out-of-service telephone. Furiously commanding his imaginary operatives to locate his apparently lost dog, the former Stasi chief played out his well-worn atrocity commander's script—unaware that his wife had given the dog away when she moved out on him. The ruins of Mielke's violent life had imprisoned his own mind within the Kafkaesque fortification that he had used to incarcerate his own society: "What goes around, comes around" is the popular way of saying that those who perpetrate atrocity against others may themselves end up on the parrot's perch of their own burnout.

Burnout Postscript

We should acknowledge the potential criticism by human rights groups and atrocity victims' families for our apparent interest in the well-being of former torturers and death squad executioners. But our primary concern throughout this book has been to demonstrate the hideous consequences that flowed from the establishing of specialized Militarized and Civil Police units that encouraged, justified, and rewarded violence. However, we must also point to the troubling evidence that most of these violence workers were "ordinary" people prior to their indoctrination into the systematized sanctioning of horrendous violence against fellow citizens. That some of them have also suffered victimization from their deeds—in the long-term negative effects of job burnout—is another message that needs reiterating. Perpetrators of atrocity should recognize that they can pay a very high personal price for their violence against humanity—a price neither initially obvious nor subsequently well documented.

As scholars committed to preventing state-sponsored torture and killing throughout the world, we are concerned about what happens to the ordinary violence workers who have engaged in such deeds. If we want to prevent their recruitment in the first place and to somehow bring them back—to reintegrate them into society and not demonize them just as they themselves have been led to view "enemies of the state"—then we must open theirs and others' eyes to the consequences of carrying out atrocities and to the necessity of preventing the social and political conditions that mandate and organize atrocity.

The Alchemy of Torture and Execution

Transforming Ordinary Men into Violence Workers

No light, but rather darkness visible.

John Milton, Paradise Lost

While some people might wish to view all Nazis as simply frozen in evil, we dismiss their complexity at our own cultural and political peril.

Robert Jay Lifton, New York Times, February 25, 2001

If systematic torture and murder by men and women of their fellows represent one of the darkest sides of human nature, we hope that our research has made that darkness somewhat more visible. We began by focusing on torturers, trying to understand both their psyches and the ways they were shaped by their circumstances and contingencies. But it soon became apparent that we had to expand our analytical net to capture their comrades-in-arms who chose or were assigned to another branch of violence work, to be executioners. These two types of violence workers shared a common enemy—men, women, and children who were declared by the authorities to be threats to the country's national security. Some had to be efficiently eliminated, whereas others who might hold secret information had to be forced to yield it up and thereby confess to their sinful treason.

In carrying out this mission, some violence workers could rely in part on the creative evil long since embodied in torture devices and techniques refined and extensively utilized over centuries by officials of the church and state. But they had also to reckon with the resistance and resiliency of the particular enemy before them, who often might claim innocence and refuse to acknowledge either culpability or intimidation. Improvised torture required time and patience as well as the development of at least a primitive understanding of the human weaknesses to be exploited. By contrast, the task of the executioners, who wore hoods for anonymity and had guns and group support, could carry out their duties swiftly and impersonally. The torturers' work could not be "just business," conducted with the speed of the murderers' hit-and-run operations, but always required a degree of personal relationship—essential for understanding what kind of torture to employ, what intensity of torture to dial up or down for this particular person at this particular time. With the wrong kind or too little pressure, there might be no confession at all; with too much, the victim could die before confessing. In either case, the torturer would fail to deliver the goods, and the bosses would not be pleased. Superiors and colleagues reward the torturer who knows best how to extract the desired information or implant the right degree of terror. It is a perfectible skill in which some men take pride.

We wanted to know what kind of people could do such deeds. Did they need to rely on sadistic impulses and a history of traumatizing life experiences to rip and tear the flesh of other human beings, humiliate them, and shame them day in and day out for years on end? Did it take a special kind of psyche to gun down fellow humans, to annihilate entire families on search-and-destroy missions? Were the violence workers a breed apart from the rest of humanity, bad seeds that produced poisoned flowers? Or is it conceivable that they could be programmed to carry out their despicable acts through some identifiable and replicable programs that seasoned them for state-sanctioned violence? Could we identify and isolate a set of external conditions—ideological, organizational, and situational variables—that contributed more informally to the making of torturers and killers? How could violence workers be fashioned out of the rather mundane material that the state had at its disposal?

If their evil deeds are not traceable to inner defects—the products of organic disabilities, dysfunctional personalities, disordered temperaments—but rather attributable to outer forces—political, economic, social, historical, and experiential—then what about the rest of us? Could we also be induced, enticed, or seduced into becoming killers with no conscience or torturers plying their trade of unimaginable deeds? What would it take to move you, us, anyone, across that seemingly impermeable membrane that we want to believe separates Robert Louis Stevenson's good Dr. Jekyll from the evil monster, Mr. Hyde? What does it take to transform "ordinary" people into perpetrators of evil? How easy is it for good men to slip on the cloak of evil and wear it with pride in their work, with indifference to moral values and social approbation? Is there a fundamental, qualitative difference between those people who would and those who would not ever become torturers or executioners under any circumstances? Of course, our self-serving, self-protecting biases lead us to think we are different, special, above the norm: "Not me! I am a good person, I have never done such evil, and I can't imagine the conditions under which I ever could."

We tend to believe in the essentialness of our human natures and to assume that goodness is one of our basic traits. It is hard to imagine any circumstances that could lead us so astray from our positive self-image. For us, our past history predicts what and how we would act in various hypothetical situations. We use that same personal historical framework for establishing our sense of personality—we are what we have been doing and feeling regularly. But do we really know what we would do, how we might behave, in a totally new situation, a completely alien setting that we have never before experienced? How can we even begin to assess the power of situational forces acting on us when we are immersed in the crucible of an intense, novel behavioral context? Imagination fails us because we do not give sufficient weight to many aspects of those situations—the effect of wearing a uniform; the roles we are expected or ordered to perform; the coercive rules that govern behavior; the camaraderie and social support from peers who urge us on; the need to be liked, accepted, and respected by our cohorts and by our superiors who parcel out the system's rewards. Many of these forces taken alone are subtle and common across many daily settings, but when combined and focused on a mission, a task, a target, they are powerful and, in some cases, explode with lethal consequences. This tendency to underestimate the power of external situational forces is typically coupled with the tendency to overestimate the strength of dispositional or personality forces in guiding behavior, a pair of misattributions that has come to be known as the "fundamental attribution error" (Ross 1977).

As social science investigators, we believe that the research evidence presented in this book begins to offer some answers to these provocative and basic questions about the nature and sources of human violence. Our understanding has broadened considerably from the personal knowledge we have gained from our close encounters with this unique set of respondents, along with supplementary information from relevant documents, scholarly reports, conversations with informed colleagues, and viewing police recruit training videos. The transformations in values, attitudes, perceptions, and lifestyles of many of the violence workers described in these pages are clearly the product of a complex network of historical, political, sociological, and psychological processes. Each of our respondents may be viewed as nodal points of these multiple forces acting on them with some commonalities and, depending on their blend, with some unique twists as well.

In this final chapter, our analytical lens focuses on the ways these men experienced the factors that enabled some to move so dramatically across the line between good and evil. We elaborate some of the most critical processes responsible for such transformations, identified in much past research and summarized in earlier chapters for our own interviewees. The relevant transformative processes are organized in this chapter as historical-political, sociological-organizational, and social-psychological. Comparisons are also made between the Brazilian and the Greek cases of atrocity training and socialization to highlight underlying similarities that might prove universal in violence work and also to specify key differences between these two national cases. We use these and other relevant social-psychological studies to reveal the power of situations and structures to dominate individual dispositions and personal morality.

Huggins's research (1998) directs attention to the role that the United States has played formally and informally in facilitating and promoting atrocity and fascist governments. Governments, often military juntas, that came to power by coup d'etat rather than by democratic means often received foreign aid, training, and "technical assistance" from the United States, as long as they espoused anticommunist sentiments during the extended cold war, especially from the 1960s through the 1980s (see also Amnesty International 2001d; Klare and Arnson 1981).

Finally, we conclude that the use of torture and other inhumane practices is widespread today in many nations around the globe. Although authoritarian and totalitarian nations are more likely to engage in such practices with total impunity, torture and other forms of state-supported violence work have come to be seen as basic tools—even in democratic nations' wars on "subversives," "terrorists," "drug lords," "gangs," and common criminals. We reiterate a point illustrated earlier: once atrocity contexts are permitted to function in surreptitious civil or military policing operations, extreme forms of abuse follow predictably.

They usually gain public censure only when they become pervasive, public, and notorious, and even then at personal risk to the dissident opposition.

Formalizing Torture: Comparing Greece and Brazil

This investigation of state-sanctioned police violence during Brazil's military regime received initial insights from Mika Haritos-Fatouros's research (see Gibson and Haritos-Fatouros 1988; Haritos-Fatouros 2002) on Greek military torturers. We wanted to know the extent to which Haritos-Fatouros's findings would be generalizable to other settings; the specialized programs used by the Greek military had transformed ordinary young recruits into torturers in a matter of a few months. We discovered some unique features that characterized the Greek situation while also noting many fundamental similarities between the Greek and Brazilian atrocity systems, including especially the underlying formal processes for shaping violence workers.

As we have explained previously, in the Greek case, interviewees were military and not police. Moreover, Greece had not granted amnesty to known atrocity perpetrators, and many were tried and jailed by the courts. The Greek torturers who were interviewed not long after being publicly exposed for their deeds were perhaps eager to share their stories, in part to exonerate themselves of their evil acts by blaming the system and in part as personal catharsis. In contrast, the general amnesty granted to all former violence workers in Brazil allowed them to maintain positions in the military, police and other institutions. There was little reason for them to share their horror stories with us after having successfully reentered civil society. However, using the rationale and methodology detailed in Chapter 3, we were able to induce some former torturers and executioners to reveal personal information about their roles in repression, although as we have described, some of these men told their tales only by indirection and innuendo, forcing us to further press our efforts to unveil their pasts.

Unlike Haritos-Fatouros's research, which focused exclusively on torturers, ours examined both men who had tortured and those who had killed; they were usually quite different as individuals, but their violence very likely shared many learning, organizational, and situational factors in common even though, as we have argued, each also had its own engendering and maintaining dynamic. In our elaboration of the relevant findings from Haritos-Fatouros's study for understanding our sample of

Brazilian violence workers, we will focus specifically on the Greek torture dynamic's lessons for exposing the roots of atrocity, especially within more formal training situations.

ATROCITY TRAINING

Unique to the Greek case was highly systematized, routinized instruction that came after their graduation from regular military training. Cadets were assigned to units designed to shape them into military policemen and torturers. This journey began for the Greeks, as for the Brazilians, with entry into a special elite unit, which for the Greeks was Kentron Ekpedeyssis Stratiotikis (KESA), the Training Center for Military Police. Ordinary soldiers, typically from more rural and politically conservative backgrounds, were selected for KESA training and entry into the Military Police. But the torture training itself took place in a special prison, with KESA cadets specifically selected for such instruction. Subsequent inclusion in a torture unit automatically enhanced these soldiers' status. They wore distinctive uniforms, held rank over other soldiers with comparable tenure, and enjoyed privileges and resources not usually available to their peers. Being a KESA soldier was an honor.

However, before a recruit could relish that honor, he had to undergo intensive hazing that pushed him to the limits of his physical and psychological endurance. In the first phases of this training, recruits were treated like the enemy—humiliated and brutalized for weeks on end. The extreme hazing suffered by these Greek recruits was mirrored by Militarized Police training in Brazil. Yet whether in Brazil or Greece, such violent treatment desensitized men to pain and suffering, promoted total obedience to authority, engendered acceptance of the system's ideology, and energized their resolve to destroy designated enemies of the state. Hazing also gave a personal reality to the kind of violence that would be acceptable in the recruit's later career. For example, in both Brazil and Greece, trainees had to run the gauntlet, which involved being beaten repeatedly as they were pushed and tugged between two lines of seniors, a technique commonly used by Brazilian atrocity perpetrators themselves in their posttraining violence work. The punishment used against Jorge in the FEBEM orphanage—making him stand for hours while supporting himself by his fingers against a wall, called "the needle," was used in Greek torture training and also employed by Greek and Brazilian atrocity perpetrators in their interrogations of suspected subversives.

Bones of military-period assassination victims unearthed from a shallow grave in Dom Bôsco Cemetery, Perús, São Paulo. Photo by L. C. Leite, *Folha de São Paulo*, September 4, 1990.

SEEKING A FEW "GOOD" MEN

No evidence points to either the Greek or Brazilian torturers having been sadistic or mentally unbalanced from the start. To the contrary, selection procedures eliminated such uncontrollable recruits in favor of ordinary, normal men who could be shaped by the system into any kind of operative the regime needed. The banality of their resulting evil was made vivid during our interview with Jorge—the former DOI/CODI operative in prison for a homicide committed after the amnesty deadline. Jorge must have sensed that we were distressed when he casually mentioned that his murder toll for each of two years was about eighty. We asked if that meant he had personally killed eighty people, "Oh, no," he replied, "eighty *incidents*. I am counting a whole family just once!" He then left the interview room only to return soon with one of his paintings and poems as gifts to each of our female researchers. These presents were meant to reassure us that he was not a brutal monster but a sensitive, creative person who just happened to have had an interlude of murdering men, women, and children.

REFINING ATROCITY

Among Greek and Brazilian recruits, the more sensitive and fragile men were weeded out, leaving the rest to become atrocity perpetrators. Then for the Greek trainees came the general training in torture strategies, tactics, and technologies as well as a gradual phasing into the "art" of effective torture. To start, a recruit would simply watch a torture session. Soon, he would join a small group of torturers, where he would at first be just one of a pair of interrogators at a "tea party." Finally the recruit— whether at the center of the torture group or alone—was charged with obtaining a confession.

We found no comparable torture training organization in the backgrounds of the Brazilian torturers. Most of these men were civil police, who did not receive formal preservice training and very little in-service instruction; we assume that their attitudes and learning outcomes were derived primarily from the on-duty, informal socialization that was described in Chapter 10. Indeed, as with their Greek counterparts, Brazilian torturers' informal socialization was sometimes made mundane by testing on real people. But these could not be bona fide enemies who might have valuable information that might be lost by a novice torturer botching the job. In Brazil, for example, some "pretesting" was done on the poor: "Torture [training]...was practical, with persons used as guinea pigs" in this gruesome learning process. One of the first to introduce this practice into Brazil was U.S. police officer Daniel Mitrione, who "took beggars off the streets and tortured them in classrooms" (Archdiocese of São Paulo 1998: 14; Huggins 1998). Torture became a "scientific method" during the military regime in Brazil and was included in training curricula for certain ranks of military personnel. But as we have just seen, learning how to extract confessions and information was not merely theoretical. The Tortura Nunca Mais human rights record includes an account of a young female student who was obliged to serve as a guinea pig for teaching police torture techniques:

She was stripped naked and subjected to beatings and electric shocks and other torments, such as the "Parrot's Perch." After being taken to her cell, the [woman] was assisted by a doctor and, after a while, was again tortured with exquisite cruelty in a demonstration of how torture should be carried out. (Archdiocese of São Paulo 1998: 14–15)

We have no way of knowing how widespread such training practices were or still are. But we do know that the kinds of atrocity work perfected in the service of such long-past dictatorial regimes as Greece and Brazil are present today throughout the world, even in some democracies.

NATIONAL SECURITY

The national security ideology, largely comparable in both countries, portrayed communists, socialists, leftists, and intellectual liberals as enemies of the state. Yet although blaming these victims was common among both groups of atrocity perpetrators, the Brazilian group also scapegoated disreputable police officials, "bad" victims, and aspects of "deviant" Brazilian culture for their atrocities. The point is that atrocity perpetrators in Brazil and Greece were activated, energized, and excused through abstract blaming of others.

Ordinary Men Doing Evil Deeds

Before summarizing the factors and processes that contributed to creating violence workers in Brazil, focusing especially on the era of the repressive military regime, let us again dismiss the hypothesis that these men were initially different from the normal population. From all that we have seen, the violence workers were quite ordinary, showing no evidence of premorbid personalities that would have predisposed them to such careers. Neither anything we have heard from our respondents nor any other evidence we have reviewed about them suggests the presence of sadistic predispositions in these violence workers prior to their immersion in an atrocity unit. Indeed, to the contrary, where torture was concerned, authorities were likely to redirect those with obviously cruel tendencies out of this work. Likewise, the trainers or supervisors of operations teams (i.e., murderers) sought to mold their recruits into "cool-headed" men who could predictably and dispassionately follow orders. Men who could not be readily controlled by their supervisors—who let their hostile impulses override the detachment necessary for intense field operations or for carrying out prolonged torture sessions—either were not assigned to this work or were transferred from these units. Of course, for such men there was always employment in an informal death squad where their being out of control could always be explained as the act of an abnormal vigilante, albeit one covertly supported by elements of the larger formal system.

The Brazilian system's formal preference for "rational" atrocity workers does not mean that officials did not know about, and did not sometimes even encourage and tolerate, some apparently barbaric atrocity work, as we have seen especially in the case of the informal death squads that operated within Brazil's military and postmilitary police systems. What statements of Brazilian officials suggest is that they did not want to *begin* preparation for atrocity work with someone who was *initially* psychologically uncontrollable or with someone who could not be shaped into a predictable performer of designated atrocity tasks. As one French interrogator said about his nation's torturers during the Algerian War: "Those who got the best results were those who neither got angry nor had pity on their victims" (Book of French torture resurfaces 2000: 6). The practice of effective torture clearly had no place for those whose emotions got in the way of coolly meting out violence, as we saw in the case of Ignácio, who was laughed at and warned by a colleague not to "cry with criminals." The most rational torturers, according to several of our Brazilian interviewees, were those without "character disorders." These men could be shaped into predictable torture functionaries. If in the process of carrying out atrocity work, the violent team or unit spun outside the system—largely by virtue of the autonomy and insularity of the atrocity work process—it does not follow that atrocity groups recruited out-of-control sadists. Group dynamics are more than the sum of their individual parts; there are also emergent phenomena, as social psychology has long demonstrated.

A similar conclusion emerged from research by sociologist John Steiner (see Steiner and Fahrenberg 2000), who analyzed a variety of data on hundreds of Nazi Schutzstaffel (SS) concentration camp guards both before and after their guard duty. Like our own respondents, they showed no prior history of violence, sadism, or abnormal personalities. The only difference found between these guards and a matched comparison group of German soldiers was the guards' higher level of authoritarianism. Interestingly, Steiner's research also revealed that after years of treating prison inmates inhumanely, the guards were subsequently found to be leading the rest of their lives in ways that could best be described as totally normal, without incidents of violence, crime, or physical abuse to others. So again, we are confronted with Hannah Arendt's conclusion (1963) about the nature of Adolph Eichmann's personality, the quintessential commander of battalions of soldiers who engaged in some of the most evil deeds the world has ever known. Eichmann was "terrifyingly normal," so much so that even the psychiatrists who examined him could assert that his personality and demeanor were socially "desirable." Arendt's postscript echoes our own feelings: knowing the enormity of the acts perpetrated by men who appeared so normal is frightening precisely because they could be anyone's son. What they became could not be predicted from knowing what they had been. What they had done could not be imagined by what they were later. They were not monsters whose facial or physical appearance could be readily identified and used to give them special treatment or to avoid or oppose them. Rather, Eichmann, like our violence workers, looked and acted like our neighbor, brother, uncle, son, or father. A frightening thought to be sure!

The title of Christopher Browning's book *Ordinary Men* (1993) refers to the select group of German police who, near the end of World War II, were assigned to murder thousands of Jewish men, women, and children by gunning them down at point-blank range. By all accounts, these cold-blooded murderers were essentially normal at the beginning of their atrocity work. The battalion of men that Browning describes were from a Hamburg reserve police battalion, not trained soldiers at all. Many of them, in fact, initially refused to carry out their officers' search-and-destroy orders: they saw themselves as fathers and grandfathers and too old to fight in their nation's war. Some cried at the thought of executing people; others were emotional at seeing the wholesale murder of innocent families. Yet, over time, as their peers modeled the required repellent behavior—by obeying authority, shooting victims in the head, demonstrating emotional calm—more and more of the reserve police battalion followed suit, going from village to village searching out and destroying their prey. These once ordinary men soon lost their empathy, suppressed their sympathy, and joined comrades in efficiently killing with detached involvement. We have seen that some of the same individual- and group-shaping processes that operated to create these killers also helped to mold our Brazilian police interviewees into violence workers. These normalizing processes eased each of these sets of violence workers across that elusive line between good and evil to do the unthinkable, over and over again.

Multiple Systems for Creating Perpetrators: Interplay and Interdependence

If we cannot rely on personality or abnormal psychology for understanding how so many men become perpetrators of evil, then we must consider the systems that operated on them to facilitate their conversion careers. In earlier chapters we illustrated how a variety of different processes within broader systems played out in the cases of our particular respondents. Now we reorganize these processes within three categories: historical and political, sociological and organizational, and social-psychological. These sometimes work in tandem, sometimes sequentially, and sometimes synchronously, creating the scaffolding that makes other shaping forces work more effectively.

Embedded in historical and emerging political settings, state bureaucracies advocate and carry out their regime's ideological imperatives. They empower authority structures to permit and encourage a variety of organizations to emerge, assisting the various relevant sociological group and organizational mechanisms to operate. In the process, these bureaucratic systems trigger a host of social-psychological variables that shape the values, thoughts, perceptions, and behaviors of functionaries and operatives within each of the systems. Their behaviors have both desirable and undesirable consequences for the actors themselves, for their directors, for their audience, and for their victims in the "theatrical genre" of torture and execution work, as was shown earlier, and as will be retold here.

Historical and Political Influences

Torture and extrajudicial killing in Brazil of course did not begin with the 1964 military coup. These had long been a part of Brazilian history, typically manifested as violent mistreatment of the poor and the politically suspect. Such violence was amplified in the corporatist, semifascist Getulio Vargas political regime and has continued since the end of military rule in the form of murders by police operatives of hundreds of rural, landless poor people and urban street children; summary executions in slum raids; and widespread torture in police stations, prisons, and orphanages—despite the presence of Brazil's formally democratic government. Violence continues to be used in Brazil to control the populace, instill fear, extract labor, and demonstrate the might and authority of the state.

What perhaps stands out about the 1964–1985 military regime, compared with earlier and subsequent governments that sponsored violence against Brazilian citizens, was its extent and intensity—especially against social classes previously spared such violence—and its justification in national security ideology, as well as the development of elaborate supporting organizational structures to more effectively carry out repression.

One need look no further than the accounts of cruel, inhuman, and degrading punishments detailed in *Brasil: Nunca Mais* (Archdiocese of São Paulo 1998) to support this claim. This elaboration of torture and executions during Brazil's military period, made possible by the courageous work of the Catholic Archdiocese of São Paulo, uses the Brazilian military's own court records as its evidentiary source and makes clear that the repressive and murderous practices of Brazil's security forces were part and parcel of national security organization itself. Reviewing and summarizing over a million pages of court documents from over 700 trials, including many fragmentary trial reports, with their testimonies from military officials and police personnel about abductions, torture, and disappearances, the BNM project incriminated hundreds of individuals, as well as the military and police systems they served and in particular the military justice system that provided a legal scaffolding for such crimes against humanity. The report supports the argument that the extent and nature of torture and murder during the military period were extreme enough to qualify as being essentially discontinuous with any prior historical legacy of Brazilian state violence—except, perhaps, for what occurred during 300 years of Brazilian slavery.

The use of torture for interrogation and punishment, though employed by earlier regimes as well, assumed a special status during Brazil's military period. As the Archdiocese of São Paulo report (1998) explains:

Torture was planned and even budgeted for by the police and military agencies charged with interrogating political prisoners. Its efficient execution, moreover, depended on a sophisticated investigative apparatus that included not only adequate sites for carrying out torture [as well as] technologically advanced equipment, but also the direct participation of nurses and doctors who advised torturers in their grisly labors. (33)

During this period, the political foundation supporting violence work in all its myriad forms was rooted in a national security ideology that viewed communists and socialists as subversives who threatened the Brazilian way of life. The military regime did what most repressive governments do: it created enemies of the state who must be identified, searched out, collected in secure settings, interrogated if they might have information of value, tortured if they do not comply, and executed when they are of no further value to the state's mission. In the lives of those who would carry out the state's dirty work, the national security ideology advanced the message that such state violence was necessary and appropriate. Examining how such ideologies come to be socially implanted and facilitate violence, social philosopher Sam Keen (1986), in his analysis of national propaganda images from around the world, makes evident that before a soldier can kill, he must internalize an image of a hated or feared enemy. That image is provided in the psychology of effective propaganda. A national rhetoric projects the widespread presence of secretive enemies to justify repressive actions by government for the good of law-abiding citizens; it establishes the sense of a state under siege. This image was fostered in Brazil's general society via the media and in its military and police academies, as Huggins's research (1998) has demonstrated.

State repression in Brazil was not only ideologically justified but also legally sanctioned and supported operationally by specialized internal security organizations and squads. Once in place, the national security ideology could be used by people of all kinds to motivate, justify, defend, and hide their own ordering, guarding, recording, or medically authorizing and disguising atrocities. These atrocity facilitators included many professionals hired by the regime to pervert their professional ethics, education, and skills in service of the authoritarian state: physicians advised when and how to torture, helped revive unconscious victims for more torture, and signed bogus death certificates; nurses administered harmful drugs; architects designed and engineered the apparatuses of pain and death; notaries falsified records; lawyers legally defended the evil empire. Political ideology, bureaucracy, and the resources for administering rewards and punishments, especially when dominated by charismatic or feared leaders, open a broad umbrella under which once good citizens would be able to do evil deeds without concern for their own or others' contrary moral evaluations.

Sociological and Organizational Influences

Institutional and group processes also played a role in transforming ordinary Brazilian policemen into atrocity perpetrators. First, the military transformed police departments into tightly controlled institutional bureaucracies that could more carefully monitor other security force and citizen conduct. Repression's division of labor then compartmentalized and Taylorized the police process of assault, capture, interrogation, and execution into units of men, each with a specifically dedicated mission. This segmented process allowed violence workers to reshape their consciousness into misrecognizing the moral repulsiveness of their own coercive behavior.

Within this violent assembly line of repression, the probability of being a particular kind of atrocity perpetrator—torturer or murderer—was largely a function of the type of police unit to which a man was assigned. Such assignments were rarely a personal choice but were allotted by chance or by being perceived by officers as "trustworthy" or as having some special talent that would be useful to a particular department or senior staffer. The perpetration of atrocity thus began with assignment to a specialized police organization or squad and was then elaborated with the in-service training that some men in such units received.

ATROCITY PREPARATION: DANGER AND MISTRUST

Both militarized and civil police were taught informally through work socialization to recognize and guard against the ever-present, pervasive danger that had put Brazil in the midst of a national security emergency, but militarized policed learned this in formal training as well. In either force, the anxieties associated with such beliefs nurtured a paranoid, hostile climate in which operatives were taught formally and informally to predict and detect that danger everywhere, not only during their missions but also by estimating their partners' reactions to potential threats. Their lives could be jeopardized by a peer who was too interested in saving his own skin, too insensitive to threats, too slow to react, or simply unprepared to act violently when violence was called for. Socializing police to be mistrustful of one another and of an ever-expanding set of dangerous others created a mind-set in which everyone was under suspicion until proven otherwise. This further contributed to manufacturing and solidifying a pervasive atrocity climate.

Given the prevalence of perceived danger and the resulting mistrust that it produced, operatives needed to learn to be persistent in finding, uncovering, and defanging the enemy—even ones who might appear innocent. There could be no special dispensation for women, the elderly, or children because they could just as readily be subversives as adult men. Such fear-induced resolve painted all suspects with the same broad brush. Not even the tears and screams of torture victims could be trusted as indicators of extreme pain and distress, as several of the Brazilian violence workers asserted with conviction. The atrocity climate allowed no sympathy or compassion. Perpetrators had to learn to suppress their own emotions to enable them to act without feeling. Emotions other than measured amounts of anger and rage were to be distrusted as signs of weakness or potential vulnerabilities.

The work environment of perpetrators further contributed to lowering their thresholds for atrocity. The advocacy of and social rewards for the use of violence and force were both the means and the message of the learning curriculum in this social control setting. Group dynamics were important in powering group support and neutralizing sanctions for a range of violent behaviors that are ordinarily condemned by Brazilian society and its primary religion, Catholicism. As we illustrated in Chapter 10, the emergent norms of special police units enabled the formerly unimaginable to become actualized in daily practice—to degrade, despoil, and destroy human beings, or rather to do so by first rendering them subhuman.

A sense of urgency further contributed to carrying out violent actions without contemplation. In Brazil's war against subversion and crime, victory depended on the speed with which security forces could make captives confess vital information about enemy plans. This speed-driven mind-set was described by one of the generals already quoted: "We all lived in a race against time and against the unknown. Speed was vital to discover and neutralize [terrorist] actions that could cause deaths and great material damage." Such a view obviously reinforced taking risks, making hasty judgments, justifying mistaken identification of enemies as preferable to the error of misjudging a guilty enemy as innocent, and carrying out torture and murder on anyone under suspicion. It legitimated casting a wide net of distrust so as not to allow a single possible subversive to roam freely. The police's violent missions increased solidarity within the squad by establishing pride in the drama of their shared, intense actions for a common cause.

FORMAL TRAINING

Formal training imparted some of the skills that refined atrocities and systemized and shaped attitudes toward police violence. Although we ourselves found no evidence among interviewees' testimonies of a specialized military or police unit dedicated in Brazil to formal instruction in the art of torture, we recall that Jorge reported having been initially prepared to enter a torture unit by watching torture sessions. However, besides such in-service sessions for shaping atrocity outcomes, there was formal, selective preservice training for the militarized police. Although such police were more likely to become murderers than torturers—largely because of the jurisdictional mission of their force—there are elements in their training that could have set a foundation for committing either torture or murder.

Militarized Police preservice training modeled violence as useful and acceptable and fostered a mentality that inured men to their own pain and to the suffering of others. In a secretly filmed video, we saw dramatic violence by trainers against recruits in scene after scene. It was very easy to confuse the police trainees with torture victims themselves: they were humiliated, cursed, slapped, hit, knocked down, and stepped on; they had sand thrown in their faces, were forced to do excruciating exercises, and were pushed to near exhaustion. Each trainee was forced to crawl through a long metal tube filled with a stream of oil, blood, and urine and then was blasted with water from a fire hose as he emerged.

This general training model clearly prepares police to become more effective at carrying out atrocities. Their own threshold for pain is raised to make them less sensitive to the pain they experience or that they inflict on others. There is no room for the "unmasculine" emotions of compassion, caring, concern, or empathy with a victim's plight or pleas. Mindless obedience to authority at whatever cost becomes the primary operating principle. Cognitive dissonance is created from the contrast between the suffering and humiliation experienced at the hands of superiors and the need to respect those superiors and depend on them for survival and promotion. Recognizing that people come to love what they suffer for and then go on to advocate its virtues (Aronson and Mills 1959), it is clear that Militarized Police preservice training set the stage for atrocity, which often manifested itself as quick-fire slaughter of anyone designated as an enemy of the Brazilian state.

INSULARITY

A feature of the daily work climate of repression was the insularity that enveloped violence workers as individuals and as members of atrocity groups. The sense of uniqueness in their nationally directed mission—of repressing and controlling subversion and crime—served to seal police operatives in a tightly wound cocoon. This insularity established the autonomous structure of their police organization, helping to create its performance expectations, nurturing and hiding coercive power, while protecting the atrocity unit from discovery by outsiders. The isolation of individual police units and squads increased the invisibility of the violence system as whole. When solidly in place, this insularity ensured that each man's acts of violence would be indistinguishable from the group's and thus carried out without serious concerns about notoriety, censure, or personal responsibility.

Over time, this insularity spread to protect atrocity perpetrators by shielding them from oversight by legal and religious systems, from the public, from their families, and eventually from their own prior values. Group insularity further ensured control by specialized units over operatives who came to live only for the system with little time for life apart from their unit and its repressive mission. The continuous nature of atrocity work was all-consuming for many of the men we interviewed, straining relationships with family and former friends. Many of these atrocity perpetrators in fact kept their violent work entirely secret from family and nonpolice friends. By rarely talking about what they were doing, these men seem to have stopped thinking about their violence within any abstract or conceptual framework, either legal, moral, or ethical. When that happens, the insularity reaches inside the individual's being, isolating behavior, cognition, and affect from each other. Such mental defenses, when overutilized, often have dysfunctional psychological consequences. For the violence workers we interviewed, these defenses eliminated concerns about moral responsibility for their deeds. Consequently, these deeds could get done routinely and reflexively but not without some personal costs.

MASCULINITY NORMS

Another organizational feature we discovered, which both arose out of the structures of repressive social control and also made these structures work better, is group masculinity. Although Brazil's repressive social control system segmented police tasks and promoted efficient social control through a kind of competitive assembly-line dynamic, nevertheless, within that organizational framework, violence may have also been a product of wider social masculinity expectations and performances. The violence system was powered by men and structured to promote "masculine" forms of power—emphasizing competition, dominance, and control. Atrocity was boosted by normal masculine competition, which was further exaggerated by its functioning within a competitive bureaucracy powered by a climate of war. Violence in general and atrocity in particular may be an inevitable outcome of daily operations in which men are enmeshed within a social control system of specialized internal security units that are in competition with one another for the system's political, economic, and social rewards. Ordinary masculine competitiveness is augmented when demanded by superiors in an elite atrocity unit that insulates actions from negative external consequences.

Within such a secret, clublike atmosphere, norms of highly concentrated masculinity may empower and reward violence as the primary means of demonstrating one's over-the-top maleness to others and to oneself.

Social-Psychological Processes

Ultimately, violence work is carried out by individuals against other individuals. A social-psychological analysis focuses on how individuals respond psychologically to features of their behavioral setting and, in turn, how these mind-sets influence the thoughts, feelings, and actions of others. At this final level, ideology is internalized as a personal set of values and beliefs, training pays its dividends to the system by molding mentalities to do the bidding of superiors, organizational structures guide individual actions, and group strategies get translated into the individual tactics and self-perceptions of violence workers. The transformative processes that helped our ordinary police interviewees become atrocity perpetrators are similar to those that operate in comparable situations where people have engaged in ego-alien deeds. It becomes easier for good people to do evil where (1) previous moral considerations are overridden, (2) blind obedience is mandated, (3) victims are dehumanized, and (4) personal and social accountability are neutralized. In and through each of these processes, moral disengagement is activated.

MORAL TRANSFORMATION

We learn to internalize a positive moral code through the course of socialization by developing personal standards that guide our behavior and deter us from acting inhumanely. These internal standards are followed because they provide a sense of self-satisfaction and self-worth; behavior becomes self-regulated even in the absence of external surveillance or authority controls by means of our own moral compass. Thus, self-sanction and concerns for social approval can reduce inhumane conduct by deterring what are widely considered reprehensible actions. However, these restraints can be removed by minimizing moral conscience and other forms of self-evaluation, a process Bandura (1990a, 1990b) calls moral disengagement. It is possible to uncouple self-regard from one's standards and one's conduct; when that happens, previously good and moral people can behave in ways that they would ordinarily regard as bad and immoral. The mechanisms of moral disengagement then allow extraordinarily aggressive behavior to be enacted by only ordinarily aggressive people or by those who are not aggressive at all. The moral disengagement process that enabled our Brazilian policemen to become atrocity perpetrators changed and distorted their perceptions of reprehensible conduct, of their victims' humanity, of the negative consequences for behavior, and of the locus and identification of responsibility.

BLIND OBEDIENCE

Every authoritarian system hinges on total, unquestioning obedience. Coercive rules and imposed roles prescribe and limit the behavioral options of the system's operatives. At every level in social and political hierarchies, obedience to superiors is demanded of subordinates, with subordinates in turn demanding it of those beneath them. Such obedience greases the machinery of top-down operations and allows functionaries to perform their actions without any feelings of responsibility, another example of moral disengagement. The hierarchy of authority and of tasks obviates individual decision-making and therefore individual responsibility for action. Each operative is only following orders and only carrying out a small part of the total operation in any case.

Orders need not even be explicitly stated; they can be implicitly communicated by superiors and assumed by followers—a process that at the very least allows leaders to have plausible deniability about their subordinates' actions. Recall the episode when Jorge—as a recent graduate from Militarized Police preservice training—was on guard duty with a buddy in a cemetery. When they spied a strange-looking apparition coming out of the cemetery, Jorge's buddy panicked and began shooting. Upon realizing that the apparition was a religious Candomblé procession, Jorge ran to report the incident to his superiors. He assumed that there would be trouble if the public and media found out about the mass shooting, and he wanted his superiors to view the atrocity scene. As soon as his superior got to the scene, without a word, he took his gun and handed it to his lieutenant, who clicked off the safety and passed it to the sergeant, who in turn gave it to Jorge. Jorge then shot point-blank into the heads of each of the half dozen or so wounded Candomblé devotees. After completing this implicitly ordered task, Jorge passed the weapon back up the line of authority. The officers could now go on their way without worrying that they had directly ordered Jorge to shoot but knowing that in the future he would very likely follow any and all of their orders to kill.

One of the most dramatic laboratory demonstrations of the power of situational forces to overcome dispositional tendencies is Stanley Milgram's paradigmatic staging of obedience to authority (1974). Could ordinary North Americans behave as mindlessly as so many ordinary Germans had under Hitler's rule by inflicting grave harm on an innocent victim just because an authority figure told them to do so? Milgram created a laboratory-controlled authority setting where naive subjects (the "teachers"—male college students at Yale) were led to believe that they were helping another person (the "learner") improve memory by punishing that person's learning errors. Each participant teacher was told that his punishment of a learner had to be swift and follow a strict pattern of gradual escalation. He was to press buttons on a shock apparatus that allegedly delivered a jolt from mild (15 volts) to dangerous (450 volts) every time his learner made an error. The learner (an experimental confederate) was strapped to his "electric chair" in an adjacent room, where his acted-out reactions could be heard by the teacher over an intercom. As the mock learner's errors mounted, the teacher had to administer what he was told would be increasingly painful levels of shock until the learner could accurately recall a list of words. Because the learner was instructed to never master this list, the teacher had to increase the intensity of the ersatz shocks, with the learner giving off louder and more persistent groans and screams each time.

When the teacher became concerned about the pain being expressed over the intercom and questioned whether the experiment should continue, the authority figure—dressed in a white laboratory coat—insisted that the teacher follow the rules, honor the verbal contract, and continue the teaching task. When the supposed shock level exceeded 375 volts, the learner screamed and a loud thud—like a body hitting the floor—could be heard over the intercom. After that, no sounds came from the learner's chamber. At this point, most of the teachers expressed dismay, but the authority figure warned that failure to continue the learning task would jeopardize the experiment and result in the teacher's own punishment. When the teacher demanded to know who would be responsible if something bad happened to the learner, the authority figure replied that he would assume full responsibility. In the vast majority of cases, the teacher continued with the experiment—escalating the shocks administered to the now apparently unconscious victim.

Who would go all the way on the shock scale and deliver the highest, perhaps even lethal, level of shocks to a learner who had ceased to even respond to the teacher's questions? What kind of person would risk harming someone already unconscious and maybe even dead? When Milgram invited forty psychiatrists to offer their estimate of the likelihood of someone's going to the maximum shock level, their average estimate was that less than 1 percent of experimental subjects would do this—only sadists would engage in such behavior, they believed. In fact, at Yale, a whopping 65 percent—nearly two-thirds—of his participants went all the way—believing that they were shocking their subjects to the maximum! Although all participants asserted that they could not harm innocent people, few went as far as to challenge or disobey authority and totally refuse to continue the experiment. Virtually all dissented verbally but obeyed behaviorally.

In nineteen subsequent studies, Milgram replicated the paradigm using about 1,000 U.S. participants from all walks of life, educational backgrounds, ages, and genders. In each replication, he varied one aspect of the situation to see if obedience levels would change with such manipulations. Milgram's experimental variations revealed the power of situational and environmental forces to shape behavioral obedience (Blass 2000). In some replications, the teacher's obedience level could be pushed to 90 percent, whereas in others, it fell to 10 percent just by changing a particular authority aspect of the experimental setting. Maximum compliance occurred where the teacher watched another peer carry out (model) the expected behavior—as when Jacob observed his glamorous civil policeman cousin as a guide for how to behave in violent conflicts.

In Milgram's experiments, most teachers refused to shock at all when the students themselves insisted that they be given a shock. After all, they did not consider themselves sadists who would indulge another's masochistic desires. This kind of assertion by a teacher, suggesting the necessity of his ultimately controlling the emotional dynamic of a torture situation, can be seen among our interviewees, although in reverse, by the Brazilian violence workers who asserted that their victims could have avoided torture if they had just cooperated in the right way with the police interrogator. Both kinds of assertions point to the interactive, controlled, and interpersonal nature of torture environments, a system that in its operation is much more than the sum of its parts.

The failure of psychiatrists to predict accurately the outcome of Milgram's powerful demonstrations is an example of the fundamental attribution error (Ross 1977). Individualistic cultures typically focus on the actor and disregard the behavioral features of the setting: effects are thus attributed to the actor's personal characteristics. The training of psychiatrists, like that of many other medical-model professionals, focuses their scientific and clinical gaze on problems within individual psyches and away from environmental determinants of behavior. A public health orientation, by contrast, seeks environmental vectors that shape individual pathologies.

Many features of Milgram's paradigm are worth mentioning in connection with our Brazilian violence workers, but one interesting parallel is the gradual escalation of harm in both cases. Milgram arranged this by offering an individual the apparent ability to produce increasingly higher shock levels. Likewise, the training procedures experienced by some Brazilian violence workers relied on a gradual escalation of violence and a systematic and increasing desensitization to the brutality they were administering. In a more informal socialization setting, some interviewees reported going on missions first as observers not directly involved in atrocity and graduating to more lethal levels of involvement after that. In a parallel to this progressive desensitization, U.S. soldiers were prepared for bayoneting the enemy in hand-to-hand combat during World War II by having them first practice their moves on straw-filled dummies decorated to look like enemy soldiers. Next, the trainees practiced ripping into animal carcasses as blood and internal organs spilled out.

A primary mechanism in Brazil for implanting obedience to authority was the formal pre- and in-service training given to militarized police. Such training was said to eliminate those with "fragile spirits." It focused on shaping men to display strength and fortitude—new values that would supersede all former moral and behavioral codes. The extreme forms of physical punishment experienced by trainees were described as "attracting a man's will to fight." Men were challenged to "look for their limits" when as trainees they were "sent to the woods" to be brutally beaten by officers. The repeated exposure of these survivors to psychological and physical abuse increased their tolerance for these states. Having learned how to survive their own violent police training, these men developed psychic numbing against others' suffering and death. We have characterized this process as disconnecting traditional masculinities.

In addition to developing new values and anti-empathetic numbing, a key to being an effective Civil Police torturer was to have a sufficiently high degree of personal and emotional control. The good torturer had to be aware of the specific objective of each torture session; his selection of appropriate forms and levels of torture had to be guided by a recognized formula involving a calculus of making victims suffer sufficiently to confess while not causing permanent injuries or premature death. The personal qualities necessary for effective torture were ones that superiors and fellow police could apparently recognize, appreciate, and reward. At the very least, officers plucked men out of a "torture track" if they demonstrated an inability to be rational, controlled, and cool. At the same time, the civil policeman who demonstrated appropriate levels of self-control could, through informal socialization, become more coolly calculating when administering pain and be guided on how to get over his own uneasiness about victims' pain and suffering.

DEHUMANIZING VICTIMS

We noted earlier the roles of dehumanization and blaming in the kinds of moral disengagement that reduce a person's perception of the negative consequences of their behavior. Most of us feel no compunction about swatting away an annoying insect. When people are viewed in the same fashion—as less than human—restraints are lifted or suspended on what is permissible to do to them. We act in self-interest, without concern for either their feelings or lives, without concern for any societal sanctions. Those who are morally wrong or are only "animals" do not deserve humane treatment as humans.

Euphemistic labeling, which involves semantic distortions and word-play that makes evil deeds innocuous or even seem worthy, erases the humanity of victims. The personhood of the victims is obscured when their murder is disguised as an "elimination" or "disappearance." A victim loses any presence at all when described as a "contract that is fulfilled." There are no bleeding, maimed, or dead people where mass murder is hygienically sanitized as "ethnic cleansing," where bombing is portrayed as a "clean, surgical strike" with only "collateral damage." This euphemistic bureaucratese either eliminates victims altogether or casts them as a disease or other pollutant to be removed from the body politic. The executioners who rationally carry this out without questioning are an organization's team players.

Hitler's propaganda machine delivered a message to Germans in films and posters that Jews and anti-Nazis were less than human: Jews were depicted as vermin eating away at the granary of the nation's resources and communists as insanely destructive. In Brazil, potential victims of the state were dehumanized by being characterized as something to fear—"subversives," "terrorists," and "communist guerrillas." As such, they needed not be accorded any of the respect and dignity that normally is supposed to govern human relationships. This socially constructed image very likely helps to explain the ability of lower-status police during the military period to commit violence against higher-status political dissidents. General social prejudices add to the effectiveness of dehumanization with their stereotyped conceptions and negative labels for a marginalized or despised group, even becoming part of the vocabulary of the society: people still warn each other, "don't get gypped," unaware that this turn of phrase derogates Gypsies. Labeling an individual or a group in a way that dehumanizes them can result in horrendous consequences when the political and organizational situation gives permission for violence.

This process has been demonstrated in a controlled laboratory study in which college students believed that they were trying to help a group of students from another school by punishing them whenever they made errors in their alleged learning task (Bandura, Underwood, and Fromson 1975). The punishments took the form of escalating levels of allegedly painful shocks administered by each innocent participant to one of the male "students" in an adjoining "learning" room. Depictions of the students to be shocked were manipulated by having those who were administering the fake electrical shocks overhear a research assistant say either that the other school's student "seems like a nice guy," "seems like an animal," or nothing at all.

With no more information than these observations and having no personal contact with their potential victims, the college students adjusted their mock electric current to significantly higher levels for those labeled "animals" than for those whose likeability status was unspecified. Humanizing the victims by depicting them as nice guys was associated with significantly lower levels of punishment. In contrast, once the dehumanized victims had received a higher level of shock, the punishment levels given by the teacher significantly escalated with each wrong answer. The authors concluded that "dehumanization fostered self-absolving justifications that were in turn associated with increased punitiveness" (Bandura, Underwood, and Fromson 1975: 253). These results demonstrate the disinhibiting power on aggressive behavior of labels that divest people of human qualities. This seems to be the case even without the added force of external justifications or preexisting, obviously negative attitudes toward the social position of potential victims.

As our Brazilian case study illustrates, one way that agents of aggression can exonerate themselves for the consequences of their actions is by blaming their victims or by pointing to negative causative environmental or cultural circumstances. For example, some victims of perpetrators' moral disengagement were seen as having brought their suffering on themselves by not doing what they were told to do. As social-psychologists point out, when those present see victims suffer maltreatment for which they themselves are totally or partly to blame, they tend to derogate the victims (Lerner 1980). Having devalued the victim and indignant at his or her ascribed culpability, the perpetrators feel moral justification for even greater maltreatment. It is thus easy to blame the poor for their poverty, the mentally ill for not trying to get better, and subversives for bringing down the wrath of the state on their heads. In the end, violence workers can feel self-righteous about having carried out their "worthy" deeds against inhuman or unworthy adversaries. In this instance, the perpetrator does not deny his own values at all but accuses the victim of having the wrong values: "If she had only confessed, she could have spared herself being tortured" were the desensitized words of one Brazilian violence worker.

NEUTRALIZING ACCOUNTABILITY

Conditions that allow individuals to feel a sense of anonymity—"no one knows who I am" and "no one cares what I do"—result in what social-psychologists call "deindividuation" (See Zimbardo 1970, Diener 1979). This can lower normal personal and social concerns about carrying out atrocity and thus reduce responsibility for such action. Self-sanctions can be neutralized by anything that induces a present-oriented focus— alcohol and drugs, intense emotional and physical involvement in the violent act itself, or shared excitement in intense team activities. All of these processes help to deindividuate participants through the sense of anonymity that they help to create.

Under conditions of anonymity, behavioral restraints are lifted; the actor then may behave in response to immediate situational forces and suspend cognitive processes of evaluation. Behavior is no longer guided by a previously rational cost-benefit analysis because past and future personal references have become distant and insignificant; it becomes locked in an expanded present time zone and is situationally determined by immediate feelings and perceptions and by what others at that moment are doing and encouraging. It is as if the usual cognitive controls on behavior—especially those involving planning and its imagined consequences or promises as well as the existing codes of moral and legal conduct—

have been blocked out or suspended. In place of these conventional, ha-bitual tendencies and restraints, we find an individual dominated by proximal demands and personal urgencies. His behavior, being anony-mous, is rendered invisible to himself and others. This violent actor is submerged in groups, acting in the dark, wearing a uniform, mask, hood, or painted face. Under such circumstances, responsibility for ac-tion is minimized: we are not socially accountable if unidentifiable.

How anonymity in the group nurtures the ability to carry out vio-lence was illustrated when choirboys stranded on a desert island in Wil-liam Golding's *Lord of the Flies* (1959) were able to kill pigs for food and thus survive only after changing their appearance by painting their faces. Much previous research supports our view that the anonymity experi-enced among Brazilian violence workers—derived from a variety of in-puts into their work and daily lives—had the effect of facilitating the ex-treme atrocities they carried out. The Brazilian police were almost always in a group, often acting in the dark, sometimes in a common uni-form, and sometimes masked or hooded. These props in the theater of repression helped to produce the deindividuating anonymity for Brazil-ian violence workers that assisted their carrying out horrific duties. Taken together, all four processes that we have covered in the previous pages—creating new moralities, instilling blind obedience, dehumaniz-ing victims, and neutralizing personal and social responsibility for vio-lence—are central to creating moral disengagement.

MORAL DISENGAGEMENT

The hypothesis that altering external appearance can help modify internal restraints and disengage responsibility for violence by liberating behavior from learned controls was scientifically demonstrated in an experiment with college women who were assigned to administer apparently painful (actually nonexistent) "shocks" to other women (Zimbardo 1970). Those female participants who had been made to feel anonymous were twice as aggressive in their behavior as women who were made to feel identifi-able. The relationship between being anonymous in appearance and be-ing able to engage in ordinarily taboo acts of violence has been shown to have cross-cultural connections as well. It is easier to get men to harm and kill other men in warfare when the killers disguise their appearance and step out of their usual persona. And this phenomenon is not limited to people in Western cultures. For example, a cross-cultural investigation using data from the *Human Relations Area Files* identified twenty-three separate cultures for which two bits of information were available: whether warriors changed their appearance before going into battle and how they treated the enemy. Eighty percent of the cultures where warriors altered how they looked before battle were also very likely to torture, mutilate, and kill their victims. Only 12 percent of the warriors who went into battle with an unchanged appearance carried out such extreme violence (Watson 1973). Although Watson did not discuss the relevance of body ornamentation and violence to masculinity presentations, we wonder whether a warrior's painting and decorating his body also nurtured violence through hypermasculinization of his persona. This appeared to be the case for some of our atrocity perpetrators.

In any case, Jorge reported that he felt safer because his murder team went to great lengths to ensure its members' anonymity. He told us that on raids the squad members made themselves indistinguishable from one another by calling each another "Pompeu." They were like the people from Pompeii, whom no one could identify from their ashes. Jorge, who was switched from a torture unit to an execution squad, pointed to another layer of anonymity when he explained what he liked best about that new role: Jorge the executioner could just put a hood over his head—or over that of his victim—and eliminate his enemy as part of business as usual, unlike Jorge the torturer, who had to establish some sort of personal involvement with the victim. The consequences of such moral disengagement is a diffusion of responsibility for violence: "You act; they take the hit if there is trouble." This kind of mentality frees up inhibitions about getting caught, about being exposed, and removes morality from the grip of self-regulatory controls. Recall our earlier analysis of the factors that combined to grant violence workers a clear conscience about their conduct. Central to their not recognizing personal responsibility was that such conduct was supported, assisted, and bolstered by an array of legitimate facilitators: prison guards, doctors, nurses, notaries, and a cast of occupational and political superiors. Then, by subdividing even the violence work itself into a variety of tasks performed by individuals taking certain roles, each actor could fail to recognize his own personal responsibility for the outcomes. Responsibility for atrocity was dissipated like a drop of poison in the sea. Immoral conduct and moral standards could exist side by side but in compartments that were psychologically impermeable.

The success of the Brazilian violence workers' moral disengagement from conventional values was illustrated earlier in Chapter 11: only one of the direct perpetrators of atrocity actually confessed openly to his crimes against humanity, but largely without attributing his atrocities to a higher moral cause. The other thirteen diffused responsibility onto victims, a few "bad" perpetrators, and professional mandates, with only four actually appealing to the "higher" moral value of national security to justify their past atrocities. The important lesson is not that atrocity is always justified by a higher moral cause but that politically such a cause needs to exist to provide the energy and moral background for atrocities, even though those carrying them out may cite more proximate ideological values and themes.

NEGATIVE CONSEQUENCES: JOB BURNOUT

Sometimes work makes those who do it into something they were not before. The nature of violent police work—sanctioned, rewarded, and repeatedly practiced—often came back to torture the Brazilian policemen who did it. Cardinal Arns (Archdiocese of São Paulo 1998: xxvii) of São Paulo recognizes this when he repeats a Brazilian general's observation that "whoever tortures once becomes changed as a result of the demoralization he has inflicted upon others. Whoever repeats torture four or more times becomes a beast." But Arns and the general may be wrong in declaring that inevitably this "torturer feels such physical and emotional pleasure that he is capable of torturing even the frailest members of his own family"! Some of those to whom this general refers were unable to sustain the necessary engagement with their horrendous work despite the many forms of insularity and the moral disengagement that were available to them. These violence workers experienced job burnout, a syndrome of emotional exhaustion, cynicism, and reduced efficacy that grows much more from excessive and inappropriate situational demands on workers than from the workers' personal weaknesses or dysfunctionality. Maslach and Leiter (1997) and Schaufeli, Maslach, and Marek (1993) describe burnout as a mismatch between worker and the work situation along six dimensions: work overload, lack of control, insufficient rewards, breakdown of community, absence of fairness, and conflicting values. These combined in a number of ways among Brazilian violence workers to produce the greatest burnout among torturers and slightly less burnout among the less personally involved executioners.

The violence workers among our interviewees who experienced the greatest burnout felt used and abused by the system and came to realize that they had given up so much of their personal and professional lives to their endlessly demanding jobs without adequate recognition or reward. Their marriages suffered, as did their relationships with their children and friends. Psychosomatic symptoms plagued their health, as did chronic fatigue and insomnia. They manifested ample use of such ultimately damaging ego-defense mechanisms as rationalization, denial, and compartmentalization. By presenting these findings, we do not advocate sympathy for the sad plight of torturers and murderers; rather, we are documenting the old aphorism that what goes around, comes around. Violence work can impair atrocity perpetrators, just as their violence destroys the lives of their victims—although not to the same extent and certainly not with the same moral, ethical, or legal implications.

The Stanford Prison Experiment: Parallels with Brazil

Many of the processes that have been described so far were powerfully illustrated in the Stanford Prison Experiment (Zimbardo, Haney, Banks, and Jaffe 1973). Although controlled social-psychological laboratory experiments can never fully portray the realities of real-world violence settings, they can offer parallels that highlight the operation of relevant dynamic processes. Although analyses of the Stanford Prison Experiment have focused on the social-psychological variables involved in transforming healthy, normal, young male research participants into pathological prisoners or guards, from the new perspective provided by our study of Brazilian atrocity workers, a more interesting analytical focus emerges. Although much of the Stanford Prison Experiment deals with the direct perpetrators as the central point of reference, it can now be argued that they are but actors in a larger drama that includes directors, producers, and audiences, without whom the drama would lose its intensity and perhaps even its significance.

The actions of perpetrators of atrocity are encouraged and validated by three sets of facilitators: (1) international governments and their representatives, along with the international corporations that supply atrocity technologies and resources; (2) national governments that provide the ideology, the cast of auxiliary actors, and the system of rewards and sanctions as well as the legal and financial structure that supports and excuses atrocity; and (3) bystander communities, both in the perpetrators' society and in the broader world, who watch the play unfold in silence.

It is as if the international level were the executive producer; the national level, the director and playwright; and the bystander community, the audiences that sees, hears, and applauds or remains silent. Each of these constituencies plays a vital role in the final product—giving the play its thematic structure; providing the sets, costumes, casting, and motivations for the actors; and creating community support or indifference. The perpetrators are but the smallest unit in this drama, much like the actors in a repertory company; to appreciate what they do requires understanding the contributions of each of the larger components of the system that contains and creates their identities. Let us briefly review the Stanford Prison Experiment and then illustrate how facilitator and perpetrator roles interacted and reinforced one another.

In the Stanford Prison Experiment, "good" young men were put in a bad place—a prisonlike setting—to determine if dispositions or the situation would win in the confrontation between two institutionally structured role relationships. College student volunteers—who were assessed to be normal on the basis of a battery of psychological tests, clinical interviews, and background reports—were randomly assigned to play the role of either prisoner or prison guard. The students who had been randomly assigned as guards were in no way different from the prisoners at the start of the experiment. However, the complementary institutional roles of each set of participants led to totally contrasting behaviors by the end of the experiment.

Those to be prisoners were arrested by the city police at their homes or dormitories in a series of surprise raids. The prisoners were then booked at the police station for various felonies and put in a detention cell. Later they were transported to a mock prison in the basement of the building housing Stanford University's psychology department, where they were issued a uniform and given rules developed by the guards that they were required to learn and follow. They experienced a variety of degradation rituals typical of such institutionalized settings as fraternities, secret clubs, prisons, and the military. The prisoners lived in their cells and performed duties in the "prison yard" day and night with no respite. The guards, however, worked eight-hour shifts, returning home afterward. Interestingly, although neither group was given instructions on how to act, each group soon began to get into their roles stereotypically—probably in part on the basis of movies and books about prison life and in part from a basic understanding of what it means to be a guard or a prisoner. But as our analysis of the interaction of facilitator and perpetrator roles will illustrate, this interaction itself also generated definitions of the behavior considered situationally appropriate for prisoners and guards.

The Stanford Prison Experiment was designed to run for two weeks, but it had to be terminated after only six days: the simulated

prison had become too real. Within a matter of days, the guards became authoritarian and even sadistic in some cases, while the prisoners
became passive and totally submissive. The prisoners—young men
chosen for their normality and good health—were having such extreme stress reactions that five of them had to be released prematurely,
the first one after only thirty-six hours. Their peers, who were acting
out the roles of guards, had become so dominated by their own potential power, use of arbitrary rules, and escalating levels of aggression
that they felt limited by the constraints of the prison superintendent's
(Zimbardo's) demands not to use physical violence against the inmates.

The guards dehumanized prisoners in many ways through punishment and harassment. During the long night shifts, guards relieved their
boredom by tormenting prisoners whom they treated as playthings.
Some of the young men began to act sadistically toward the prisoners,
taking apparent pleasure in their own inventive cruelty. As processes of
deindividuation, dehumanization, and moral disengagement unfolded,
it no longer mattered to the guards that they were just in an experiment
with other college boys who had been randomly assigned to play prisoner. In the end, the guards perceived the prisoners as dangerous—so
much so that they decided some needed to be kept chained or in solitary
confinement for longer than the maximum allowable duration while
torturing other prisoners to keep them in line or force them to obey
their authority. Some guards felt they were in a real prison, albeit run by
psychologists rather than by the state. The distortions of reality was so
extreme that prisoners forgot they could say, "I quit this experiment."
Instead, they worked within the confines of the system and only requested parole, which was denied.

The results of the Stanford Prison Experiment, when combined with
those of Milgram's, Bandura's, and other related experiments, point to a
psychology of evil in which ordinary, even above-average men and
women can harm and degrade totally innocent people. These studies
suggest that a situational power can induce good people to behave in
ways that violate their preexisting moral and ethical standards (Zimbardo, Maslach, and Haney 2000). We have used this research as an analytical backdrop for the transformations of Brazilian policemen into
brutal torturers and murderers. Now we wish to recast even further the
Stanford Prison Experiment's examination of obedience to authority,
using that study to illustrate similarities with Brazilian atrocity through
our model that places atrocity actors on a broad stage with many different facilitators.

Setting the Stage for Violence

Science represents the international level of facilitation with its quest for objective knowledge using experimental paradigms and approved analytical tools for evaluating the validity of the obtained data. The national level of facilitation comes in the form of a local institution, in this case, Stanford University and its psychology department. They are background facilitators that sanctioned the research and lent institutional credibility to its researchers and to the research itself; they provided the physical space for the mock prison and the technicians to help construct it. The principal experimenter and his research associates, who designed the study and planned the details of its execution and analysis, represented more direct facilitators. But within the context of the experiment itself, the principal investigator also played the role of prison superintendent, a tactical error that confused the dispassionate scientist-researcher with the passionate prison official who was concerned primarily with maintaining the functioning of his institution. Lending credibility to the legitimacy of the experiment and creating confusion in the minds of prisoners and guards alike were the many auxiliary facilitators whose very presence imparted a mundane realism to this artificial experience and setting.

These active and bystander facilitators came in a host of forms. The city police arrested students assigned the prisoner role using the same tactics and procedures as would be employed with real criminals. The city police backing for the experiment lent authority to the surprise arrest. Having these arrests recorded by a local TV station photographer as shocked neighbors watched nurtured the reality of this illusion even further.

Other bystander facilitators came in a host of forms. A Catholic priest interviewed the prisoners in the presence of the guards, heard their complaints, saw one break down and cry, and went away telling them that they needed to get a lawyer if they wanted to be released. A "public defender" took accounts of abuse from prisoners and told them he would consider deciding on their case in a few days. Parents and friends visited during planned visiting hours and, despite the ragged appearance of their sons or buddies, did nothing to force their release. A "parole board" heard their pleas and sided with the guards and the parole board "chief," an ex-convict himself. The parole board consisted of a variety of people not connected with the study in any direct way—secretaries and graduate students—and was not under the authority of either the principal investigator or the prison superintendent. In addition, many psychologists came to view the experiment and also did not challenge its premises. Finally, the extremely abusive, even sadistic behavior of some guards was typically supported by at least one other guard on that same shift. Although the good guards never openly challenged the bad guards—and never even complained to the authorities about their colleagues' violations of prison rules—these good guards also never left early or arrived late for their shift. They seemed content to be liked by the inmates and enjoyed the positive comparison between themselves and the bad guards, a phenomenon we pointed out for Brazilian violence workers as well (see Chapter 8).

It becomes evident that the actions of the atrocity perpetrators in the Stanford Prison Experiment must be appreciated within the concentric contexts created, provided, and maintained by the many direct and auxiliary facilitators. The same is absolutely the case among Brazil's atrocity perpetrators, whose solitary actions were always embedded in and circumscribed by legions of facilitators operating at the multiple levels outlined previously.

Human Rights and Wrongs

Annual reports by Amnesty International and the United Nations make evident the pervasiveness of torture and other forms of inhuman and degrading treatment of citizens by state-linked security forces throughout the world. A recent news release by the international secretariat of Amnesty International (2001c) summarized its global survey on torture: over 150 countries were identified as practicing torture or ill treatment by state agents, with more than 70 having widespread torture. Furthermore, "most victims of torture by state agents are criminal suspects from the poorest or most marginalized sectors of society. Most of their torturers are police officers" (Amnesty International 2001a). The Amnesty International report asserts that torture could be stopped but that governments continue to ignore the practices of their security agencies. In its call to action, Amnesty International concludes that only public pressure can force governments to stop torture. The organization aims "to turn public indifference into outrage, and outrage into action."

Similarly, Forrest's collection (1999) of reports on torture worldwide reveals the insidiousness of torture primarily to control dangerous "aliens" and threatening "subversives." Armed with an all-purpose ideology of preserving the security and integrity of religion, nation, way of life, an economic system, or family values, governments go to "war" to ensure that these abstract ideals will not be tarnished at the hands of the enemy.

Abuses become common especially where the facilitating conditions that we have previously identified are present—a sense of emergency, dehumanization of enemies, victim blaming, secret operations without external oversight or review, perpetrator anonymity, and overall moral disengagement. Dictatorships embrace these conditions more explicitly than democracies because they need have less concern about citizen opposition. Democracies have to be more controlled and secret in their violence work so as not to raise the ire of opposing political parties or citizen watchdog groups. Democracies must hope that citizens will not believe that torture occurs, that the media will not disclose torture, that the police will not investigate allegations of it, and that lawyers and the courts will not press charges against those who commit torture yet will accept evidence from its use in securing confessions. It has been said that the nearly universal lack of accountability for torture makes it the perfect crime in most societies.

Indeed, atrocities abound—whether in authoritarian, democratizing, or democratic countries. Israeli soldiers beat Palestinian men. Palestinian police torture Israeli citizens. British "peacekeeper" police in Northern Ireland torture Catholic suspects. Chicago police brutally abuse murder suspects with burns and electric shocks. These are just a few of the recent cases of torture and inhuman treatment documented by journalist John Conroy in *Unspeakable Acts, Ordinary People* (2000). Conroy argues that torturers act out the will of the larger community in suppressing its foes; this community of citizens ignores, minimizes, and tolerates the torturer's evil deeds. Conroy endorses another primary finding of our research, that men who engage in extraordinarily evil deeds are not monsters, even though their actions are monstrous. These men are able to rationalize their unspeakable acts by functioning within a subsystem that provides appropriate positive supports, justifications, and sanctions. Their normality and ordinariness is so unsettling because they seem so much like any one of us yet they have done, and still do, things we want to believe are unimaginable acts for us ever to commit.

Like Conroy, the authors of the present study believe that a society's failure to challenge human rights abuses offers support for such conduct. Nonintervention against evil in one society, or in the world at large, sustains abusers and maintains their abuses: "Throughout history, it has been the inaction of those who could have acted, the indifference of those who should have known better, the silence of the voice of justice when it mattered most that has made it possible for evil to triumph," proclaimed Ethiopian Emperor Haile Selassie in 1963 at the U.N. General Assembly opening. That powerful assertion is no less true today.

As social scientists, we tried hard to preserve our mantle of objectivity and professional detachment during the discovery phase of this investigation. And we strove to be fair and evenhanded in reporting our findings to the extent that it was possible for us to do so. But now, as citizens, we feel obligated to move into an advocacy role: knowing how perpetrators of violence are made does not excuse their violence, and understanding the situational determinants of atrocity work in Brazil, in Greece, and elsewhere does not absolve atrocity workers from moral condemnation for violating human rights. It is a moral imperative to use the kind of knowledge that our research has generated to help fuel concerted action against further violence work. Our work and that of our colleagues makes clear that anyone could become a torturer or an executioner under a set of quite well-known conditions. Therefore, we must collectively strive to first expose these sociopolitical conditions wherever they appear and then to join others in denouncing and challenging them.

Evil of the kind documented in this book must be recognized and treated as a public health problem—as a social and political illness that can escalate into an epidemic. Prevention of its spread begins with public inoculations through information about its causes, prevalence, and vectors of transmission. Prevention requires vigilant media, nongovernmental and governmental human rights monitoring organizations, legal systems, and legislatures all willing to systematically monitor, expose, and condemn human rights abuses. If we allow the deeds of human rights abusers to go unchallenged and unpunished, we are all responsible for the evils they commit. Ultimately, therefore, supporting, engaging in, and justifying violence work is a personal and moral decision. It cannot be explained away as only the result of special training, bureaucratic systems, ideological imperatives, or social situational forces. Alexander Solzhenitsyn (1974), a prisoner of Soviet repression in the camps of the Gulag Archipelago, locates the origin of evil within the human heart. He tells that the line between good and evil should not be traced through states, classes, or political parties but rather passes through each and every one of us. Thus, the decision to engage in evil is essentially one that each human must make—to become a perpetrator or to resist powerful situational pressures and choose the path of goodness.

References

Adler, C., and K. Polk
    1996 "Masculinity and child homicide." In *Masculinities, social relations, and crime*. Spec. issue of *British Journal of Criminology* 36 (3), pp. 396–411.

Alencar, Frei Tito de
    1969 Letter from a Brazilian jail. Senator James Abourezk Papers, Richardson Archives. I. D. Weeks Library. University of South Dakota, Vermillion.

Alves, M. H.
    1985 *State and opposition in military Brazil*. Austin: University of Texas Press.

Amnesty International
    1984 *Torture in the eighties*. London: Amnesty International.
    2001a http://www.stoptorture.org. MDE 0/006/2000. January 22.
    2001b *Brazil: Commentary on Brazil's first report to the UN Committee Against Torture*. AMR 19/016/2001.
    2001c News release issued by the International Secretariat of Amnesty International. January 22.
    2001d *Stopping the torture trade*. London: AI Publications.

Arendt, Hannah
    1951 *The origins of totalitarianism*. New York: Harcourt, Brace.
    1963 *Eichmann in Jerusalem: A report on the banality of evil*. New York: Viking Press.

Archdiocese of São Paulo
    1998 *Torture in Brazil*. New York: Vintage.

Aronson, E., and J. Mills
    1959 The effect of severity of initiation on liking for a group. *Journal of Abnormal and Social Psychology* 59, pp. 177–181.

Bandura, Albert

1990a "Mechanisms of moral disengagement." In *Origins of terrorism: Psychologies, ideologies, theologies, states of mind,* edited by W. Reich. New York: Cambridge University Press.

1990b Selective activation and disengagement of moral control. *Journal of Social Issues* 46 (1), pp. 27–46.

1999 Moral disengagement in the perpetration of inhumanities. *Personality and Social Psychology Review* 3 (3), pp. 193–209.

Bandura, A., B. Underwood, and M. F. Fromson

1975 Disinhibition of aggression through diffusion of responsibility and dehumanization of victims. *Journal of Research in Personality* 9 (4), pp. 253–261.

Bayley, David, and Egon Bittner

1984 Learning the skills of policing. *Law and Contemporary Problems* 47 (4), pp. 35–59.

Beck, Bernard

1970 "Cooking welfare stew." In *Pathways to data: Field methods for studying on-going social organizations,* edited by Robert Habenstein. Chicago: Aldine.

Becker, Howard S.

1967 Whose side are we on? *Social Problems* 14 (Winter), pp. 239–247.

Bellman, B. L.

1984 *The language secrecy.* New Brunswick, NJ: Rutgers University Press.

Benjamin, Jessica, and Anson Rabinbach

1989 Foreword to *Male fantasies, male bodies: Psychoanalyzing the white terror,* edited by Klaus Theweleit. Volume 2. Minneapolis: University of Minnesota Press.

Benjamin, Walter

1968 *Illuminations.* New York: Schockan.

Bittner, Egon

1993 *The police on skid row: A study of peace keeping.* New York: Irvington Publications.

Black, Jan K.

1977 *United States penetration of Brazil.* Manchester: Manchester University Press.

Blass, T.

2000 *Obedience to authority: Current perspectives on the Milgram paradigm.* Mahwah, NJ: Erlbaum.

Bledstein, Burton J.

1976 *The culture of professionalism: The middle class and the development of higher education in America.* New York: Norton.

Book of French torture resurfaces

2000 *Japan Times,* December 6.

Botello, Nelson Arteaga, and Adrian Lopez Rivera
    2000 Everything in this job is money: Inside the Mexican police. *World Policy Journal* 17 (3), pp. 61–70.

Bourdieu, Pierre
    1977 *Outline of a theory of practice.* Cambridge, UK: Cambridge University Press.

Bourgeois, Philippe
    1995 *In search of respect: Selling crack in el barrio.* Cambridge, UK: Cambridge University Press.

Brazil: Toward profound change
    1964 *Time Magazine,* April 17, pp. 49–50.

Brittan, A.
    1989 *Masculinity and power.* Oxford, UK: Blackwell.

Browning, Christopher
    1992 *Ordinary men: Reserve Police Battalion 101 and the final solution in Poland.* New York: HarperCollins.

Caldeira, Teresa P.R.
    2001 *City of walls: Crime, segregation, and citizenship in São Paulo.* Berkeley and Los Angeles: University of California Press.

Cannon, Lou
    2000 One bad cop. *New York Times,* October 1.

Caruth, Cathy
    1995 *Trauma: Explorations in memory.* Washington, DC: Johns Hopkins University Press.

Cava, Ralph Della
    1970 Torture in Brazil. *Commonwealth* 24 (April), pp. 135–41.

Chandler, David
    1999 *Voices from S-21: Terror and history in Pol Pot's secret prison.* Berkeley and Los Angeles: University of California Press.

Chevigny, Paul
    1995 *Edge of the knife: Police violence in the Americas.* New York: New York Press.

Clendinnen, Inga
    1998 *Reading the Holocaust.* New York: Cambridge University Press.

Cohen, Elie
    1954 *Human behavior in the concentration camp.* London: Jonathan Cape.

Cohen, Stan
    1993 Human rights and crimes of the state: The culture of denial. *Australian and New Zealand Journal of Criminology* 26 (July), pp. 97–115.

Collins, John M.
    1998 Fixing the past: Stockpiling, storytelling, and Palestinian political strategy in the wake of the "peace process." Paper presented at "Legacies of au-

thoritarianism: Cultural production, collective trauma, and global justice," University of Wisconsin, Madison, April.

Conroy, John
2000 *Unspeakable acts, ordinary people: The dynamics of torture*. New York: Alfred A. Knopf.

Crank, John P.
1998 *Understanding police culture*. Cincinnati: Anderson.

Crelinsten, Ronald D.
1993 The World of Torture: A Constructed Reality. Unpublished paper.

Cronin, Karena
1999 Women's solidarity: Methodological and theoretical obstacles to understanding prostitutes' lived experience. Honors senior thesis, Departments of Sociology and Political Science, Union College, June.

Departamento de Ordem Político e Social.
1969 São Paulo: Operação Bandeirantes, central de difusão. Contra propaganda anti-terrorista. Proposta para ação psychològica. September. Records of the Departamento de Ordem Político e Social, 50-Z-910210. Arquivo Público de São Paulo.
1974 Operação Bandeirante, organização do CODI/II ex. Memorandum by Jose Canavarro Pereira, June 17. Records of the Departamento de Ordem Político e Social, 50-D-19280. Arquivo Público de São Paulo.
1977 Depoimento de Aldo Avantes, December 16. Records of the Departamento de Ordem Político e Social, 50-K-6263. Arquivo Publico de São Paulo.

Diener, E.
1979 Deindividuation, self-awareness and disinhibition. *Journal of Personality and Social Psychology* 37 (7), pp. 1160–1171.

Dossiê da repressão
1978 *Isto È*, September 27.

Dulles, John W.
1978 *Castello Branco: The making of a Brazilian president*. College Station, TX: A & M University Press.

Durkheim, Emile
1933 *The division of labor in society*. New York: Macmillan.

Excerpts from sentencing hearing in the Louima torture case
1999 *New York Times,* December 14.

Fanon, F.
1963 *The wretched of the earth*. New York: Ballantine Books.

Feitlowitz, Marguerite
1998 *A lexicon of terror: Argentina and the legacies of torture*. New York: Oxford University Press.

Fundação Getulio Vargas
1997 *Ernesto Geisal,* edited by Maria Celina D'Araújo and Celso Castro. Rio de Janeiro: Editora Fundação Getulio Vargas.

Fon, Antonio Carlos
1986 *A tortura: A història da repressão política no Brasil.* São Paulo: Editora Global.

Forrest, D., ed.
1999 *A glimpse of hell: Reports on torture worldwide.* New York: New York University Press/Amnesty International.

Foucault, Michel
1979 *Discipline and punish: The birth of the prison.* New York: Vintage.

Frank, Arthur W.
1995 *The wounded storyteller: Body, illness, and ethics.* Chicago: University of Chicago Press.

Friedman, P.
1967 "Suicide among police." In *Essays in self-destruction,* edited by E. Schneidrean. New York: Science House.

Flynn, Peter
1978 *Brazil: A political analysis.* Boulder: Westview Press.

Geer, Blanche
1970 "Studying a college." In *Pathways to data: Field methods for studying ongoing social organizations,* edited by Robert W. Habenstein. Chicago, IL: Aldine Publishing.

Gibson, Janice, and Mika Haritos-Fatouros
1988 The official torturer: A learning model for obedience to an authority of violence. *Journal of Applied Social Psychology* 18, pp. 1107–1120.

Glebbeek, Marie-Louise
2000 The police reform and the peace process in Guatemala: The fifth promotion of the new National Civilian Police into action. Paper presented at the Latin American Studies Association, Miami, Florida, March 16–18.

Goffman, Irving
1961 *Encounters.* Indianapolis: Bobbs-Merrill.

Gold, Hal
1996 *Unit 731 Testimony.* Singapore: Yen Books.

Golding, William
1959 *Lord of the Flies.* New York: Aeonian Press.

Gordon, Diana
1990 *The justice juggernaut: Fighting street crime, controlling citizens.* New Brunswick, NJ: Rutgers University Press.

Guimarães, E.
1978 *A chancela do crime.* Rio de Janeiro: Âmbito Cultural.

Gunn, Janet Varner
  1997 Autobiography in the "emergency zone": Reading as witnessing. Paper presented at the Modern Languages Association conference, Toronto, December 29.

Guralnick, L.
  1963 Mortality by occupation and cause of death among men 20–64 years of age. U.S. 1950, Vital Statistics—Special Report no. 53. Washington, DC: U.S. Government Printing Office.

Habenstein, Robert
  1970 "The ways of pathways." In *Pathways to data: Field methods for studying ongoing social organizations,* edited by Robert W. Habenstein. Chicago, IL: Aldine Publishing.

Haney, C., W. C. Banks, and P. G. Zimbardo
  1973 Interpersonal dynamics in a simulated prison. *International Journal of Criminology and Penology* 1 (February), pp. 69–97.

Haney, Craig, and P. G. Zimbardo
  1977 "The socialization into criminality: On becoming a prisoner and a guard." In *Law, justice and the individual in society: Psychological and legal issues,* edited by J. L. Tapp and F. J. Levine. New York: Holt, Rinehart & Winston.

Haritos-Fatouros, Mika
  2002 *The psychological origins of institutionalized torture.* New York and London: Routledge.

Haritos-Fatouros, Mika, Martha Huggins, and Nicos Bozatzis
  2000 Identity characteristics as expressed by policemen torturers and killers who served under the Brazilian dictatorship. Paper presented at the Political Psychology Annual Conference, Seattle, Washington, July 1–4.

Harris, Richard N.
  1961 *The police academy: An inside view.* New York: John Wiley & Sons.

Hecht, Tobias
  1998 *At home in the street: Street children of northeast Brazil.* Cambridge, UK: Cambridge University Press.

Huggins, Martha K.
  1992 Violência institucionalizada e democracia: Ligações perigosas. Lecture given at the Núcleo de Estudos da Violência, Universidade de São Paulo, November 21.
  1998 *Political policing: The United States and Latin America.* Durham, NC: Duke University Press.
  2000a Legacies of authoritarianism: Brazilian torturers and murderers' reformulation of memory. *Latin American Perspectives* 27 (2), pp. 57–78.
  2000b "Modernity and devolution: The making of police death squads in modern Brazil." In *Death squads in global perspective: Murder with deniability,* edited by Arthur D. Brenner and Bruce B. Campbell. New York: St. Martin's Press.

Huggins, Martha K., and Mika Haritos-Fatouros
1998 "Bureaucratizing masculinities among Brazilian torturers and murderers." In *Masculinities and violence,* edited by Lee H. Bowker. Beverly Hills, CA: Sage.

Huggins, Martha K., and Myriam Mesquita
1995 Scapegoating outsiders: The murders of street youth in modern Brazil. *Policing and Society* 4 (4), pp. 265–279.

Jefferson, T.
1996 "Introduction." In *Masculinities, social relations, and crime.* Spec. issue of *British Journal of Criminology* 36 (3), pp. 337–347.

Jenkins, Brian Michael
2000 Elite units troublesome but useful. *Los Angeles Times,* March 27.

Johnson, Robert
1997 *Death work: A study of the modern execution process.* Belmont, CA: Wadsworth.

Jovem photografado em "pau-de-arara" confirma tortura
1985 *Jornal do Brasil,* August 10.

Keen, S.
1986 *Faces of the enemy: Reflections on the hostile imagination.* New York: Harper & Row.

Kelling, G., and M. Pate
1975 The person-role fit in policing: Current knowledge. In *Job stress and the police officer: Identifying stress reduction techniques,* edited by W. Kroes and J. Hurrell. Washington, DC: U.S. Department of Health, Education, and Welfare.

Kersten, J.
1996 Culture, masculinities and violence against women." In *Masculinities, social relations, and crime.* Spec. issue of *British Journal of Criminology* 36 (3), pp. 381–395.

Klare, Michael T., and Cynthia Arnson
1981 *Supplying repression: U.S. support for authoritarian regimes abroad.* Washington, DC: Institute for Policy Studies.

Kroes, W.
1976 *Society's victim: The policeman.* Springfield, IL: Charles Thomas.

Lago, Henrique, and Ana Lagoa
1979 A repressão a guerrilha urbana no Brasil. *Folha de São Paulo,* January 28.

Langguth, A. J.
1978 *Hidden terrors.* New York: Pantheon.

Lee, M., P. Zimbardo, and M. Bertholf
1977 Shy murderers. *Psychology Today* 11 (6), pp. 69–70, 76, 148.

A lei da bárbarie
1992 *Veja,* November 18, p. 30.

Lerner, M. J.
   1980 *Belief in a just world: A fundamental delusion.* New York: Plenum.
Lernoux, Penny
   1982 *Cry of the people: The struggle for human rights in Latin America—the Catholic Church conflict with U.S. policy.* New York: Penguin Books.
Levi, Primo
   1995 *Survival in Auschwitz: The Nazi assault on humanity.* NewYork: Collier Books.
Liddle, A. M.
   1996 "State, masculinities, and law: Some comments on gender and English state-formation." In *Masculinities, social relations, and crime.* Spec. issue of *British Journal of Criminology* 36 (3), pp. 361–380.
Lifton, R.
   1986 *The Nazi doctors: Medical killing and the psychology of genocide.* New York: Basic Books.
Lynd, Helen
   1958 *On shame and the search for identity.* New York: Harcourt.
MacCormack, Carol, and Marilyn Strathern
   1980 *Nature, culture, and gender.* Cambridge, UK: Cambridge University Press.
Machell, David F.
   1993 Combat post-traumatic stress disorder, alcoholism, and the police officer. *Journal of Alcohol and Drug Education* 38 (2), pp. 23–33.
Manning, Peter K.
   1978 "The police: Mandate, strategies, and appearances," In *Policing: A view from the street,* edited by P. K. Manning and J. van Maanen. Santa Monica, CA: Goodyear.
Martin, Aldo
   1995 Individual depression after an active role in violations of human rights. Paper read at the Seventh International Symposium on Caring for Survivors of Torture. Cape Town, South Africa.
Maslach, Christina
   1981 "Burnout: A Social Psychological Analysis." *The Burnout Syndrome: Current Research, Theory, Interventions,* ed. J.W. Jones. Park Ridge, Ill.: London House Press.
   1982 *Burnout: The cost of caring.* Englewood Cliffs, NJ: Prentice Hall.
   1998 "A multidimensional theory of burnout." In *Theories of organizational stress,* edited by C. L. Cooper. Oxford, UK: Oxford University Press.
Maslach, Christina, and S. Jackson
   1979 Burnout cops and their families. *Psychology Today* 12 (12), pp. 59–62.
   1986 *Maslach burnout inventory manual.* Palo Alto, CA. Consulting Psychologists Press.

Maslach, C., and M. P. Leiter
1997 *The truth about burnout: How organizations cause personal stress and what to do about it.* San Francisco: Jossey-Bass.

Messerschmidt, J.
1993 *Masculinities and crime: Critique and reconceptualization of theory.* Lanham, MD: Rowman and Littlefield.

Milgram, S.
1974 *Obedience to authority.* New York: Harper & Row.

Mills, C. Wright
1940 Situated actions and vocabularies of motive. *American Sociological Review* 6, pp. 904–913.

Mingardi, Guaracy
1991 *Tiras, gansos, e trutas: Cotidiano e reforma na Policia Civil.* São Paulo: Editora Scritta.

Morales, Frank
1999 The militarization of the police. *Covert Action Quarterly* 67 (Spring-Summer), p. 67.

Nordstrom, C., and A. Robben
1995 *Field work under fire: Contemporary studies of violence and survival.* Los Angeles: University of California Press.

Ortner, Sherry B., and Harriett Whitehead
1981 *Sexual meanings: The cultural construction of gender and sexuality.* Cambridge, UK: Cambridge University Press.

Parker, Phyllis R.
1979 *Brazil and the quiet intervention.* Austin: University of Texas Press.

Paton, D., and J. M. Violanti
1996 *Traumatic stress in critical incidents: Recognition, consequences, and treatment.* Springfield, IL: Charles C. Thomas.

Payne, Leigh A.
1999 Confessions of torturers: Reflections on cases from Argentina. *Social Justice* (July).
2000a Collaborators and the politics of memory in Chile. *Human Rights Review* 2 (3).
2000b *Uncivil movements: The armed right wing and democracy in Latin America.* Baltimore: Johns Hopkins University Press.

Pinheiro, Paulo Sérgio
1991 "Police and political crisis: The case of the military police." In *Vigilantism and the state in modern Latin America,* edited by Martha K. Huggins. New York: Praeger.

Piot, C.
1993 Secrecy, ambiguity, and the everyday in Kabre culture. *American Anthropologist* 95 (2), pp. 353–370.

O poder da pauleira e do chocque
   1995 *Veja,* November 1, pp. 28–35.

Porão iluminado
   1998 *Veja,* December 9, pp. 42–53.

Pratto, F.
   1999 "The puzzle of continuing group inequality: Piecing together psychological, social, and cultural forces in social dominance theory." In *Advances
   in Experimental Social Psychology,* edited by M. P. Zanna. New York: Academic Press.

Prenzler, T.
   1997 Is there a police culture? *Australian Journal of Public Administration* 56
   (4), pp. 47–56.

Ramirez, R.
   1999 *What it means to be a man: Reflections on Puerto Rican masculinity.* New
   Brunswick, NJ: Rutgers University Press.

Robben, A.
   1995 "The politics of truth and emotion among victims and perpetrators of
   violence." In *Fieldwork under fire: Contemporary studies of violence and survival,* edited by C. Nordstrom and A. Robben. Berkeley and Los Angeles:
   University of California Press.

Rodrigues, Sandra, and Martha Huggins
   1999 Working kids on São Paulo's Paulista Avenue: Unbounded labor and
   delinquency stereotypes. Unpublished paper.

Rosen, Ruth
   1982 *The lost sisterhood.* Washington, DC: Johns Hopkins University Press.

Ross, L.
   1977 "The intuitive psychologist and his shortcomings: Distortions in the attribution process." In *Advances in experimental social psychology,* edited by
   L. Berkowitz. New York: Academic Press.

Rubenstein, Jonathan
   1973 *City police.* New York: Noonday Press.

Rudi não moudou na volta
   1969 *Estado de São Paulo,* March 27.

Sargento do DOI matou colega antes de desaparecer
   1985 *Jornal do Brasil,* November 3.

Saxe-Fernandez, Ivan
   1972 The Vietnamization of Latin America. *North American Congress on Latin
   America and Empire Report* 7 (5).

Schaufeli, W. B., C. Maslach, and T. Marek
   1993 *Professional burnout: Recent developments in theory and research.* Washington, DC: Taylor & Francis.

Schneider, Peter
    2001 The enemy within. *New York Times Magazine,* January 7, p. 32.

Scott, Marvin, and Stanford M. Lyman
    1968 Accounts. *American Sociological Review* 33 (1), pp. 46–62.

Scully, D., and J. Marolla
    1984 Convicted rapists' vocabulary of motive: Excuses and justifications. *Social Problems* 31 (5), pp. 530–544.

Selassie, Haile
    1963 Lecture to United Nations General Assembly, October 4.

Seligman, M.E.P.
    1974 "Depression and learned helplessness." In *The psychology of depression: Contemporary theory and research,* edited by R.J. Friedman and M.M. Katz. New York: John Wiley & Sons.

Sheridan, Alan
    1980 *Michel Foucault: The will to truth.* New York: Tavistock.

Sidanius, J., and F. Pratto
    1999 *Social dominance: An intergroup theory of social hierarchy and oppression.* New York: Cambridge University Press.

Simmel, George
    1950 *The sociology of George Simmel.* Glencoe: Free Press.

Skidmore, Thomas
    1988 *The politics of military rule in Brazil, 1964–1985.* New York: Oxford University Press.

Skolnick, Jerome
    1966 *Justice without trial.* New York: John Wiley & Sons.

Skolnick, Jerome, and James Fyfe
    1993 *Above the law: Police and the excessive use of force.* New York: The Free Press.

Skovholt, T.M., D. Moore, and M. Haritos-Fatouros
    n.d. The 180-degree bind: Trained for war, expected to nurture. Unpublished paper.

Solzhenitsyn, Alexander
    1974 *The gulag archipelago.* New York: Harper & Row.

Stack, Carol
    1974 *All our kin: Strategies for survival in a black community.* New York: Harper & Row.

Steiner, J.M., and J. Fahrenbert
    2000 Authoritarianism and social status of former members of the Waffen-SS and SS of the Wehrmacht: An extension and reanalysis of the study published in 1970. *Kolner-Zeitschrift fur Soziologie and Sozialpsychologie* 52 (June), pp. 329–348.

Stevens, Dennis

  1999 Stress and the American police officer. *The Police Journal* 73 (3), pp. 247–259.

Sykes, Gresham, and David Matza

  1957 Techniques of neutralization: a theory of delinquency. *American Sociological Review* 22 (6), pp. 664–670.

Tefft, S.

  1980a "Secrecy, disclosure and social theory." In *Secrecy: A cross-cultural perspective,* edited by S. Tefft. New York: Human Sciences.

  1980b "Secrecy as a social and political process." In *Secrecy: A cross-cultural perspective,* edited by S. Tefft. New York: Human Sciences.

Theweleit, Klaus

  1989 *Male fantasies, male bodies: Psychoanalyzing the white terror.* Vol. 2. Minneapolis: University of Minnesota Press.

TOAID

  1969 Public Safety Report for November, 23 December. A-1259. OPS-Brazil. Washington, DC: FOIA: Agency for International Development.

Toch, Hans

  1969. *Violent men: An inquiry into the psychology of violence.* Chicago, IL: Aldine.

  1996 "The violence-prone police officer." In *Police violence: Understanding and controlling police abuse of force,* edited by William A. Geller and Hans Toch. New Haven, CT: Yale University Press.

Tortura Nunca Mais Archive

  n.d. Torture in Brazil: A shocking report of the pervasive use of torture by Brazilian military governments, 1964–1979. Austin: University of Texas.

United Nations Commission on Human Rights

  2000 Civil and political rights, including the questions of torture and detention. Report of the Special Rapporteur Sir Nigel Rodley, submitted pursuant to Commission on Human Rights Resolution 2000/43.

Uildriks, Niels, and Hans van Mastrigt

  1991 *Policing police violence.* Deventer, The Netherlands: Klewer.

Ustra, Carlos Alberto Brilhante

  1987 *Rompendo o silêncio.* Brasília: Editora Editorial.

Van Gennep, A.

  1960 *The rites of passage.* London: Routledge and Kegan Paul.

Verbitsky, H.

  1996 *The flight: Confessions of an Argentine dirty warrior.* New York: The New Press.

Watson, J.

  1973 Deindividuation and changing appearance before battle. *Journal of Abnormal and Social Psychology* 25, pp. 342–345.

Weber, Max
   2001 *The Protestant ethic and the spirit of capitalism.* Los Angeles: Roxbury.

Weschler, Lawrence
   1987 A reporter at large: A miracle, a universe II. *The New Yorker,* June, pp. 72–93.
   1998 *A miracle, a universe: Settling accounts with torturers.* Chicago and London: University of Chicago Press.

Willison, Andrea Klein
   1998 *The only true power is in connection.* Schenectady, NY: White Wing Press.

Wright, Jaime
   1987 Taped interview by Martha K. Huggins, São Paulo, November 20.

Zimbardo, P. G.
   1970 "The human choice: Individuation, reason, and order versus deindividuation, impulse, and chaos." In *1969 Nebraska symposium on motivation,* edited by W. J. Arnold and D. Levine. Lincoln: University of Nebraska Press.
   1972 Comment: Pathology of imprisonment. *Society* 4 (April), pp. 4, 6, 8.

Zimbardo, P. G.., C. Haney, W. C. Banks, and D. Jaffe
   1973 The mind is a formidable jailer: A Pirandellian prison. *New York Times Magazine,* April 8, 38ff.

Zimbardo, Philip, C. Maslach, and C. Haney
   2000 "Reflections on the Stanford Prison Experiment: Genesis, transformations, consequences." In *Obedience to authority: Current perspectives on the Milgram paradigm,* edited by T. Blass. Mahwah, NJ: Erlbaum.

Index

accountability. *See* moral universes of tor-
turers and murderers; secrecy, man-
agement of
Adler, C., 87
Agent Orange, 131
AIDS, labeling victims and perpetrators,
24
alcoholism, stress-related, 10–11
Alencar, Tito, torture of, 73–74, 112
Algerian War, 241
Aliança Libertação Nacional (ALN), 73
Amnesty International: on Carandiru
Prison massacre, xvii; reports on human abuses and torture, 265
Arendt, Hannah, 241–42
Arns, Cardinal, 260
assembly-line violence, 178–82
atrocity: anonymity and insularity between
violence workers, 185–88, 248–49,
266; assembly-line violence, 178–82;
atrocity training of violence workers,
153–55, 168–71, 237; competitive masculinity within division of violence
labor, 180, 181–82; conceptualizing
atrocity, 138–40; continuum of police
inviolability, 189–91; dehumanizing
victims, 255–57; distinguishing torturers and murderers, 144; elaborate division of violence labor, 178–82; in
emergency-charged environments,
175–77, 266; euphemistic labeling of,
255–56; and exposure to childhood

and adolescent trauma and violence,
141; facilitator police roles in, 138; formula for, 137; hazing and violence in
militarized police training, 156–60;
historical and political influences in,
243–45; insularity of violence workers, 185–88, 248–49, 266; internal
security politics of, 168; learning
through oral tradition, 174; masculinity norms and, 249–50; moral disengagement from violence implications
and outcomes, 153, 183–84, 258–60,
266; motivations of perpetrators,
15–16; moving into society after Hell
Week, 155–56; multiple systems for
creating perpetrators, 242–61; murders, Militarized Police role in, 144,
145–47; national security ideology in,
240; nature versus nurture: being or
becoming a violence worker, 140–43;
neutralizing accountability, 257–58;
"normal" violence in, 188–89; on-the-
job learning, 174–75; ordinary men
doing evil deeds, 240–42; personal
transformation and, 188; policeman's
"working personality" and, 189; policemen as teacher, 173–74; preservice
socialization and, 143–45; prevention
of, 267; reasons for recruits joining
the police force, 141–42; refining torture strategies, 239–40; remaining in
a special unit and, 166–67; routinizing

Compositor:	Impressions Book and Journal Services, Inc.
Text:	10/13 Galliard
Display:	Galliard
Printer and Binder:	Sheridan Books, Inc.

sociological and organizational influences on, 245–50; third generation of, 8; torture training using human guinea pigs, 239; transforming ordinary men into, 232–67; variable masculinity, compartments of, 89–90; violent life themes of perpetrators, 15–16. *See also* atrocity. *See also* locating torturers and murderers. *See also* Stanford Prison Experiment

Volpe, Justin A., 191

water torture: full-body water torture, 93; used by a "rational" torturer, 104

Weber, Max, 105

Weschler, Lawrence, 78

White Hand death squad, 80, 126

women: male sexual domination of, 85; in torture roles, 81

Wretched of the Earth, The (Fanon), 212

Zimbardo, P., 81, 137